International Political Economy Series

General Editor: **Timothy M. Shaw**, Professor of Commonwealth Governance and Development, and Director of the Institute of Commonwealth Studies, School of Advanced Study, University of London

Titles include:

Vijay S. Makhan
ECONOMIC RECOVERY IN AFRICA
The Paradox of Financial Flows

Clever Mumbengegwi (*editor*)
MACROECONOMIC AND STRUCTURAL ADJUSTMENT POLICIES IN
ZIMBABWE

Nana Poku
REGIONALIZATION AND SECURITY IN SOUTHERN AFRICA

Howard Stein, Olu Ajakaiye and Peter Lewis (*editors*)
DEREGULATION AND THE BANKING CRISIS IN NIGERIA
A Comparative Study

Peter Vale, Larry A. Swatuk and Bertil Oden (*editors*)
THEORY, CHANGE AND SOUTHERN AFRICA'S FUTURE

International Political Economy Series
Series Standing Order ISBN 0–333–71708–2 hardback
Series Standing Order ISBN 0–333–71110–6 paperback
(*outside North America only*)

You can receive future titles in this series as they are published by placing a
standing order.

Please contact your bookseller or, in case of difficulty, write to us at the address
below with your name and address, the title of the series and one of the ISBNs
quoted above.

Customer Services Department, Macmillan Distribution Ltd, Houndmills,
Basingstoke, Hampshire RG21 6XS, England

Twenty Years of Independence in Zimbabwe

From Liberation to Authoritarianism

Edited by

Staffan Darnolf
Adviser to the European Commission on Elections in Nigeria

and

Liisa Laakso
Department of Political Science, University of Helsinki

First published 2003 by
PALGRAVE MACMILLAN
Houndmills, Basingstoke, Hampshire RG21 6XS and
175 Fifth Avenue, New York, N.Y. 10010
Companies and representatives throughout the world

PALGRAVE MACMILLAN is the global academic imprint of the Palgrave
Macmillan division of St. Martin's Press, LLC and of Palgrave Macmillan Ltd.
Macmillan® is a registered trademark in the United States, the United Kingdom
and other countries. Palgrave is a registered trademark in the European
Union and other countries.

ISBN 0–333–80453–8

This book is printed on paper suitable for recycling and made from fully
managed and sustained forest sources.

A catalogue record for this book is available from the British Library.

Library of Congress Cataloging-in-Publication Data
Twenty years of independence in Zimbabwe : from liberation to
authoritarianism/edited by Staffan Darnolf and Liisa Laakso.
      p. cm. — (International political economy)
   Includes bibliographical references and index.
   ISBN 0–333–80453–8
   1. Zimbabwe—Politics and government—1980– I. Darnolf, Staffan.
   II. Laakso, Liisa. III. International political economy series (Palgrave (Firm))
   DT2996.T85 2003
   968.9105—dc21   2003049806

10   9   8   7   6   5   4   3   2   1
12 11 10 09 08 07 06 05 04 03

Printed and bound in Great Britain by
Antony Rowe Ltd, Chippenham and Eastbourne

Contents

Tables and Figures

Tables

Figures

List of Abbreviations

AAG	Affirmative Action Group
ACP	African, Caribbean and Pacific Group of States
AEC	African Economic Community
AFC	Agricultural Finance Corporation
AEOS	Agricultural Extension Officers
AGRITEX	Agricultural Technical and Extension Services
ANC	African National Congress
ANZ	Associated Newspapers of Zimbabwe
CAP	Community Action Project
CEAN	Centre for African Studies
CCJP	Catholic Commission for Justice and Peace
CFU	Commercial Farmers' Union
CIO	Central Intelligence Organization
CODESRIA	Council for the Development of Social Science Research in Africa
COMESA	Common Market for Eastern and Southern Africa
CSO	Central Statistical Office
CUSO	Canadian University Service Overseas
CZI	Confederation of Zimbabwe Industries
DDC	District Development Committee
DERUDE	Department of Rural Development
DRC	Democratic Republic of Congo
ECOWAS	Economic Community of West African States
EIU	Economist Intelligence Unit
ERF	Export Revolving Fund
ERP	Economic Reform Programme
ESAF	Enhanced Structural Adjustment Facility
ESAP	Economic Structural Adjustment Programme
ESPP	Enhanced Social Protection Programme
EwP	Education with Production
EWS	Extension Workers
FCA	Foreign Currency Account
FTLS	Farmer Training Leaders
GAC	Grants Allocation Committee
GDP	Gross Domestic Product
IBDC	Indigenous Business Development Centre

ICFU	Indigenous Commercial Farmers Union
ILO	International Labour Organization
IMF	International Monetary Fund
ISDSC	Inter-State Defence and Security Committee
LAC	Loans Allocation Committee
LRF	Legal Resources Foundation
MDC	Movement for Democratic Change
MERP	Millennium Economic Recovery Plan
MFI	Micro-finance Institutions
MIGA	Multilateral Investment Guarantee Agency
MISA	Media Institute of Southern Africa
MMPZ	Media Monitoring Project
MOI	Minister of Information, Posts and Telecommunications
MZRDP	Mid-Zambezi Rural Development Project
NAM	Non-Aligned Movement
NCA	National Constitutional Assembly
NCC	National Convention for Change
NECF	National Economic Consultative Forum
NFC	National Foundation Certificate
NGO	non-governmental organization
NIT	National Investment Trust
NOCZIM	National Oil Company of Zimbabwe
NRZ	National Railways of Zimbabwe
NUST	National University for Science and Technology
OAU	Organization of African Unity
OCCZIM	Organization of Collective Co-operatives of Zimbabwe
OPIC	Overseas Private Investment Corporation
PAAP	Poverty Alleviation Action Plan
PAC	Pan African Congress
PASS	Poverty Assessment Study Survey
PDL	Poverty Datum Line
PF-ZAPU	Patriotic Front-Zimbabwe African People's Union
PTA	Preferential Trade Agreement
PTC	Posts and Telecommunications Corporation
RBC	Rhodesia Broadcasting Corporation
RDC	Rural District Councils
RENAMO	Resistência Nacional Moçambicana/Mozambican National Resistance
RF	Rhodesian Front
SADC	Southern African Development Community

SADCC	Southern African Development Co-operation Conference
SAMDEF	Southern Africa Media Development Fund
SAPEM	*Southern African Political and Economic Monthly*
SAPRI	Structural Adjustment Participatory Review Initiative
SDF	Social Developments Fund
SEDCO	Small Enterprise Development Corporation
SMS	Subject Matter Specialists
SSMA	Small-scale Miners Association
SWAPO	South West Africa People's Organization
TNDP	Transitional National Development Plan
TTL	Tribal Trust Land
UDI	Unilateral Declaration of Independence
UNDP	United Nations Development Programme
UNIDO	United Nations Industrial Development Organization
UNITA	União Nacional para a Independência Total de Angola/National Union for the Total Independence of Angola
UNTAG	United Nations Transition Group
UPE	Universal Primary Education
VIDCO	Village Development Committee
WAD	Women and Development
WADCO	Ward Development Committee
WID	Women in Development
WOTRO	Netherlands Foundation for the Advancement of Tropical Research
WTO	World Trade Organization
ZANLA	Zimbabwe African National Liberation Army
ZANU	Zimbabwe African National Union
ZANU-PF	Zimbabwe African National Union – Patriotic Front
ZAPU	Zimbabwe African People's Union,
ZBC	Zimbabwe Broadcasting Corporation
ZCTU	Zimbabwe Congress of Trade Unions
ZESA	Zimbabwe Electricity Supply Authority
ZIMASCO	Zimbabwe Mining and Smelting Company
ZIMCORD	Zimbabwe Conference on Reconstruction and Development
ZIMFEP	Zimbabwe Foundation for Education with Production
ZIMPREST	Zimbabwe Programme for Economic and Social Transformation
ZINTEC	Zimbabwe National Teacher Education Course

ZIPRA	Zimbabwe People's Revolutionary Army
ZISCO	Zimbabwe Iron and Steel Company
ZMMT	Zimbabwe Mass Media Trust
ZNA	Zimbabwe National Army
ZNCC	Zimbabwe National Craft Certificate
ZNLWVA	Zimbabwe National Liberation War Veterans' Association
ZUM	Zimbabwe Unity Movement

Notes on the Contributors

Donald Chimanikire is the Chair of International Relations and Social Development Studies Department at the Institute of Development Studies, University of Zimbabwe. He has carried out research on South Africa's destabilization policy and more recently on regional peace and security issues and democratization. His articles have been published in *Africa Development, Peace Review* and *Review of International Affairs*. He has held positions in the Zimbabwe Chapter of the African Association of Political Science, Zimbabwe National Commission for UNESCO and the Organization of Social Science Research in Eastern and Southern Africa.

Daniel Compagnon is a Professor of Political Science at Sciences Po Bordeaux, and a researcher at the Center for African Studies (CEAN), as well as a former director of the French Institute for Research in Africa's branch in Harare from 1994 to 1997. He has published several articles in French on Zimbabwe and a book with John Makumbe, *Behind the Smokescreen: The Politics of Zimbabwe's 1995 General Elections* (2000). His other areas of scientific interest include public policy (especially environmental policies and comparative analysis of the post-colonial state). He has conducted fieldwork in Botswana and Somalia as well.

Staffan Darnolf holds a PhD in Political Science from Göteborg University, Sweden. He has worked as a scholar and practitioner within the field of elections and election administration since the early 1990s. He has written on media, electioneering and party development in Zimbabwe and Botswana. His publications include *Democratic Electioneering in Southern Africa: The Contrasting Cases of Botswana and Zimbabwe* (1997). During 2000, he was the Senior Advisor to OSCE's (the Organization for Security and Co-operation in Europe) Director of Elections in Kosovo. He currently works as an adviser to the European Commission on Elections in Nigeria.

Godfrey Kanyenze is the Chief Economist at the Zimbabwe Congress of Trade Unions (ZCTU), where he has been employed since 1986. He has conducted consultancy work on youth unemployment, wages, productivity, vocational education and training, the Social Contract among others. He sits on the boards of the Zimbabwe Open University,

National Manpower Council, Poverty Reduction Forum, Non-State Actors Forum, and Structural Adjustment Participatory Review Initiative (SAPRI).

Norma Kriger is a Visiting Professor at Goucher College, Baltimore. She is the author of *Zimbabwe's Guerrilla War: Peasant Voices* (1992) and of *Power and Privilege in Zimbabwe: Guerrilla Voices* (forthcoming). She has published articles in journals such as *Journal of Southern African Studies*, *African Studies Review*, *Peace Review* and *Review of African Political Economy*.

Liisa Laakso teaches at the Department of Political Science, University of Helsinki. She is author of *Voting Without Choosing: State Making and Elections in Zimbabwe* (1999), co-editor and contributor of *Challenges to the Nation-state in Africa* (1996) and *Multi-party Elections in Africa* (2001). Her articles have appeared in the *Journal of Commonwealth and Comparative Studies*, *Journal of Modern African Studies*, *The Nordic Journal of African Affairs* and *Current Research on Peace and Violence*.

Anders Närman is an Assistant Professor at the Department of Human and Economic Geography at Göteborg University. He is also the Director of the Centre for Africa Studies at the same university. His research area covers education, but also more general development issues. Regionally his research has been based on Eastern and Southern Africa and lately also Sri Lanka. Among other publications, he has been the co-editor for *Development as Theory and Practice* (1999).

Brian Raftopoulos is an Associate Professor at IDS, University of Zimbabwe. He has published on labour history, urban history, historiography, democratization, civil society, indigenization, poverty and human resource utilization in Zimbabwe. His work has appeared in the *Review of African Political Economy*, the *Journal of Southern African Studies*, *Southern African Report*, the *East African Social Science Review* and *Zambezia*. Between 1997 and 1999 he was a member of the first executive of the National Constitutional Assembly, and is currently the Editor of the NCA journal *Agenda*. He has also served as an advisor to the labour movement and several NGOs in Zimbabwe.

Helge Rønning is Professor of Media Studies at University of Oslo. He has carried out research on and in Africa since studying at SOAS in London and at Oslo University in the late 1960s. Since the mid-1980s he has worked on research and media projects in Southern Africa, particularly Zimbabwe and Mozambique. The main areas of research have been media and democratic change, media and globalization, and cultural impacts of the media. His work has been published in Africa, Europe and the Nordic countries.

Marja Spierenburg has studied social psychology and anthropology at the University of Utrecht. At present she is affiliated to the Amsterdam School for Social Science Research. She has conducted extensive fieldwork in Zimbabwe dating back to 1989. Her publications include articles on the conservation of the environment and development in Northern Zimbabwe. She is a co-editor of *The Quest for Fruition Through Ngoma, the Political Aspects of Healing in Southern Africa* (2000).

Christine Sylvester is a Professor at the Institute of Social Studies in The Hague. She is the author of *Zimbabwe: The Terrain of Contradictory Development* (1991) and *Producing Women and Progress in Zimbabwe: Narratives of Identity and Work from the 1980s* (2000). She has also written about Zimbabwe in the *Journal of Modern African Studies*, *Review of Southern African Studies*, *African Studies Review*, *Signs*, *Differences*, and the *International Feminist Journal of Politics*.

Preface

The country that we now know as Zimbabwe has made the headlines of the international media for more than four decades. The Unilateral Declaration of Independence in 1965, announced by the whites governing Rhodesia at that time, resulted not only in a racist regime and economic sanctions from the international community, but eventually also in a bloody civil war between the government of the white settler state and the liberation movements. Following independence in 1980, in spite of grave concerns and outright scepticism towards the new government in some quarters, racial tolerance and reconciliation was promoted. In addition, the economy was recuperating after the lifting of sanctions and re-direction of the war economy to the betterment of the Africans. Social developments also showed a positive trend; the literacy level increased, and so did average life expectancy. In spite of violence in Matabeleland in the middle of the 1980s, Zimbabwe was heralded as an African showcase.

The economic development, however, came to a standstill and the implementation of structural adjustment from 1991 onwards did not manage to bring investments to the country. Import liberalization and high interest rates resulting from financial liberalization led to bankruptcies, increasing unemployment, inflation and grievances. From then on, the headlines became more critical. During the last decade, Zimbabweans have experienced increasing political tension between the Mugabe administration and anyone who opposes him and his party. The private media has experienced a hostile climate resulting in bombed-out offices, manhandled journalists and prosecution. The days of racial reconciliation are also gone. Although President Mugabe has always played the 'white-settler-card' come elections, his unwillingness to react to the so-called War Veterans' occupation of land, which started shortly before the 2000 general elections, was a serious blow to the reconciliation process. Furthermore Mugabe decided to intervene into the one institution that so far has been the democratic beacon in the Zimbabwean society: the judiciary. The courts have time and again resisted the government's many attempts to politicize the judiciary, and instead have upheld the constitution. This development is probably one explanation as to why Zimbabwe's twentieth anniversary as an independent state in April 2000 passed without any great celebrations.

Events leading up to the 2002 presidential election did not herald any dramatic improvements in the status of the Mugabe regime internationally. Even though some African leaders still stood firmly behind ZANU(PF), actions taken by the incumbent government in the run-up to the presidential poll tended to alienate President Mugabe and his ministers even further from the international community, eventually resulting in economic sanctions imposed on the Mugabe regime by the European Union and the country's one-year-long suspension from the Commonwealth. The people of Zimbabwe, however, were the ones to suffer the most from this negative development.

The parliamentary elections of 2000 brought Zimbabwe back on to the international agenda, and actions taken by Mugabe in the two most recent years in power made it practically impossible for foreign politicians and media representatives to ignore developments inside its borders. The economy has suffered immensely as a direct effect of the so-called land redistribution programme. Many farmers saw no reason to cultivate their land when they were not sure if they would still be on the farm come harvesting. The value of the Zimbabwean dollar has also plummeted even further making it increasingly difficult for factories and producers to afford imported spare parts and other commodities necessary to keep operating. As a result, the number of unemployed and underemployed has risen sharply joining an ever-growing cadre of unemployed youths who face a dismal future in the labour market. Zimbabweans looking for an alternative future in neighbouring South Africa as illegal immigrants are on the increase, though owing to the contracting economy there, xenophobia has surfaced, of which Zimbabweans have become a prime target.

The run-up to the 2002 presidential elections revealed that President Mugabe had no intention of abandoning the electioneering concept of intimidation by violence that made the ZANU(PF) victorious at the polls in 2000. However, since the political climate was even more antagonistic this time around, he and ZANU(PF) stalwarts decided to be even more diligent in implementing this strategy. Their prime target on the political scene was Mugabe's main rival for the Presidency, Morgan Tsvangirai, a former union leader and now leader of the main opposition party, the Movement for Democratic Change (MDC). Tsvangirai had already proved to have a large and enthusiastic support base necessitating an array of semi-legal and blatantly illegal actions by the Mugabe regime to ensure victory at the presidential poll. The ruling party didn't stop at harassing the MDC leadership. Members of various civil society organizations also experienced the iron fist of ZANU(PF) supporters and the regime's official security apparatus.

The international observers made deviating statements at various stages of the electoral process; some were highly critical of the ruling party for its actions, while others were much more accommodating. Up until polling day, non-African countries and organizations were much more vocal and critical, while representatives from the continent were more moderate. The ZANU(PF) government had a particularly difficult time accepting the European Union's election observation mission, partly owing to the fact that it was widely perceived by the regime as a front for their former colonial masters, and partly because the mission was headed by the Swedish Ambassador to the United Nations, Pierre Schori. Ambassador Schori also headed the EU's observation mission to the Zimbabwean parliamentary elections in 2002, which resulted in a highly critical report denouncing those elections as undemocratic.

President Mugabe's tactics to defuse international criticism of the 2002 presidential election by overtly accusing his critics of racial discrimination and being non-Africans were effectively neutralized when the African continent's most influential countries, Nigeria and South Africa, both supported the Commonwealth election observation report condemning the presidential poll and stating that it was neither free nor fair.

The Commonwealth's harsh statement and subsequent suspension of Zimbabwe from the organization did little to change President Mugabe. In fact, recent developments indicate that the present regime is determined to complete the land reform and hold on to power, even if that means curtailing the free press, making a mockery of the once-independent judiciary and jailing people who dare to question and challenge Mugabe's authority. The terrible consequence of the present regime's war on democracy is not just that the rights and the liberties that so many true war veterans fought for are being trampled upon, but that their leader is now willing to let millions of Zimbabweans starve to death just to satisfy his own personal needs.

We hope that this collection encompassing scholars representing a wide academic spectrum and range of nationalities is able to shed light not only on the social, political and economic complexities behind the current turmoil but also on the many possibilities available to Zimbabweans for overcoming the current crisis. This collection covers a wide range of topics where the actual achievements and disillusionments of the independence era can be examined. Our specific attempt has been to look at the whole period in its political context by addressing actual changes taking place in different high-profile policy fields since independence.

We are grateful for the support given by the Nordic Foundation for Research on Southern Africa and the Department of Political Science at the University of Helsinki. James Murray provided valuable help in checking the language usage and Lalli Metsola in the editing of this book. Finally we want to thank Tim Shaw, as well as Nicola Viinikka and Amanda Watkins from Palgrave Macmillan, for their patience with our project.

STAFFAN DARNOLF
LIISA LAAKSO

1
Research Debates in Zimbabwe: From Analysis to Practice
Liisa Laakso[1]

Introduction

For the new government of Zimbabwe independence meant enormous expectations concerning social and economic equality, which in the increasingly harsh international economic environment were anything but easy to achieve. While the government wanted to adjust to the capitalist world economy, build on the state it inherited from the minority rule and reconcile itself with the white minority, it also called for a radical socialist and racial transformation. It is not surprising that high expectations and the opposing challenges of the new situation have also characterized the research on Zimbabwe's performance.

From the beginning, this research was heavily influenced by the political economy approach, which has dominated critical studies on development since the late 1970s. And indeed Zimbabwe, with its extremely unbalanced but still at least apparently dynamic national economy, provided an interesting instance of the interplay between political and economic pressures. The interpretations of how much room the government actually had to manoeuvre and what its real choices were, however, show great variation. It is useful to divide the research into three categories: those analysing (1) the transition of government power and the prospects of an independent Zimbabwe; (2) the pressure of democratization; and (3) authoritarianism in the country. While there are overlaps in individual contributions, these categories roughly follow the periods of (1) consolidation of the power of the ruling party during the 1980s, (2) World Bank and IMF sponsored economic liberalization during the first half of the 1990s and (3) the deepening economic crisis since the end of the 1990s.

The transition of power

When Zimbabwe finally gained its independence in 1980 the perform-ance of the new regime in consolidating its power was researched in detail. Before independence, concern over the prolonged minority rule and liberation struggle had already inspired research focusing on the racial imbalances and injustice in Southern Rhodesia, both among Zimbabwean scholars and internationally. This research played a not inconsiderable role in building this young nation and its image. Analysis of Zimbabwe's opportunities and constraints in creating a coherent economic and political strategy in the changing international and regional setting was considered relevant beyond its borders – not least with regard to the future of South Africa, still under apartheid. By the same token the continuing struggle in South Africa made this research immediately political at least as far as its approach to majority rule was concerned. Criticism of the new rulers was moderate or indir-ect only. Three significant collections edited over a short period and including both Zimbabwean nationals and researchers who had con-ducted field studies in Zimbabwe should be mentioned: Michael Schatzberg's *The Political Economy of Zimbabwe* (1984); Ibbo Mandaza's *Zimbabwe: The Political Economy of Transition 1980–1986* (1986b); and Colin Stoneman's *Zimbabwe's Prospects: Issues of Race, Class, State and Capital in Southern Africa* (1988).

The Rhodesian-made state apparatus efficiently controlled the econ-omy, which was now intended to serve the interests of the African majority. In the research, however, it was not development policy in general that was significant, but rather the relationship between the socialist ideology of the new regime and the interests of private capital. While Andre Astrow (1983) criticized the 'petty bourgeois' character of the new ruling elite, another debate divided this elite into 'technocrats' and 'populists' or 'nationalists'. According to Stoneman and Lionel Cliffe, at independence the predominant element in the government was the 'old guard' of the nationalists who had been in the movement since the 1950s and 1960s and many of whom had spent long periods in detention. But the government was also able to utilize the numerous Zimbabweans who had obtained university degrees while in exile. Such people were seen to represent more technocratic views (Stoneman and Cliffe 1989, 35). The 'pragmatic' approach of the new regime towards the realities of the capitalist world economy was understood to be largely owing to these technocrats (see especially Libby 1987; Herbst 1990.) However, Timothy Shaw's notion that in the 1980s economic changes were 'marginal rather than fundamental' (1989, 152) was probably widely shared among these scholars as well.

Soon after independence the state launched ambitious plans to develop the rural areas, especially for resettlement. As the early resettlement plans proved far too optimistic, explanations were needed. An obvious one concerned the constitutional provision of a 'willing seller – willing buyer' principle that was agreed on at the Lancaster House peace negotiations. The white commercial farmers simply were not willing to sell their property at prices the government could afford. Stoneman and Cliffe blamed Britain for having betrayed the promise it had made during the negotiations to fund the purchase of land (1989, 33). On the other hand, the state was also accused of not using all available constitutional means to define what 'adequate compensation' for the large-scale farmers was (see Sylvester 1991a, 73). Herbst argued that the high cost of resettlement was not only because of the 'willing seller' principle but also because of the need to construct roads, clinics and schools for large numbers of people moving to new areas. The government's failure to implement its resettlement programme was then manifest in its political difficulty in responding to illegal squatting by peasants, which further complicated the promotion of a coherent and transparent resettlement policy (Herbst 1990, 63–81). There were also grounds for arguing that the government in fact wanted to avoid the risk of disbanding the large-scale production that was generating the bulk of the country's export revenues. Nick Amin argued that because the state was not able to invest adequately in large-scale agriculture, its strategic choice was rather to develop African small-scale farming in the Communal Areas (CAs, formerly Tribal Trust Lands) instead of massive resettlement (see Amin 1992).

Meanwhile, it has to be noted that the government was successful in its attempt to support and encourage small-scale farming, even in the poor agricultural areas, by providing the CA farmers with loans and access to marketing boards with competitive prices and transportation facilities, which had been almost inaccessible to them in Rhodesia (Amin 1992). Besides, after the economic boom of the first two years, the country had faced severe droughts, which made the government introduce drought relief programmes in the CAs. Through these programmes and the delivery of seed and fertilizer, the government gradually assumed a new role in the CAs, where the majority of Zimbabweans lived.

Indeed, instead of resettlement it was the new government policy in smallholder agriculture that attracted the attention of researchers. Michael Bratton's article (1986) on farmer organizations and the expanding small-farmer credit system is a good example. William Masters's study (1994) showed how the government helped smallholders triple their grain sales in the early 1980s, although he also points out shortcomings that left them vulnerable to drought. Even as late as 1997 Stephen Burgess argued that the transformation in the smallholder sector made the small-scale farmers politically influential. According to him the ability of farmers to organize as well as the multi-party system in the country pushed the government to distribute social services in the rural areas (Burgess 1997).

The very repressive government reactions to opposition or criticism were not important to research during the first decade. In this regard the government offensive in Matabeleland is particularly noteworthy. With hindsight it is easy to explain this by the regional support of the 'junior' government party, the Zimbabwe African People's Union, ZAPU, and its leader Joshua Nkomo among the Ndebele. Nkomo, 'Father Zimbabwe', had seniority over the then Prime Minister Robert Mugabe as the original leader of the liberation movement. Besides, the politically powerful position the Ndebele had held before Rhodesian rule was still remembered. However, in the collection edited by Mandaza (1986b) the violent conflict in Matabeleland was hardly mentioned, although published information was already available about the atrocities and human rights violations committed by government forces (the first report by the CCJP came out in April 1983). The same applies to Stoneman's edition, in which Joseph Hanlon analysed the conflict only through the South African destabilization policy (see Hanlon 1988). This was perhaps understandable in the context of the recently ended liberation struggle, the security threats from apartheid South Africa and the devastating civil wars in Angola and neighbouring Mozambique, which were fuelled by cold war rivalry. Inside Zimbabwe the situation was very tense, while the outside world, the research community included, was not willing to question the legitimacy of the new majority rule. There were very real fears that any such involvement could exacerbate rather than mitigate conflicts in Southern Africa.

What the world needed was a peaceful Zimbabwe which could play a constructive role in the region as a whole. In the 1980s, Zimbabwe's foreign and regional policy attracted more interest than its internal stability. It was a key player among the Frontline States against minority rule in the region (see Thompson 1984). Zimbabwean nationalists themselves had enjoyed the support of the Frontline leaders during their own struggle. The country soon adopted a leading role in the Southern African Development Co-operation Conference (SADCC), which was formed after its independence and also included Angola, Botswana, Mozambique, Tanzania, Zambia, Lesotho, Swaziland and Malawi.[2] Furthermore, in sharp contrast to what happened in Matabeleland, the government was praised for its policy of tolerance and reconciliation with regard to the white minority. While this was primarily explained by the government's willingness to avoid a sudden exodus of the economically skilled white minority, a lesson learned from the experience of Mozambique, or by the opportunism of the new ruling elite (Astrow 1983), there were also those who emphasized elements of forgiveness in the Shona culture (de Waal 1990).

Two monographs utilized extensive empirical material to clarify the interplay between the government, popular pressure and interest groups in independent Zimbabwe. Jeffrey Herbst's *State Politics in Zimbabwe* (1990) and Tor Skålnes's *The Politics of Economic Reform in Zimbabwe* (1995) challenged much of the literature on African politics by showing that rational interest-based action and institutional settings rather than deinstitutionalized 'patrimonial' relations explain many of the choices made by the government. Skålnes's analysis was particularly rich because of the historical approach he adopted. In independent Zimbabwe, party politics had only limited significance and the most important economic interest groups were able to interact and influence the government directly, because the economy was characterized by state intervention in almost every sector. In Southern Rhodesia the government regulation of production and marketing had been particularly crucial in agriculture and mining and since the international sanctions, during the period of the Unilateral Declaration of Independence (1965) of Ian Smith's regime, it had also applied to manufacturing industry. Although some authors such as Peter von Blanckenburg based their analysis on the assumption that the large-scale farmers, in spite of their important role in the economy, had lost their political influence since independence (von Blanckenburg 1994), Skålnes pointed out that white vested interests were still politically very important. It was rather the labour unions that the government attempted to control. This also clarifies much of the difficulty of liberalization since 1991 and the fact that the government had been the brake on reform rather than its instigator.

The analyses of Herbst and Skålnes predicted that the next phase in research on Zimbabwe would concentrate on the state of democracy. In general, however, the literature looking at the transition period in

Zimbabwe helped to create an image of pragmatic, reconciliatory and relatively strong government.

Democratization

During the first decade, the state of democracy in Zimbabwe had raised little interest among the researchers apart from a few articles on the 1985 elections (Sithole 1986; Sylvester 1986; and Lemon 1988). The general approach to the political system had merely been concerned with the prospects for a one-party state in Zimbabwe (see, for example, Shaw 1986). However, in 1988 Zimbabwe was included in the comparative four-volume work *Democracy in Developing Countries* (1988) edited by Larry Diamond, Juan Linz and Seymour Martin Lipset. In this collection Masipula Sithole argued that democracy in Zimbabwe was unstable owing to the antagonistic relationship between the Zimbabwe African National Union (ZANU) and the Zimbabwe African People's Union (ZAPU), and the conflict in Matabeleland. Sithole saw unity between these parties as imperative for democratization. He noted Zimbabwe's ability to learn from the experiences of other African states as a positive factor, the undemocratic era of colonialism and independence struggle as a negative one (Sithole 1988, 249–251). The editors of *Democracy in Developing Countries* classified Zimbabwe as a 'semidemocracy' on qualitative grounds (Diamond, Linz and Lipset 1988, xvii).

Similar classification was frequently employed in many quantitative comparative studies. Tatu Vanhanen regarded Zimbabwe as a deviant democracy after independence but dropped it to the category of semidemocracy at the end of the decade (Vanhanen 1990, 76–99). Zimbabwe's position in the middle of the democracy scale in Axel Hadenius's study was atypical, since the majority of the developing countries in Hadenius's sample were either in the lowest or the highest third on the scale (Hadenius 1993). As late as 1997, Michael Bratton and Nicolas van de Walle argued that in 1989 Zimbabwe was one of the rare 'hybrid regimes' in Africa since it combined neopatrimonialism with a 'competitive' multi-party system (Bratton and van de Walle 1997, 79, 82).

For the Zimbabweans it was all too clear that the question was one of a *de facto* one-party state. The Matabeleland offensive had left ZAPU with few alternatives other than to join ZANU, which happened in 1987. However, this did not imply a monolithic 'neopatrimonial' power structure. First of all, the judiciary in Zimbabwe was quite independent of the executive and was able to open up and safeguard space for civil society in spite of the strengthening executive. Civic organizations managed to come together and bring issues to the agenda, mostly via the independent press but also through the government-controlled media, so that the ruling party could not ignore them completely. It was apparent that there were different political views inside the ruling party too, especially after the unity between ZANU and ZAPU. Most importantly, however, the unity made room for critics simply by ending the war in Matabeleland. As a result, academics, journalists, writers and NGO activists were able to conduct a thorough discussion on the pros and cons of the one-party state and come to the conclusion that finally made it unpopular even in the ranks of the ruling party. This more nuanced picture of the state of democracy in Zimbabwe was reflected in two Zimbabwean collections of articles from that time.

The first was edited by the former president Canaan Banana under the title *Turmoil and Tenacity: Zimbabwe 1890–1990* (Banana 1989). In that collection President Mugabe characterized the significance of the Unity Accord between the two liberation parties as a step towards political stability and a one-party state. However, he also admitted that there were both bourgeois and socialist economic agendas among the party membership (see Mugabe 1989). A legal scholar and university teacher Welshman Ncube also emphasized the Unity Accord as an encouragement to the emerging democratic culture. But he included in that culture the formation of new opposition parties, and gave a detailed overview of the ruling party's suppression of that culture and the government's overreactions toward all critics (Ncube 1989).

A critical approach to Zimbabwean democracy was central to *The One-party State and Democracy* published in 1991 and edited by Ibbo Mandaza and Lloyd M. Sachikonye. Most of the contributors favoured a multi-party system. But contrary ideas were expressed as well. Andries Rukobo argued that 'the economic question should be posed first in the discussion of democracy' (1991, 122), claiming that promotion of multi-party democracy was used ideologically by 'imperialist powers' to weaken the socialist strategy of the government. Mandaza and Sachikonye's collection included an article by Ncube about human rights violations by ZANU activists and government forces. Ncube concluded that 'the challenges of democratic government require the total dismantling of Rhodesia's "trademarks of tyranny" and a concerted effort towards the creation of a culture of political tolerance' (1991, 173).

The conduct of the 1990 elections received much attention among Zimbabwean scholars. John Makumbe considered the 1990 general elections as not free and fair because the opposition parties had not been given equal opportunity to outline their programmes in the media or in public rallies, and because there was violent harassment of opposition candidates by ruling party activists. Furthermore, he pointed out the increasing level of apathy among the Zimbabwean voters, only 54 per cent of the registered electorate having voted (Makumbe 1991a). Jonathan Moyo, who, in 2000 as an official spokesperson of the ruling party, later adopted a high profile in defending campaigning by the ruling party, developed his in-depth knowledge of the Zimbabwean electoral system through a comprehensive study of the 1990 elections (Moyo 1992). In spite of the fact that almost 80 per cent of the votes were cast for the ruling party, which was committed to a one-party state, Moyo found out that about 60 per cent of the voters opposed the one-party state (1992, 144). He also made a detailed analysis of government malpractice in the organization of the elections.

John Makumbe and Daniel Compagnon wrote an even more detailed analysis of the 1995 general elections (2000). Quite remarkably, their book came out during the campaigning for the 2000 elections and was soon sold out on the Zimbabwean market. In much the same tone as Moyo had adopted with regard to the 1990 elections, the authors pointed out several legal and institutional constraints on the conduct of free and fair elections. Their surveys of electoral rolls provided indisputable evidence of rigging. They were also looking at the conduct of primary elections, an often forgotten but in practice the most important forum, in which the actual competition takes place in a *de facto* one-party system. This was especially true in 1995 when the number of uncontested seats was a record high. Makumbe and Compagnon collected much of the material on the shortcomings in the democratic process in Zimbabwe from local observer groups and newspapers. What their study also demonstrated was that the facade of Zimbabwean democracy was clearly recognized by Zimbabwean civil society, the independent media and civic groups.

Internal factors related to the expiry of the Lancaster House agreement, which stipulated the multi-party system, and an increasingly vocal civil society help to understand why democracy had become such a topical theme in Zimbabwe since 1990, but there were also external factors. The era of one-partyism was virtually coming to its end elsewhere, such as in Eastern Europe and more importantly in other African countries, including Zimbabwe's neighbour Zambia. Perhaps even more importantly, Zimbabwe was starting to liberalize its economy according to the model advocated by the World Bank and the International Monetary Fund. This both rendered the socialist ideal of a one-party state anomalous and implied more or less open abandonment of the cause of the working poor by the ruling party. After the Economic Structural Adjustment Programme (ESAP) was launched in 1991, it became increasingly difficult for the government to rely on its earlier rhetoric to justify the control of the workers.

As in many other African states, the hardships caused by structural adjustment were accompanied by a revival of civil society, making the role of the trade unions and civil society important to research. With increasing unemployment and inflation, the living standards of the rural and urban poor and the urban middle class deteriorated rapidly. Added to the government-level corruption scandal revealed by the press in 1989, this eroded the legitimacy of the government. Norbert Tengende's (1994) and Per Nordlund's (1996) studies on civil society in Zimbabwe focused particularly on its potential to democratize the entire political system. Nordlund concluded that the state in Zimbabwe interacted with civil society in an authoritarian manner, which constrained the emergence of a democratic system. Tengende argued that towards the end of the 1980s a major rupture had occurred, the workers and the students becoming able to unite and successfully resist the government. But although this had contributed to support for a new opposition party in the urban areas in the 1990 elections, it was still too weak to challenge the position of the ruling party. Labour relations, albeit from an intra-organizational angle, were discussed by Mark Shadur (1994) who argued that corporatism was the key to understanding the situation.

However, with respect to the intensified civic attempts to transform the state and the politically active role adopted by the labour unions during the late 1990s, it is possible that the seeds of a politically active civil society had already been sown in the 1990 elections. Although there were serious setbacks, it can be argued that the 1990s have been a period of strengthening civil society. This has been evident in its frequent ability to resist the government's attempts to co-opt it. More recently, the complex relationship between the state and civil society and the role of NGOs in the struggle for democratization have been discussed by Sam Moyo, John Makumbe and Brian Raftopoulos (2000).

As far as the implementation of structural adjustment was concerned, it needs to be noted that during the 1980s the government had not been able to promote investments outside the agricultural sector and thus liberalization of the economy seemed to be the only way to attract (especially foreign) investment. A major weaknesses of Zimbabwe's economic policy had been the decline of gross fixed capital formation, which fell from 28 per cent in 1975 to an average of 13 per cent in 1983–86, while net investment averaged only 3.6 per cent of GNP

(Raftopoulos 1992, 64). Stoneman noted, however, that post-independence Zimbabwe had developed a coherent, successful economy and been 'surprisingly successful economically in the 1980s despite severe constraints' (1993). The situation stimulated debate over whether Zimbabwe had been forced to liberalize or whether it volunteered to introduce ESAP, whose 'homegrown' nature was frequently emphasized, especially inside Zimbabwe in the early 1990s (see Cliffe 1991; Dashwood 1996; also Bond 1998, 340). Although research from the 1980s had largely questioned the socialist direction of economic policy,[3] socialism had been an ideologically essential element of the legitimacy of the ZANU(PF) regime. ESAP not only brought this idea of socialism to an end, but also pressured the decades-old state interventionism in the various sectors of the economy. For the still-protected economy, the measures adopted proved to be too drastic. The simultaneous increase of competition in the domestic markets and increasing interest rates led to a wave of bankruptcies in Zimbabwean manufacturing industry. The findings of Jørn Rattsø and Ragnar Torvik suggest that the comparative advantages of trade liberalization for Zimbabwe are not related to advanced manufacturing production but only to raw materials, mining, agriculture and horticulture (1998). If this is the case, deindustrialization and growing unemployment are not short-term problems of the adjustment but its logical end result.

Miscalculations in ESAP seemed obvious. In spite of the full support of ESAP in the government, its implementation followed the advice of the IMF and the World Bank. Thus it was these institutions that the literature blamed. The detailed empirical research done within the Nordic Africa Institute's programme on *The Political and Social Context of Structural Adjustment in Sub-Saharan Africa* (1990–2000), led by Peter Gibbon and Adebayo Olukoshi, is particularly noteworthy. Chapters on Zimbabwe were included in all the major publications of the project and one collection edited by Gibbon (1995) was devoted to Zimbabwe alone. Two reports written by Leon Bijlmakers, Mary Bassett and David Sanders dealt with the performance of the health sector (1996 and 1998); Rodrick Mupedziswa and Perpetua Gumbo's report dealt with women informal traders (1998); Rudo Gaidzanwa's report with the migrating health sector labour (1999); and Lloyd Sachikonye's report with the fate of textile and metals industries in the country (1999). Sam Moyo argued in his book *Land Reform under Structural Adjustment in Zimbabwe* (2000) that new land use patterns and production oriented towards global markets fuelled the struggle for redistribution, changing the relations between landholders, land seekers and the government.

Local publishing houses also produced critical analysis of ESAP (see, for instance, Mlambo 1997).

But whatever the responsibility of the IMF and the World Bank in the initial introduction of ESAP, toward the later part of the 1990s the relationship between the government and these financial institutions became very difficult. The problems had already started in 1995/96, when ESAP expired and the IMF withheld disbursement of a remaining loan because of the budget deficit and delayed parastatal reforms.

The authoritarian state

Paradoxically, when the government of Zimbabwe started to lose its economic power *vis-à-vis* international financial institutions in the 1990s, it was internally more powerful than ever before measured by concentration of power and the weakness of its opposition. But it was simultaneously becoming less popular. In other words, government power was consolidated with regard to internal political opposition and divisions, but this did not prevent the deepening legitimacy crisis and state decay.

Thus it is not surprising that government repression of civil society and opposition continued. Until 1994 the government's involvement in the war in Mozambique and its fight against RENAMO (Mozambican National Resistance) had given it some excuse to repress domestic opposition especially along the Eastern border. This had reflected a similar inability to distinguish between political and armed opposition, as in Matabeleland during the 1980s, though not on the same scale. The Matabeleland era was still not addressed by the government, but continued to trouble state–society relations. It was only in 1997 that the Catholic Commission for Justice and Peace (CCJP) in Zimbabwe and the Legal Resources Foundation (LRF) published a comprehensive report of the human rights violations between 1980 and 1988 (CCJP/LRF 1997). But even then this publication was controversial. After it was handed to Mugabe and he refused to respond to it, the Catholic Bishops' Conference did not want to make the report public. Consequently the LRF decided to print and circulate it alone. Consequently the bishops, who traditionally have had close relations with Mugabe, broke their ties with LRF (*Zimbabwe Independent*, 6–12 June 1997; and 22–28 August 1997). Only after the death of Joshua Nkomo in July 1999 did the government announce that it would compensate those who suffered during the atrocities (*Moto*, August 1999, 1). A comprehensive and scholarly historical study of the Matabeleland covering government repression following independence by Jocelyn Alexander, Joanne McGregor and Terence Ranger (2000) is important to note, too.

Ronald Weitzer was one of the early authors who conducted systematic research on authoritarianism in Zimbabwe (1990). His particular emphasis was on the role of police, military and intelligence agencies in shaping political developments. He showed that the government of Zimbabwe had retained and fortified basic features of the repressive Rhodesian security apparatus, and used this apparatus to create a one-party state. By comparing Zimbabwe to Northern Ireland he concluded that thoroughgoing transformation of this security apparatus would have been an essential precondition for democracy. Much along the same lines, John Hatchard (1993) analysed the relation between individual freedoms and the repressive legislation, especially that giving the authorities emergency powers to detain people without trial introduced in 1965 a few days before UDI. Although the Zimbabwean government claimed it was keen to end the state of emergency, it was in force for a quarter of a century, until July 1990. During the first ten years of independence, the government justified it each time by pointing out the South African threat. According to Hatchard, South African destabilization in independent Zimbabwe was not a threat which could have explained the continuation of emergency powers. However, after political changes started to take place in South Africa, the Zimbabwean government ceased to renew the state of emergency.

A third important field of critical research clarifying the authoritarian power structures concerns the state in the rural areas. Norma Kriger challenged the common view that ZANU's and ZANLA's success was based on popular support among the peasants (1992). Kriger showed the coercive character of the ZANU mobilization in the rural communities, which were often split along generational lines. Michael Drinkwater (1991) analysed how government agricultural officials with their 'technocratic rationality' ignored the local knowledge of the peasants, which then created mistrust. Jocelyn Alexander (1996) argued that the reason why the new local government structures failed to become accountable to the local communities was their arbitrary nature *vis-à-vis* the traditional local organizations. But when the government changed its early policy of stripping traditional chiefs of their powers, the chiefs, in most cases, only helped in bringing the local communities under party control.

The ruling party was structured in the rural areas through centralising and strengthening its power over the local people's committees. During the liberation war, many of these committees had been created around local grievances such as land distribution. William Munro argues that, if not structured under the party hierarchy, these bodies could have continued to provide an autonomous base for putting local demands to the government (Munro 1998, 241). In the end the organization of local authorities and their relation with the ruling party became a hindrance to effective decentralization of power (Makumbe 1999). Such analyses suggested a very different rationale to that presented by Burgess, for instance (1997). It was not the small-scale farmers who were able to present their demands to the state but the government that was able to tighten its political control over the farmers by responding to their apparent needs, including delivery services, seed, fertilizer and drought relief. In this sense it was not the multi-party system that prevailed, but an authoritarian state, giving the peasants no alternative but to turn to the ruling party with their grievances or to develop survival strategies completely outside the state competence (see Mararike 1999).

Toward an understanding of the crisis

Much of the literature points to the conclusion that contradictory tendencies characterized the post-independence era in Zimbabwe. Sometimes this was explicitly stated. Christine Sylvester's book *Zimbabwe: The Terrain of Contradictory Development* (1991a) even carried the idea in its title. David Moore argued that the post-independence era was a contradictory process of constructing a hegemony for a new group of rulers (1992). Carolyn Jenkins (1997) stated that during the 1980s Zimbabwe protected existing economic interests with 'a little nationalization' and 'a little land resettlement' (see Sylvester in this collection). Implicitly these 'contradictions' outlined a dynamic system that only responded to the different challenges and pressures on it. The serious decay in the late 1990s does not fit such a picture.

However, the development of the economic crisis had been recognized early on – not least by the government itself and by its main economic advisors. Since the mid-1980s the Ministry of Finance had warned of the fragility of the economy. For instance, the government noted that after the post-independence boom, drought alone was able to drop the annual economic growth to −4.2 per cent by 1983, while in 1985 the growth rate was as much as 9.3 per cent (Government of Zimbabwe 1986b, 2). Such volatility did not facilitate long-term economic planning. Zimbabwe devalued its currency by 20 per cent in 1982 and in 1983 the government signed a standby agreement with the IMF. The World Bank studies noted the very unusual combination of a balanced current account with high public deficit and low levels of investment and growth. These studies showed that fiscal policy was pivotal to the size of deficit (see Morande and Schmidt-Hebbel 1991; 1994).

Patrick Bond's study (1998) on the interplay between the domestic financial markets and speculation helps one to understand the development of the crisis further. By looking at the tendencies of accumulation within a society where the poor majority was not able to consume and which thus provided fewer and fewer opportunities for profitable investment, Bond is able to tackle many 'contradictions' in Zimbabwe. Thus the seemingly dynamic economic opening up in 1991 with a stock market growing at a record pace was only one manifestation of the inherently unbalanced capitalist development, which had been established during minority rule and continued since then. Bond notes, however, that the policy makers could have chosen an alternative way of development. Why then was it not chosen and what are the opportunities of making a new choice now?

A simple way around this question is to look at the leader. '[T]he gifted Mugabe inherited a well-run, well-off territory. He robbed Zimbabwe of its potential', writes Robert Rotberg in *Foreign Affairs* (2000, 51). But the current leadership inherited very little: it gained power only through armed struggle. It is no wonder that critical historiography on the liberation struggle and more generally on nationalism is becoming an important part of the democratization debate in Zimbabwe (an excellent overview is given by Raftopoulos 2000). Contested notions of the liberation help one to understand why Mugabe has chosen the nationalist discourse in his attempt to protect the hegemony of the ruling party. Paradoxically nationalist discourse is needed, because the party has not been able to fulfil even its own expectations, and the difficult process of democratization is crystallized in the banal question of how long the independence regime itself believes in its leadership.

Notes

1. The author is grateful for comments given by Jeffrey Herbst and Brian Raftopoulos.
2. Independent Namibia joined in 1990. In 1992 SADCC was replaced by SADC (the Southern African Development Community), which has been joined by majority-rule South Africa and more lately also by the Democratic Republic of Congo.
3. Stoneman, who as late as 1988 interpreted the situation in the country as one 'that could eventually lead to a socialist society in line with government pronouncement', was somewhat exceptional (1988a, 4; cited in Bond 1998, 156).

2
Indigenization, the State Bourgeoisie and Neo-authoritarian Politics

Brian Raftopoulos and Daniel Compagnon[1]

Introduction

When a liberated Zimbabwe came into being in 1980, a political injustice was finally redressed with the establishment of majority rule, but not the economic and social imbalances between the white and the black communities, in particular the glaringly unequal distribution of economic capital. Very little has changed in the twenty years since independence: although the civil service was Africanized within the first five years.[2] The state gained control of a significant section of the national economy, both in the financial and productive sectors, but the private sector is still largely owned by the 70 000 white Zimbabweans (out of 12 million citizens) or by international companies such as Lonrho and the Anglo-American Corporation. Indeed, whites are preponderant among the 4000 commercial farmers and largely dominate the manufacturing and mining sectors. However, there are no statistics for the racial composition of local company ownership, and since independence many blacks – including ruling party cadres – were co-opted into business by sections of white capital.[3] However, figures from the early 1990s show that 63 per cent of senior management in the corporate sector are still white (Strachan 1993, 41).[4]

Today's racial imbalances are, for the most part, a legacy of colonialism. They have been nurtured by successive policies biased against the indigenous inhabitants of the country. Discrimination commenced with the founding of the British South Africa Company in 1889, and the subsequent land-grabbing it legitimized. This trend endured until the end of the segregationist policies of Ian Smith's illegal regime. The colonial power had stimulated the formation of a white settler bourgeoisie with its agrarian and urban components having strong connections with British and South African industrial and banking capital (Bond 1998). Throughout the

1960s and 70s, the white minority regime prevented blacks from entering certain professions and trading in the areas reserved for Europeans. There was also limited access to finance, since the white-controlled banking sector was reluctant to lend money to black entrepreneurs. These restrictions frustrated the African petty bourgeoisie's economic aspirations.

Under colonial rule, therefore, the vast majority of the black people of Zimbabwe were socially marginalized and economically impoverished. They were denied equal access to social services – especially in health care and education. Until the mid-1950s, there was very limited access to secondary and tertiary education. For a handful of black students, access to higher and tertiary education was obtainable in South Africa until the University College of South Rhodesia opened in 1957. Thus, in the early 1960s, the significant minority of educated blacks who entered the formal labour market did so in a subordinate position, as teachers, clerks, and so on. They formed the core of the nationalist movement's cadre. At the same time, petty trade and transport in the African townships and the rural Tribal Trust Lands (TTLs) offered some opportunities for upward mobility to a small group of black entrepreneurs. Thus, during the last decades of white rule, a small indigenous business class was in a formative stage and provided some financial support for the nationalist parties led by the more educated among the African petty bourgeoisie.

One might therefore have expected that when independence from colonial rule was achieved, the black, nationalist government would hasten to adopt a proactive strategy of black empowerment in the economy, providing support and encouragement in priority to the existing black entrepreneurs. This chapter will examine why this did not take place in the 1980s, and then focus on the indigenization discourse and lobbying efforts in the 1990s. It will attempt to explain how indigenization became subject to political manipulation from the ruling party's leaders. Finally, it will be suggested that the lack of an effective indigenization policy served and continues to serve the interests of the ruling class or aspirant 'state bourgeoisie',[5] whose members perceive authentic indigenous businessmen as a threat to their economic as well as political ambitions.

The lack of a pro-active strategy of Black empowerment in the 1980s

The fact that there has been no dramatic change in the distribution of economic capital since ZANU(PF) assumed power in 1980 is often attributed to the Lancaster House agreement, which legally entrenched the property rights of the white minority, especially in agriculture. White settlers and their British protectors feared that because ZANU's political mobilization during the war was based on black peasants' hunger for land (Kriger 1992, Ranger 1985a), its government would confiscate settlers' properties. As a matter of fact, such a policy would have been generally understood if not unanimously accepted at the onset of majority rule. However, ten years later, it was perceived as illegitimate, and the Land Acquisition Act (1992) authorizing the designation of commercial farms without proper compensation was widely seen as a violation of Human Rights and a threat to the whole economy.[6] This perception was solidified with the rejection from many quarters, including the majority of the electorate in the February 2000 referendum, of the compulsory acquisition of land as a provision of the government's constitutional draft. After that the violence associated with farm invasions did nothing to improve the government policy's image.

Yet, constraints imposed by the Lancaster House agreement provided a convenient excuse for a highly symbolic but practically limited programme of land appropriation and resettlement, which represented a token response to popular expectations in the former TTLs. The fact that the government could buy land only at the market price from willing sellers was certainly an impediment and, by 1996, only 71 000 families had been resettled (Adams *et al.* 1996, 7). But legal and financial constraints do not account for all policy shortcomings, in particular the government's inability to provide enabling conditions for resettlement operations to succeed as crucial factors were overlooked (Herbst 1990, 37–62; Palmer 1990; Herbst 1992; Moyo 1995; Maposa 1995). In addition, resettlement procedures ignored the modest but vibrant black small-scale farming sector, which should have been supported and strengthened to help blacks penetrate the large commercial farms but were excluded from land distribution. Indeed, the rationale of the resettlement policy was not the promotion of a genuine economic empowerment agenda, but rather the consolidation of ZANU(PF)'s political power-base in the rural areas. Later on it provided a smoke-screen for land-grabbing by powerful politicians, army generals and state officials.

Beyond Lancaster House's constitutional constraints, Mugabe had good reason to compromise on white capital – foreign and local – instead of adopting a confrontational attitude. His most publicized 'reconciliation policy' was partly driven by a sense of 'economic realism', that is his understanding that Zimbabwe suffered from a double dependence, i.e. on world markets of minerals and agricultural products (especially tobacco) on the one hand, and on external industrial and banking capital on the other. Warned by the then Mozambican president Samora Machel about the adverse economic impact of the white exodus experienced by his country in 1975, Mugabe managed to convince most white civil servants and entrepreneurs to stay in Zimbabwe by pledging to pay pensions and to build a non-racial society. The fundamental flaw in this clever tactical move – that is the contradiction between his then socialist/statist stance and white private business interests – was partly obliterated by rhetorical contortions.

However, at that time Mugabe was primarily concerned with imposing his complete hegemony on the polity and getting rid of political competition within the nationalist camp – a potential impediment to the establishment of a one-party state. Therefore he carefully planned the political elimination of PF-ZAPU, whose leaders were arrested or forced to flee in 1982, being accused of plotting Mugabe's downfall on the basis of a perceived threat to the new state both at a national and regional level. Massive and deliberate killings in Matabeleland and the Midlands between 1982 and 1985 were meant to destroy ZAPU's political base once and for all (CCJP/LRF 1997). Joshua Nkomo, PF-ZAPU's leader, whose seniority in the nationalist struggle and his backing by the USSR and the OAU made him, still then, a potential challenger to Mugabe, went into exile.

In this context, Mugabe's rather lenient attitude towards local whites and the safeguarding of their economic interests under the guise of 'reconciliation' not only attracted support from various countries and donor agencies, but gave him a free hand in Matabeleland as US and British intelligence services looked the other way. The Western powers welcomed 'reconciliation' as a departure from Mugabe's rigid communist/nationalist leanings – his image in the Western press before 1979 – and they perceived him as a stabilizing factor in the region (after all, his proclaimed hostility to apartheid had not been followed by an aggressive military policy against his neighbour). Some disputable domestic policies could be tolerated as long as he stuck to the Lancaster House provisions.

Moreover, Mugabe's 'reconciliation' policy divided the shrinking white community into those who were prepared to collaborate fully and supported the Cabinet in Parliament and the unrepentant Rhodesian Front conservatives. Hence, by 1987, when Nkomo's PF-ZAPU was forcefully merged into a 'united' ZANU(PF), ostensibly paving the way for the one-party state, the white minority had lost its political privileges formerly entrenched in the constitution and had ceased to play a significant role in national politics. The prospect of an alliance between white politicians and PF-ZAPU to form a credible opposition to ZANU(PF) was more remote than ever.

Through the years, an implicit co-operation – both political and economical – developed between the Zimbabwe state and white economic capital, what Taylor calls the 'alliance between white settlers and the state' (Taylor 1999, 244). It was rather an 'historical compromise' reached by black nationalists in the government and sections of the white economic establishment. It stemmed from political expediency as noted above but evolved into numerous business links between members of the embryonic state bourgeoisie and the white corporate sector. Many former civil servants and ZANU(PF)'s political clients were recruited during the 1980s as middlemen for white-owned corporations at a time when political connections had become vital to operate a business,[7] and were later co-opted as junior partners in the same companies.

Through the state control of various economic sectors, opportunities were created for members of the ruling class to enrich themselves and position themselves for co-option. A large body of parastatals regulated the trade of commodities (grain, beef, dairy products, etc.), and ZANU(PF)'s government seized control of various industrial and financial conglomerates at every opportunity,[8] using various techniques to persuade British or South African companies to sell the shares of their local subsidiaries to the government. Currency regulations were enforced to prevent the repatriation of profits by foreign-owned companies, wage and pricing policies were used to squeeze foreign investors who could not run their businesses profitably,[9] drastic fiscal policies discouraged foreign investment (Robertson 1992, 71, 72; Wild 1997, 260). The point that many of these regulations were originally introduced by Smith's regime after his UDI made open resistance from white capital politically risky.

A paradoxical situation developed: despite prevalent socialist rhetoric, Zimbabwe's mixed economy remained dependent on white-controlled market forces, while parastatals were run – inefficiently – according to bureaucratic principles. However, for the new power elite, the long-term socialist transformation of the economy was no longer the primary aim of state control: the bloated public sector was, above anything else, a valuable resource for Mugabe's political patronage, as it offered a good number of lucrative positions for party cadres, political cronies and family members. Those 'who had sacrificed for the struggle', so they said, thought that they deserved some rewards and should be the first to benefit from black empowerment, which was not, at this stage, called 'indigenization'. However, as the upsurge of the War Veterans' movement in 1996–97 revealed, benefits from patronage were not equitably distributed among former 'freedom fighters'. Moreover, many vocal indigenization activists have no war record at all.[10]

Rhetorical socialism also led to the condemnation of the existing 'black bourgeoisie', that is the small group of pre-independence African entrepreneurs. The nationalist leaders had no particular sympathy for the blacks who ran successful businesses – however modest – while the former were in exile or fighting 'in the bush'. Moreover, the nationalist's own project to capture the economy through state control was inherently antagonist to the entrepreneurial ethos of the black businesspeople. The latter's practice of market economy was indeed closer to nineteenth-century capitalism – no trade unions, no minimum wages and no labour laws – than to even a diluted form of socialism. In other words, the populist-oriented labour policies of the first half of the 1980s did nothing to bring together the two sections of the black elite (Wild 1997, 258). Government also feared that an autonomous black private sector would provide alternative power-bases (Raftopoulos 1992). As a result, the publicized policy of promoting small- and medium-scale black businesses through the Small Enterprise Development Corporation (SEDCO) was at best half-hearted (Wild 1997, 259).

However, by the end of the first decade of ZANU(PF)'s regime, the failure of the statist/command economy system became obvious. First of all, the recurrent mismanagement of the parastatals, and to a lesser extent of an over-sized bureaucracy, increased budget deficits and the public debt. Secondly, state control over the economy was self-defeating in view of Zimbabwe's dependence on external markets when, for example, the scarcity of spare parts strangled the export-led commercial agriculture and mining sector. Finally, private investment dried up and the state was not in a position to sustain its investment effort at the level of the early 1980s, despite the contribution of foreign aid. Therefore unemployment began to rise when the state bureaucracy could no longer absorb new generations of university and school graduates and various businesses had to retrench workers.

The launch of the IMF-inspired economic structural adjustment programme (ESAP) in 1991 sanctioned these fundamental faults of the original economic strategy, subsequently abandoned by the govern-ment. Nevertheless, the command economy had facilitated the emergence from within the new black ruling elite of a state bourgeoisie whose appetite for capital accumulation had been exacerbated rather than quenched by a decade of privileged access – through the state – to various resources.[11] This aspirant class adjusted itself quickly to the drastic changes in economic conditions and espoused liberalization and privatization as a means to pursue its drive for capital accumulation during the following decade.

The manipulation of the indigenization debate and survival politics in the 1990s

The indefinite postponement of the establishment of a one-party state, the implicit abandonment of socialism, both as an ideal and as a devel-opment strategy, and the concomitant adoption of the IMF/World Bank agenda on the liberalization of trade, deregulation and privatization of loss-making parastatals created a serious crisis of legitimacy for Mugabe's regime in the early 1990s. In this context, the indigenization thrust was to serve as an important theme of the renewed populist rhet-oric, as the would-be political ideology to keep a discredited ZANU(PF) leadership in power until the year 2000 (Wetherell 1994). From then on the ruling elite supported indigenization for its promising short-term rewards, both political and financial, and not as a long-term develop-ment strategy. This narrow-minded utilitarian agenda was bound to conflict with genuine indigenous businessmen's aspirations.

When originally approached by a group of black entrepreneurs as early as 1988, Mugabe jumped at the idea to act as an official godfather to the creation of the Indigenous Business Development Centre (IBDC) in 1990. The short history of the IBDC is widely known although limited data is available (Raftopoulos 1996 and 1999; Taylor 1999), but its most fascinating dimension is the sudden decline of IBDC after a leadership conflict emerged within the organization in 1994. Although such a conflict was to be expected in any organization growing in membership and influence, the way it was resolved (through a High Court ruling in 1996), the fact that it was perceived – correctly or not – as ethnically polarized, leading the late Joshua Nkomo to support Chemist Siziba's faction publicly, and the amount of abuse exchanged in public meetings or through government press reports suggest that there was more to it than the usual wrangling between rival ambitions. Enoch Kamushinda, who had been appointed secretary-general of the organization in April 1993 when Strive Masiyiwa resigned, apparently engineered this leadership struggle from within the IBDC board.

It seems obvious that the confrontation was precipitated if not entirely created, behind the scenes, by some high-ranking politicians in ZANU(PF) – Kamushinda apparently had close links with Mugabe and his aides. Indeed, the stimulation of factionalism is one of Mugabe's preferred techniques of control both within the ruling party and towards the civil society, as experienced by trade unions, student unions and various NGOs in the past (Nordlund 1996, 179–205; Mitchell 1997). Ruling party leaders could not tolerate an independent and increasingly popular IBDC mobilizing part of ZANU's political base – the African petty bourgeoisie – on a theme that had become the core of Mugabe's political stance. However, other factors fuelling the leadership conflict might have been IBDC's ability to attract funding from foreign donor agencies, hence its potential central role in accessing financial resources, and the perception that IBDC was a channel for political appointment within the power structure (Raftopoulos 1999, 12).[12]

Besides, as Taylor points out, the original IBDC had a vision of indigenization distinct from the aggressive and narrowly anti-white approach of many ZANU(PF) leaders: IBDC founders were more concerned with fighting unemployment by increasing the size of the economic pie through the creation of new black businesses than with taking over existing companies owned by whites (Taylor 1999, 249, 250).[13] Conversely, the state bourgeoisie was more interested in making easy money by seizing corporate properties in the name of indigenization, as it had done previously with some commercial farms. While IBDC's original emphasis was on policy measures to support small-and medium-scale African entrepreneurs in the informal sector (IBDC 1993) – a preoccupation it shared with the international donor community – the 'political businessmen'[14] were more interested in acquiring equities in large companies, foreign or local.[15]

While the divisive effects of factionalism began to weaken the IBDC, another indigenization lobby, the Affirmative Action Group (AAG), led by Philip Chiyangwa who was a close associate and a relative of Mugabe, emerged in July 1994.[16] AAG adopted from the onset an aggressive nationalist and anti-white rhetoric, reminiscent of ZANU's anti-imperialist stance of the 1970s mixed with indirect references to the Black Power Movement in the United States (Raftopoulos 1999, 14). AAG's vocal press campaigns and its blackmail tactics against

white-owned companies to force them to open their leadership structure or shareholding to members of the indigenization lobby irrevoca-
bly shifted the agenda of indigenization. The competition prompted
the alignment of what remained of the IBDC on the same polemical
line of discourse, which served Mugabe's political agenda rather than
the indigenous businesspeople's true interests. With the new wave of
politically connected leaders and the creation of satellite organizations
such as the Indigenous Business Women's Organization, the War
Veterans Association, the Small-scale Miners Association and later the
Indigenous Commercial Farmers Union, the indigenization lobby
forfeited all its autonomy to become the extension of certain factions
within the ruling party.

As a matter of fact, the net result of the indigenization lobbyists'
activities has been very limited. Most policy recommendations formulated as early as 1991 (Raftopoulos 1999, 10), especially access to cheap
finance for black entrepreneurs, were never properly implemented.
Although some funds were earmarked for indigenous emergent businesses from both government and international donors – notably the
African Development Bank and the World Bank – and the share of this
sector in the total credit dispensation rose slightly from 1993 to 1995,
these loans were processed through the established financial institutions (the IBDC and AAG demanded to play this role and vet applications, but to no avail). There was a predictable adverse impact on
black-owned businesses, since 'the status quo in the banking sector has
for the most part been retained, with small businesses having to face
conservative bank conditionalities, and, especially during the ESAP
period, exorbitant interests rates' (Raftopoulos 1999, 16).[17] Bureaucracy
impeded the disbursement of earmarked funds and the lack of transparency in the process suggests that some of these funds might have
been abused by the political clients of ZANU(PF)'s 'big men'. Therefore
there has been no serious attempt on the part of Mugabe's government
to implement a coherent indigenization policy,[18] beyond vague
programmatic statements, and despite all the rhetoric and the creation
of a Cabinet task force and later a position of Minister of State for
indigenization.[19] Heavy political pressure on foreign-owned companies
such as Lonrho and Anglo-American to localize their shareholding
through government-sanctioned deals achieved little for black entrepreneurs, but was a serious disincentive for foreign investors.

The manner in which the protracted programme of privatization
(limited in scope because Mugabe remains reluctant to part with such
sources of benefices and sinecures) was conducted by the government,

whose main concern was to raise as much money as possible in order to reduce the state budget deficit (Godana and Hlatswayo 1997, 29), is another testimony of its ingrained indifference to the demands of the indigenous entrepreneurs. Indeed, indigenous businesspeople were *de facto* left out of the sale of shares on the stock exchange market of Delta Corporation and Astra Corporation, and they were excluded as well from the attempted privatization of Hwange power station in 1996. The latter deal generated an outcry from the AAG, IBDC and public opinion,[20] since it was perceived as a betrayal of the indigenization policy and of the national economic interest. In particular, the price allegedly paid by the Malaysian Y.T.L Berhad to acquire a 5 per cent equity in the joint venture formed with the Zimbabwe Electricity Supply Authority (ZESA) was said to be far below the real value of the assets. Needless to say, the government's promise to credit all proceeds of privatization to the National Investment Trust (NIT), a public financial institution set up in 1996 – with a paltry Z$200 million capital – as a warehousing mechanism (that is withholding shares of localized or privatized companies until indigenous businessmen could repay them), was not fulfilled (Raftopoulos 1999, 18).

Besides, in Mugabe's view indigenization was above all a useful propaganda theme in the 1990s: claims that government's indigenization policy was blocked by some 'Rhodies', in other words white economic interests, featured prominently in the 1995 and 1996 electoral campaigns (Darnolf 1997; Makumbe and Compagnon 2000). By using the classical scapegoat tactic, Mugabe wanted to evade his own responsibility in the economic mismanagement and in the reversed trends of health and education services development in Zimbabwe since the late 1980s. Thus his political discourse instrumentalized the historical – political *vs* structural – economic cleavage between white and black Zimbabweans, in order to mobilize the rural and urban poor in favour of the ruling party, while downplaying increasing class differences within the black majority itself. Attributing all economic hurdles to the whites (and white-controlled institutions such as the IMF and the World Bank), such a discourse opportunely diverted the mounting criticisms of Mugabe's own policy blunders coming from the black indigenization lobby, the trade unions and numerous NGOs. Thus Mugabe was able to capitalize on the cry for indigenization in his electoral campaigns. By so doing, he succeeded brilliantly in transforming a direct challenge to his authority into a valuable political resource.

This ploy gained some momentum in 1994–95. By that time, the IBDC had become so popular that the press was full of reports on the indigenization debate, with cabinet ministers subjected to severe public criticisms for their apathy and their weak policy proposals. Simultaneously, some backbenchers vocally relayed these criticisms in Parliament, quite often linking the need for indigenization to the disastrous social impact of the ESAP.[21] ZANU(PF)'s leadership had to overcome the potential of political destabilization contained in that somewhat unexpected and sudden movement of opinion. The subjugation and control of the indigenous lobbies was not enough; there was also a need to hijack the indigenization discourse and to fine-tune it with the group interests of the ruling class.

Capital accumulation and intra-elite competition

Mugabe was less interested in promoting a broad-based indigenization project than in expanding 'crony capitalism', which serves the particularistic interest of his extended family and the families of his political allies and clients.[22] This notion of crony capitalism was first applied to Mahathir Muhammad's policy of indigenization and economic development in Malaysia, which favoured rent-seekers belonging to the clientele of the ruler rather than real entrepreneurs (Searle 1999). Indeed, the many similarities between the two neo-authoritarian regimes – in spite of the different development stages – might explain why the 'Malay model' of indigenization became so fashionable among Zimbabwean leaders, as argued elsewhere (Compagnon 1999).

For Mugabe, indigenization is a means to retain control over the polity through patronage, and arbitrate between the rival clientele networks of his long-time associates of the Politburo through the division of spoils. A case in point is his refusal to endorse Solomon Mujuru's bid on the Zimbabwe Mining and Smelting Company (ZIMASCO) in early 1997.[23] Therefore, in the post-ESAP era, business opportunities largely play, as rewards for political loyalty, the same role that lucrative positions in the parastatals and bureaucratic bribes played in the 1980s. But this must be a comprehensive control: no sector, market or lucrative opportunity which is in the realm or the reach of government – directly or through specific regulations – should be exploited outside the patronage system, even when it comes from a genuine indigenous entrepreneur.[24]

The 'cellular phone saga', as dubbed by the press, is a case in point. Mugabe and some of his close associates in the Politburo tried everything they could to prevent Strive Masiyiwa from succeeding – including repeated threats to his life and blackmailing his company's clients during the All Africa Games in 1995 in order to bankrupt him. Although Masiyiwa was a former PTC engineer and a founding member of the IBDC,[25] he had challenged the ruling elite and the President himself. It began with his criticisms of the government's economic policy as early as 1992; it went on with his challenge of the PTC monopoly in the courts.[26] More importantly, he incurred the government's wrath with his refusal to grant some Politburo members free shares in Econet, the company he had created to operate a cellular phone network. This was an open breach of the rule of the game: everything is possible if you invite the 'big men' to be 'partners' in the deal (that is they do nothing other than to provide some kind of political protection in exchange for a share of the profits).[27] It has become an institutionalized form of bribery, which goes far beyond the amateur corruption of the 1980s.

Masiyiwa did not want to play the tune because of his 'born-again' Christian strict moral principles – as he claims – but also because, like many young Zimbabwean executives of his age group, he believes in market competition and global capitalism (as opposed to a state-centred nation-bound economy). The fact that he survived his ordeal against all odds can be ascribed to several factors. First, his determination never flagged and his business acumen is remarkable: Econet Wireless, launched in July 1998 and listed three months later, is the largest cellular company in Zimbabwe and the fifth largest in Africa in terms of subscriber numbers and market capitalization, and it generated profits after only one year in operation. Secondly, Masiyiwa received some support from many friends both in business and in politics, including the late Joshua Nkomo who tried to plead Strive's case before Mugabe. The young businessman inherited good political connections through his parents, who were PF-ZAPU members during the liberation struggle, and had good contacts also within ZANU(PF)'s leadership. Thirdly, his cause was taken up by civil society and human rights activists and his court cases got good coverage in the international press. He also enjoyed some support among resident foreign diplomats. With all the publicity, it would have been politically damaging for Mugabe to suppress him. Lastly, there are significant remnants of the independence of the Judiciary in Zimbabwe and Masiyiwa won his successive legal battles in the courts.

Mugabe and other Politburo members, sometimes supporting conflicting interests (that is either their own extended family interests or the economic interests of competing political factions within the ruling party), grant some privileges to political businessmen closely related to them or clever enough to invite them, or some family members acting as straw men, as partners in their businesses. Privileges include preferential access to public funds (including state guarantee for bank loans) and foreign currency,[28] exclusive state procurement contracts, and flouted tender procedures as illustrated by the new Harare International Airport and the Hwange power plant tenders, at the expense of the national interest and public finances.[29] Many of these political businessmen began with little cash and no assets at all and became rich after only a few years, thanks to Mugabe's patronage. However, their position remains inherently weak, not only because their business skills are sometimes questionable,[30] but also because the conservation of their wealth and social status depends on the preservation of these political connections. Hence their desire to acquire equities in large and established businesses, to guarantee their social and economic reproduction once Mugabe's regime is gone.

Other crony businessmen were not political clients from the onset, since they had an independent economic base long before the indigenization crusade was launched, even before independence in the case of Roger Boka. However, the economic liberalization and Mugabe's patronage gave Boka's business ventures a tremendous boost. Political protection at the highest level saved him from public scrutiny in various shoddy deals. His method was to hide his real activities behind a smokescreen of colourful anti-white propaganda, with aggressive advertising in the government-owned press. For example, when buying gold from black gold panning workers, he would claim that he was protecting them in this way from the greed of white-owned companies, but he was once publicly accused of buying stolen gold.

Moreover, it later emerged that Boka's Merchant Bank and his oversized and loss-making Tobacco Auction Floor were built on a pyramid of loans granted to him by government-owned banks and financial institutions, or by his own companies one to each other, with limited assets for collateral or as tangible guarantees. Clearly, without political protection Boka would never have been able to muster the resources to expand his business empire so quickly or to obtain a banking licence without the proper qualifications.[31] He secured the support of the ruling class by granting generous loans to various ZANU(PF) politicians under the guise of indigenization. But this political-minded profligacy increased the mountain of his debts. To avoid insolvency, Boka resorted to forgery and sold Z$1 billion of fake commercial paper in the name of the government-owned Cold Storage Company, and at the same time illegally transferred US$21 million to an offshore bank account (*Financial Gazette*, 19 November 1998).

When the Reserve Bank governor reported this fraud in April 1998, Boka was declared a specified person and had no other option than to avoid prosecution by fleeing abroad (without serious police efforts to stop him), while his businesses were liquidated to pay creditors. Significantly, when the ailing businessman was repatriated and died upon his arrival in November 1998, several Cabinet ministers and high-level ZANU(PF) officials attended his funeral. Moreover, AAG and IBDC sycophants called him a hero in press statements, despite the fact that the Universal Merchant Bank demise had plunged Zimbabwe's financial sector into deep crisis. This was eventually overcome by the Treasury, thanks to taxpayers' money. Police investigations later revealed that a good number of ministers, political businessmen or high-ranking ZANU(PF) officials owed Boka's bank millions of dollars, but the complete list of names remains a best-kept state secret.

Therefore, segments of the parasitic state bourgeoisie succeeded in pre-empting opportunities offered by the liberalization and deregulation of the 1990s at the expense of existing black entrepreneurs – some of whom are heirs of pre-independence dynasties – thus giving birth to potential intra-class conflict.[32] Unfortunately, crony or rent-seeking capitalism amounts frequently to inefficiency and capital waste: businesses are not sustainable, employment created is short-lived and embezzled public funds evaporate or are smuggled out of the country and find their way to some hard currency accounts abroad. The respective sagas of Boka and Masiyiwa sketched above illustrate these qualitative differences between two kinds of indigenous capitalism.

Ultimately, Mugabe will always support the first type and will fight the second, not only for affective[33] or self-centred reasons – though the Leo Mugabes and the Chiyangwas serve his family interests and also fill his own coffers – but primarily for political reasons: the transformation of the ruling party into a coalition of political businessmen, who are bitter rivals but are united against perceived common enemies (whites, gays, foreigners, opposition parties, human rights activists, independent press and genuine black entrepreneurs), implies that their demands must be met for Mugabe to stay in power. As long as Mugabe can keep ZANU(PF) united – not as a political organization but as a clientele and a kind of crime syndicate – so he believes, nobody will kick him out of office or force him to accept major reforms to curb his extensive powers. In fact, he does not have too many options, since the collective control of ZANU(PF)'s apparatus on the state – for example, through the manipulation of the electoral process (Makumbe and Compagnon 2000; Laakso 1999 and 2002) – is his only chance of political survival in the twenty-first century. His stunning defeat in the constitutional referendum held in February 2000 and his narrow victory in the parliamentary elections in the following June demonstrated that even cheap politicking with racist overtones will not counterbalance a vanishing popularity.

Concluding notes

Indigenization as practised by Mugabe and his associates is not in contradiction to the neopatrimonial tendencies already at work – though not so blatant – in the 1980s. On the contrary, it is the continuation of these trends in a new international environment dominated by the IMF and World Bank's neoliberal orthodoxy, with its paraphernalia of deregulation and privatization. It reflects also a post-Cold War context with no 'elder brother' to offer military protection, provide diplomatic support and finance your state-controlled economy – even China plays the capitalistic card nowadays. One phenomenon summarizes this continuity: patronage and kinship connections which were on the rise during the 1980s, as a means for Mugabe to ensure political loyalty, remain the main channels of dispensation of wealth and opportunities in the neoliberal era.[34]

On the most superficial level of analysis, as we hinted above, indigenization is a political propaganda tool for a regime whose historical legitimacy is largely eroded. But at a deeper level, indigenization is both a methodology and a pretext to allow the emerging state bourgeoisie to further enrich itself and perpetuate its political and social hegemony. This confiscating of the theme to promote particularistic interests, instead of using it as a development tool against poverty and unemployment, confirms that indigenization in Zimbabwe is not about social justice, but about a narrowly defined deracialization of economic capital. Opposition parties fighting Mugabe's regime are still to formulate a coherent programme of genuine black economic empowerment to provide an alternative to the current political manipulation of an otherwise legitimate goal.

One of the most significant outcomes of the failure of the indigenization programme to develop a broad basis has been the land occupations that have taken place since March 2000. These occupations, led by the presidency and the war veteran's movement, have effectively eclipsed the indigenization movement of the 1990s, and combine a popular demand for land reform, with the political control and repression of opposition politics. The debate on indigenization has thus moved on to the central issue of the land question, encapsulated in the ZANU(PF) election slogan, 'The land is the economy, the economy is the land.'

Notes

1. Daniel Compagnon's field trip to Zimbabwe in July–August 1999 was funded by the French Institute in Johannesburg and the Université Antilles–Guyane. (Editors' note: this chapter was written by the authors in December of 1999.)
2. In 1980, blacks occupied only 32 per cent of the positions in the civil service, but they were 88 per cent in 1984 and 78 per cent of the high-ranking positions, including all permanent secretaries (Government of Zimbabwe 1985, 16, 17).
3. A good example is the old and strong connection between Bill Rautenbach and the former Minister of Justice Emmerson Mnangagwa. Rautenbach owns an international transport and car-sales company, Wheels of Africa, which has been a business partner of ZANU(PF) for years. More recently, Rautenbach was appointed general manager of RDC public company Gécamines by President Kabila on the recommendation of Mnangagwa directly and of Mugabe through a member of his family (see *Africa Confidential*, 23 October 1998 and 14 May 1999; *Wall Street Journal*, 9 October 1998). However, he was later demoted by Kabila.
4. However, blacks dominated the middle-grade level (66 per cent) and Strachan noted that among the new recruits appointed between 1986 and 1988, 60 per cent were black at senior level and 85 per cent at middle level. According to the author, black advancement in managerial positions is taking place partly because the number of qualified young whites available on the labour market is fast declining (Strachan 1993, 41).
5. A convenient definition of which is provided by Sandbrook (1985, 72): 'We are designating as the ruling class a political elite which aspires to become a bourgeoisie. But this aspiration itself connotes little more than an opportunistic exploitation of 'insider' privileges . . . not the development of the classic risk-taking entrepreneurial behaviour'.
6. On this debate, see Maposa (1995); Moyo (1995). The impact of the current 'fast track' resettlement programme on the economy will certainly be dramatic, though it is difficult to predict all its side effects.
7. Middlemen with no particular business acumen but good connections in the state apparatus would obtain an import licence or a foreign currency permit from corrupt civil servants, and sell them at twice or three times their nominal value to genuine entrepreneurs struggling to operate in an economic environment ridden with all sorts of regulations. James Makamba, a former Lonrho employee and a middleman in various deals in the 1980s (for example the purchase of an aircraft by Air Zimbabwe), became a prominent indigenization activist in the 1990s, an MP for Mount Darwin, a front for Solomon Mujuru's business ventures, and later a business associate of Mugabe's family. He is the likely ZANU(PF) candidate for Harare's next mayoral election.
8. For a list of government-owned companies see Bloch (1994); Wetherell (1993).
9. A good case in point is the fate of Lancaster Steel, formerly a subsidiary of British Steel, which relied on the parastatal Zimbabwe Iron and Steel Company (ZISCO) for its supply of crude steel. The government exerted pressure by fixing the price at which Lancaster bought from ZISCO and the price at which it could sell its own products, and by enforcing workers' wage increases. Soon Lancaster Steel ran into a huge loss and British Steel had no

other choice but to sell it at a low price to the state; then Lancaster Steel was merged with ZISCO (interview with independent economist John Robertson, Harare, 23 August 1999).

10. Philip Chiyangwa, Peter Pamire, Roger Boka, etc. Some others were 'sell-outs': for instance James Makamba worked for the Rhodesian government radio during the war.

11. This scenario is not peculiar to Zimbabwe in Africa (see Sandbrook 1985, chap. 4).

12. Indeed, in the 1995 Cabinet reshuffle, two IBDC members were appointed to deputy ministerial positions. Chiyengwa also made it very clear that he harboured political ambitions (see the *Zimbabwe Independent*, 28 June 1996). He was eventually elected an MP in Chinoyi in June 2000 through alleged vote-buying and intimidation.

13. According to Masiyiwa, some white businessmen supported the IBDC financially at its inception, because of its moderate and business-minded approach. Ironically, 'indigenization', as opposed to 'black empowerment' or 'Africanization', was chosen by IBDC founders to avoid racist connotations (interview with Strive Masiyiwa, Harare, 24 August 1999).

14. These are members of the indigenization lobby who rely on their connections with the inner power circle to obtain various privileges while conducting business and also to bypass competitors (interview with Strive Masiyiwa, Harare, 24 August 1999).

15. Understandably, ZCTU criticized the selfish predatory ambitions of the indigenization lobby (ZCTU 1995, 13).

16. With no known business experience prior to independence, Chiyengwa allegedly began his career in 1982 as a 'commodity broker' – that is a middleman of the kind mentioned above (the *Zimbabwe Independent*, 28 June 1996). However, he became famous in only the late 1980s as a music entertainment entrepreneur and expanded into various businesses during the 1990s. He chaired with the late Peter Pamire (his associate in AAG) the organizing committee of Mugabe's wedding in August 1996, and was a member with Ben Mucheche, Pamire and Enoch Kamushinda of the fund-raising committee of the ruling party for the 1995 and 1996 campaigns. Chiyengwa is said to work closely now with Rautenbach to oversee the extended family's economic interests in DRC.

17. The situation worsened in the late 1990s because of Mugabe's irresponsible policies. With the accelerated decline of the economy, high inflation and increased state borrowing on the money market, interest rates skyrocketed to levels unknown before.

18. However, local government is required by law to subcontract 30 per cent of all construction work, and 100 per cent of tender under Z$3 million, to indigenous entrepreneurs (Wild 1997, 271). This development lead to increased corruption at this level, as illustrated by the case of the Harare City Council.

19. Cephas Msipa, being a former ZAPU member, is a political lightweight. As a minister of state (1995–2000) without real power – not even a proper department administration – he was carrying out basically a window-dressing exercise. He was not included in the Africa Resources Investments, a committee headed by Mnangagwa and set up in 1997 by Mugabe to undertake negotiations with foreign-owned companies over indigenization mechanisms.

20. The deal was criticized by the board of ZESA, left out of the negotiations with the Malaysians, in breach of the Electricity Act. Subsequently the entire ZESA board was dismissed by Mugabe. On the Hwange deal, see the *Zimbabwe Independent*, 4, 11 and 18 October 1996; the *Financial Gazette*, 10 and 17 October 1996.
21. A Select Committee on the Indigenization of the National Economy was established in Parliament in April 1991 and provided a forum for such criticisms, which, however, was largely ineffective.
22. As in other parts of sub-Saharan Africa, the importance of family networks and kinship ties in the social life of the Shona peoples is underlined by social scientists (see Bourdillon 1991). However, its impact on post-colonial Zimbabwe has been largely downplayed by academic literature which construes 'tribalism' as a colonial-invented evil.
23. Although Mujuru's manoeuvre to secure at a discount price a 27 per cent equity in the company, as part of a plan to localize 50 per cent of the latter's capital, fulfilled the objective of indigenization, Mugabe was incensed by the *fait accompli* and dubbed the deal 'a fraud'. The government had been negotiating for months with the management of ZIMASCO, a subsidiary of Union Carbide bought in 1994 by some white members of its management through an offshore company. Eventually Mugabe forced the retired general to back off from the deal but the government has failed to date to obtain a controlling share in ZIMASCO (see *Financial Gazette*, 29 May, 5 June and 30 November 1997; *Zimbabwe Independent*, 3 December 1999).
24. Masiyiwa's harassment by the CIO began long before the cellular phone quarrel, when he tried to process an IFC loan for emergent businessmen through the Reserve Bank and the Ministry of Finance. He was accused of being in cahoots with foreign countries' intelligence since he had obtained that loan without using his political connections (interview with Masiyiwa, Harare, 24 August 1999). These methods echo the pressure exerted by CIO officers on bank managers to prevent them from lending money to opposition politicians running businesses, as in the case of Enoch Dumbutshena after the 1995 elections. As a result of this ban his farm was auctioned (interview with Dumbutshena, Harare, 5 August 1999).
25. Though not a member of the ruling party, Masiyiwa was a successful emergent entrepreneur (Businessman of the Year in 1990) and far from being estranged from, or hostile to, the government. His first company Retrofit received numerous government orders in the late 1980s (including at Mugabe's rural estate in Zvimba).
26. In 1995 the Supreme Court ruled that the government monopoly over telecommunications violated the freedom of expression as guaranteed by the constitution. Masiyiwa was entitled to run a cellular phone service. However, the President then used his emergency powers to oblige operators to secure a licence from the parastatal Posts and Telecommunications Corporation (PTC). The first licence was granted to PTC itself in a joint venture with the German company Siemens. In 1997, the tender for the second cellular phone network was flouted, on direct instructions from the President's Office, in favour of a consortium of political businessmen led by Leo Mugabe and James Makamba, the latter being very close to the Mujuru family (an obvious conflict of interest since Mrs Joyce Mujuru was then Minister of Posts and Telecommunications).

They formed a joint venture called Telecel with some Zairian and American businessmen, but the tender was declared null and void by the courts and the government was ordered to grant Masiyiwa a third licence, which it did eventually in 1998.

27. On the notion of 'big men' in such a context, see Fauré and Médard 1995.
28. For a testimony supporting this view, see Wild 1997, 278.
29. In both cases, it is understood that the President himself and/or family members and political associates in the ruling party received huge kickbacks. In the airport contract, the local representative of the Cyprus-based contractor is Mugabe's nephew Leo, so the extended family will derive a double benefit from the deal (see the *Financial Gazette*, 19 and 26 October 1995).
30. Former army chief Solomon Mujuru's Bindura business conglomerate nearly collapsed and he had to return to active politics and get a seat in Parliament, in order to start anew his accumulation drive (see *Horizon*, February 1993 and various issues of this magazine in 1995 and 1996). The fate of Xavier Kadhani whose properties were impounded, Boka's bankruptcy and more recently the mismanagement of another 'indigenous' financial institution, the Universal Merchant Bank (see *Zimbabwe Independent*, 4 February 2000), are other cases in point.
31. In his April 1998 report, the Reserve Bank governor noted that Boka had violated all known banking regulations during the time he ran UMB.
32. Some prominent young black business leaders such as Isaac Takawira, general manager of Barclays Zimbabwe, James Mushore, deputy-general manager of the First Merchant Bank, or Nigel Chanakira, executive manager of Kingdom Securities, ostensibly stay away from politics and decline to comment on indigenization issues, even when attacked by ministers or indigenization activists. At the same time, many of these successful black managers contribute to ZANU(PF)'s finances (like many of their white counterparts). However, this protective public attitude might prove untenable as the country's economy deteriorates rapidly and the race for scarcer spoils heats up. Chanakira was recently the target of a judicial inquiry into alleged insider trading triggered by Chiyangwa and other political businessmen.
33. In the sense of Hyden's 'economy of affection' (Hyden 1983).
34. Here, we concur with Wild (1997, 262): 'What is today portrayed as a break with socialism and a move towards a market economy in Zimbabwe's economic policy, proves on closer inspection to be the transition from a latent to a manifest phase of clientelistic capitalism.'

3

The Performance of the Zimbabwean Economy, 1980–2000

Godfrey Kanyenze

Introduction

This chapter traces the performance of the Zimbabwean economy during the period 1980–2000. In analysing the performance of the economy, it is important to bear in mind that the goal is to achieve development. As UNDP rightly pointed out, the concept of development goes beyond growth. In its 1996 Human Development Report, UNDP identified conditions under which economic growth will not lead to development. These are:

- jobless growth (growth which does not expand employment opportunities);
- ruthless growth (growth associated with increasing inequality and poverty);
- voiceless growth (growth in the absence of democracy or empowerment);
- rootless growth (growth that withers cultural identity); and
- futureless growth (growth that squanders resources needed by future generations (UNDP 1996).

Since the main objective of economic activity is improving welfare, then the people are the subject of development. To capture the centrality of the human being in development, UNDP has popularized the concept of 'human development'. It sees human development as 'the process of enlarging people's choices' such that they live 'long, healthy and creative lives' (UNDP 1990).

In this context, growth is seen as a means rather than an end in itself. Such an approach acknowledges that a country may achieve high levels of growth, but that does not mean it has a high level of human development. Growth does not automatically translate into parallel human development. It is a necessary, but insufficient, condition for human development.

Thus, the analysis of the performance of the Zimbabwean economy will attempt to use this broader framework to assess the extent to which (human) development has occurred in Zimbabwe. The chapter provides a chronological account of economic developments during the past twenty years of independence.

The inherited economy

Zimbabwe attained its independence relatively late, in 1980. It was therefore hoped that hindsight would enable Zimbabwe to avoid the pitfalls that befell other countries before it. In its Transitional National Development Plan (TNDP), this hope was aptly expressed:

> In some of these countries, growth and development have been impeded by a number of external and internal constraints. Some of them have adopted inappropriate policies and strategies and have misallocated much human and material resources in building costly, unproductive and often unnecessary capacity. Often the result has been uneven development, stagnation, even decline, leading to no significant and sustained improvement in living standards of the people as a whole. (Government of Zimbabwe 1982a, 1)

At independence in 1980, Zimbabwe inherited an economy that exhibited both extreme characteristics of a relatively developed economy and economic backwardness and neglect of the majority of the people. This dualism (separate development) had arisen from the policy of white supremacy that underlined the colonial era.

The relative strength of the economy lay in its diversified formal sector, with no overwhelmingly dominant sector. At independence in 1980, agriculture, manufacturing and mining together accounted for almost half the gross domestic product and 55 per cent of formal employment. Industry had developed to the extent that by 1980, the manufacturing sector consisted of some 1260 separate units producing 7000 different products.

In fact, by the advent of independence, the manufacturing sector was already contributing the most (25 per cent) to GDP. The diversified nature of the formal sector was exceptional by sub-Saharan African standards.

Whereas the share of manufacturing output in GDP in Zimbabwe averaged 23.3 per cent of GDP during the period 1980–89, the corresponding figure for sub-Saharan Africa is only 10.4 per cent. For sub-Saharan Africa, the predominance of agriculture is reflected in its high share of GDP from that sector, which averaged 31.6 per cent over the period 1980–89. The contribution of agricultural output to GDP averaged only 12.2 per cent over the same period for Zimbabwe. The relative strength of the economy is also reflected in the fairly broad export base, with agriculture accounting for 41 per cent of export earnings in 1984, followed by manufacturing at 32 per cent and mining at 27 per cent.

Notwithstanding the relatively developed nature of the inherited economy at independence, the Zimbabwe economy has a dark side to it: the underdeveloped, deprived and marginalized non-formal sector, including the peasant sector. The economy can therefore be described as characterized by enclave and dual development. The enclave nature of the economy refers to the fact that the most dynamic and efficient part of the Zimbabwean economy that accounts for the greater part of gross domestic product is the formal sector. This sector, however, only accounted for about one-fifth (one million) of the potential labour force, while the majority of the labour force, constituting about four-fifths, were either underemployed in the informal and communal sectors, or openly unemployed. The enclavity refers to the fact that the formal sector has a growth momentum of its own that is relatively isolated from the activities of those in the non-formal sectors (informal and communal).

The lack of asset entitlement on the part of the black population is clearly demonstrated with regard to the allocation of land. Through the Land Apportionment Act (1930) and the Land Tenure Act (1969), a pattern of land distribution whereby 18 million hectares were allocated to blacks (the former Tribal Trust Lands, now Communal Areas), an equal share was given to whites, with the remaining two million hectares being game reserves and government land.[1] The injustice lay in the fact that blacks made up 95 per cent, while whites represented 4.5 per cent of the population (of the 1969 population). Worse still, blacks were relegated to the agro-ecological zones with poor soil and unreliable rain, while their white counterparts occupied prime land (Stoneman 1988b; Moyo 1986; Riddell 1979). By 1980, the communal areas, with a carrying capacity of 275 000 families, were already overcrowded with 700 000 families (Riddell 1979). This situation is in sharp contrast to that prevailing in white farming areas where an estimated 60 per cent of the land was either unused or under-utilized (Jackson and Collier 1988; Stoneman 1988b; Riddell 1979).

Table 3.1 Distribution of land according to natural regions (%)

Natural region	Large scale commercial land	Communal areas	Small scale commercial land	Other land	Total
I	63	18	1	18	100
II	74	21	4	1	100
III	44	39	7	10	100
IV	27	49	4	20	100
V	35	46	1	18	100
Total	40	42	4	15	100

Source: Government of Zimbabwe 1982a, 67, Table 11.2.

Table 3.1 traces the distribution of land by natural region and land use. Clearly, large-scale commercial farms, which are predominantly white-owned, are located in the prime agro-ecological regions I and II, with communal areas mainly located in the poorer natural regions IV and V.

Owing to the inequitable distribution of resources, income distribution followed a similar pattern. Table 3.2 summarizes the distribution of income by race. While blacks represented 97.6 per cent of the population, they received a disproportionate share representing 60 per cent of wages and salaries. In contrast, whites represented only 2 per cent of the population, and accounted for a disproportionate 37 per cent of wages and salaries. On the whole, an estimated 3 per cent of the population controlled two-thirds of gross national income (Stoneman and Cliffe 1989).

The World Bank (1987) found that at independence black incomes were one-tenth of that of whites, with the wage differentials as high as 24 times for whites compared to those for blacks in agriculture. The differential stood at 7.3 times for manufacturing, with the lowest differential of 3.5 in the financial services. The observed trend is that

Table 3.2 The distribution of income by race

Group	Proportion of population, %	Share of wages & salaries, %
African	97.6	60.0
Europeans	2.0	37.0
Coloured	0.3	2.0
Asians	0.2	1.0

Source: Government of Zimbabwe 1983.

the lower the average skill level in a sector, the higher the average wage differentials between black and white, and vice versa.

Earlier, the relative diversity of the economy was presented as a strength. However, the predominance of agriculture and mining, accounting for 68 per cent of total export earnings in 1984, presents some constraints, given the dependence and vulnerability of the two sectors to exogenous factors. The weather patterns and commodity prices lie outside the control of government.[2]

The manufacturing sector presented its own contradictions. The import substitution industrialization strategy, which had performed well during the sanctions period (particularly during the fastest growth period of 1966–74), was already showing signs of severe strain by 1980. All easy and moderately hard industrialization had been exhausted by 1975 (Green and Kadhani 1986). The deliberate policy of compressing imports to contain the balance of payments situation left capital stock in an obsolete and depleted state. The manufacturing sector itself became a net user of foreign exchange. Although it contributed 32.1 per cent of export earnings in 1984, it accounted for 90.6 per cent of imports during the same year.

Furthermore, the high level of protection created a monopoly structure whereby 50.4 per cent of manufacturing products are produced by single firms, 20.6 per cent in sub-sectors with two firms and 9.7 per cent where there are three firms, implying that 80 per cent of goods produced in Zimbabwe are monopoly or oligopoly products (Ndlela 1984; UNIDO 1986). This market structure is further exacerbated by the concentration of production in the two major towns, Harare (accounting for 50 per cent of all manufactured products) and Bulawayo (accounting for 25 per cent).

Above all, the economy in 1980 was war-ravaged and hence required a substantial inflow of resources for reconstruction and rehabilitation. National ownership of the economy was very low, with over two-thirds of invested capital foreign-owned (Government of Zimbabwe 1986a). Such a structure inevitably creates pressure on the balance of payments. The Government of Zimbabwe (*ibid.*) lamented that between 1980 and 1983 as much as Z$300 million was remitted abroad in the form of dividends and profits.

Mhone (1993; 1999) utilizes a technical framework to draw out the structural implications of the inherited economy. He summarizes these inherent anomalies into four distortions or inefficiencies, that is distributive, allocative, microeconomic and dynamic inefficiencies. Distributive inefficiencies refer to the unequal or restricted access to key economic assets (such as land, education and training, finance) which undermine the participation of the majority in productive activities.

Such a distortion conditions the extent of participation and benefit from growth in the economy. The structure of the asset base therefore determines the nature of growth. The narrow base whereby a small elite owns the bulk of resources delivers a skewed distribution of income, resulting in jobless, ruthless, voiceless, rootless and futureless growth. At the other extreme, a broad-based structure will ensure that an inclusive growth pattern that is driven by, and benefits, the majority emerges.

Allocative inefficiency refers to the situation whereby a significant proportion of the labour force is under- or unemployed. This suggests resources are being wasted. Over time, it is argued that such under- or unused resources will depreciate in value and consequently impact productivity. This under- or unused labour represents forgone productive potential and incomes. Unleashing an inclusive growth path releases this potential productive energy and unravels a 'virtuous cycle' of self-reinforcing growth.

Microeconomic inefficiencies relate to the distortions at the enterprise level that undermine economic efficiency, competitiveness and employment absorption. Examples are the limitations imposed by the inherited inward-looking development strategy, and the inefficiencies of the non-formal sector. In such situations, human capabilities, value channels (work, production, management and marketing processes and capabilities) and value chains (linkages in distribution of inputs and outputs, marketing structures, financial intermediaries) undermine the productive potential of the economy. This undermines capital accumulation and overall development. This largely constrains employment creation and reinforces the enclave relationship of the sectors.

Dynamic inefficiencies result from all the other inefficiencies. These hinder the movement to an inclusive and sustainable growth pattern as the economy becomes trapped in a low-income, low-demand, low-savings, low-investment, low-growth, low-employment vicious cycle. The inequitable distribution of resources will result in the fulfilment of the needs (mainly luxuries) of the privileged (for example, importation of luxuries) at the expense of the basic needs of the majority.

Management and performance of the economy: the pre-reform period, 1980–90

Independence therefore gave the people of Zimbabwe the opportunity to redress inherited inequalities. Thus, in its first post-independence policy document entitled 'Growth With Equity: An Economic Policy Statement', of February 1981 (Government of Zimbabwe 1981), this desire is articulated. This policy statement sought 'to inform the people of Zimbabwe and to enlist their participation and active support in the development process' (Government of Zimbabwe 1981, 1). The government's objectives were to implement policies based on socialist, egalitarian and democratic principles under conditions of rapid economic growth, full employment, price stability, dynamic efficiency in the allocation of resources, and to ensure that the benefits are equitably distributed.

Embracing key tenets of good governance, the government reiterated that it was determined 'to embark on policies and programmes designed to involve fully in the development process the entire people, who are the beginning and the end of society, the very asset of the country and the *raison d' être* of Government' (Government of Zimbabwe 1981, 2). The importance of pursuing 'popular democratic participation' in the ownership and management of national resources was articulated (see Government of Zimbabwe 1981; 1982a; 1986a).

The need to redress the inequities of the past, and in particular land redistribution, was given pride of first place in government policy. Other objectives, such as minerals, were also highlighted.[3] It was clearly outlined that 'development is by people' (Government of Zimbabwe 1981, 8), a principle at the heart of good (economic) governance. On fiscal and monetary policy, the economic statement adopted the view that 'fiscal soundness is a matter of cardinal importance, especially as it will go a long way towards preserving and increasing our creditworthiness internationally, which will allow us to borrow if and when necessary' (Government of Zimbabwe 1981, 14).

It is most unfortunate that the people, through their own organizations, were not involved in the design of policy. At this stage, the government was highly suspicious of business and paternalistic with respect to mass organizations such as trade unions.

The first two years of independence

Just before the proclamation of independence, Zimbabwe was rocked by nationwide strikes, largely emanating from a crisis of expectations. Zimbabweans immediately wanted to see tangible changes to their welfare. The new government responded by intervening extensively in the labour market. That intervention was meant to:

- promote security of employment;
- raise the standard of living of the people, in particular, the low paid;
- narrow income differentials; and
- reduce inflationary pressures, especially after 1982 (Government of Zimbabwe 1986b, 90).

First, the government responded to the strikes by promulgating a Minimum Wage Act of 1980. Employers responded by retrenching workers. To forestall unwarranted retrenchments, the government promulgated the Employment Act of 1980. Sachikonye argued that this regulation was meant to stamp out the emerging 'fratricidal conflict between the working class and the bourgeoisie' (Sachikonye 1990, 4). This regulation required that ministerial approval be obtained before any retrenchment or dismissal. To discourage resort to employing casual workers as a way around the Employment Act, the rate at which such employees are remunerated was set at double that for permanent workers.

To deal with wider issues of incomes policy, the government constituted in September 1980 a commission of inquiry under the chairmanship of Roger Riddell to look at incomes, prices and conditions of service, with a view to correcting inherited anomalies. The Riddell Commission Report observed that 'the necessity for action and for the introduction of policies directed specifically at alleviating poverty and narrowing differentials is apparent when one considers the implications of a "no change" or status quo type of policy scenario' (Riddell Commission 1981, 84). According to the Commission report, there was a need for a policy shift towards 'growth with equity through planned change,' as opposed to the prevailing situation of 'growth with widening inequalities' (Riddell Commission 1981, 85).

On the minimum wage issue, the report went beyond supporting it, recommending that:

> The basis for determining minimum wages should be solely the needs of workers and their families and not the place where work is carried out or the type of work performed. It is only through adopting the principle of need that present (and future) anomalies can be removed. Thus, whether a person is employed as a domestic worker, as a factory worker, the criterion of need should determine minimum wages. (Riddell Commission 1981, 105)

On the basis of the Poverty Datum Line (PDL) of an average family of six, a father, mother and four children, the 'ideal' target income paths were plotted for both the urban and rural areas.[4] It was then recommended that the target for wage policy was to reach 90 per cent of the PDL by mid-1984 (after three-and-a-half years). The remaining 10 per cent was left to employers to reward for human capital investment.

While the Riddell Commission admitted that such a wage policy was unsustainable, it argued that its sustainability could be enhanced by freezing (in real terms) salaries at the top until the minimum wage targets were achieved. The report noted that the long-term sustainability of the redistributive wage policy lay in restructuring the economy. The Commissioners were conscious of the very specific conditions upon which the proposed redistributive policy was based, and they advised against intro-ducing a target minimum wage under conditions of economic decline. This therefore was the major weakness of the Riddell Commission, that while its redistributive incomes policy had to be implemented with immediate effect, its sustainability lay in longer-term economic restructuring. Thus, with the recession of 1982/84, and the three years of drought during the same period, the government abandoned the 'target wage' path and instead adopted a stabilization programme, with a wage restraint policy.

Informed by the Riddell Commission, the government adopted a sliding scale mechanism, whereby those at the bottom of the earnings structure received higher percentage increases, and vice versa. Maximum ceilings beyond which no increase was granted were also fixed by the government.

As a result of the opening up of the economy to the international world in 1980, the end of the war, renewed access to international aid and borrowing from abroad, favourable terms of trade, good weather conditions, excess capacity and increased aggregate demand arising from agricultural and wage incomes, the economy experienced a major boom during the first two years of independence.[5]

Table 3.3 below summarizes the performance of the economy during the period 1980–85. Real Gross Domestic Product (GDP) grew by 11 per cent in 1980 and 10 per cent in 1981. This post-independence boom resulted in increased capacity utilization from 75 per cent at inde-pendence, to 83 per cent in 1980 and 95 per cent by 1981 (Kadhani and Green 1985). However, the high levels of GDP growth did not translate into high levels of employment growth, the latter increasing at only 3 per cent in both years. A particularly encouraging development was the rise in the share of gross fixed capital formation in GDP from 14 per cent in 1979 to 15 per cent in 1980 and 19 per cent in 1981.

However, the boom of the first two years of independence created a false sense of security, resulting in the introduction of liberal policies on foreign exchange allocation, remittance of dividends and profits and an expansionary incomes policy which were to contribute towards macro-economic instability in the subsequent period. Even during the boom, these liberal policies led to the deepening of the current account deficit from Z$74 million in 1979 to Z$157 million in 1980 and Z$440 million in 1981. The capital account followed very much the same trend, moving from a surplus of Z$174 million in 1979 to a deficit of Z$44 million in 1980 before returning to a surplus of Z$134 million in 1981. The economy showed signs of overheating in 1981, with the rate of inflation rising from 7 per cent in 1980 to 14 per cent in 1981.

The Transitional National Development Plan period, 1982–85

In November 1982 the government published its first development plan, the Transitional National Development Plan (TNDP) to cover the period 1982/83–84/85. In the foreword to the Plan, the then Prime Minister (now Executive President) Mugabe gave an ambitious role for the Plan, contending: 'This Plan in essence puts our nation at the threshold of our second revolution – the socio-economic revolution designed to give greater meaning to our independence' (Government of Zimbabwe 1982a, i). TNDP was designed as a short-term guidepost. It was transitional because: (1) society was changing from war to peace; (2) data and information required to formulate a comprehensive plan based on advanced quantitative techniques were either inadequate or nonexistent; (3) the statistical series were undergoing revision and reorganization because some of these had been manipulated during the colonial period.

In terms of (economic) governance, the Plan aimed to provide 'a firm foundation for a new society based on equality of opportunity and prosperity for all Zimbabweans' (Government of Zimbabwe, 1982a. 1). The Plan recognized the existence of capitalism in Zimbabwe, which has to be 'purposefully harnessed, regulated and transformed as a partner in the overall national endeavour to achieve set national Plan goals' (Government of Zimbabwe, 1982a, 1). The underlying economic strategy was outlined as follows:

> While the inherited economy, with its institutions and infrastructure, has in the past served a minority, it would be simplistic and, indeed, naïve to suggest that it should, therefore, be destroyed in order to make a fresh start. The challenge lies in building upon and developing on what was inherited, modifying, expanding and, where necessary, radically changing structures and institutions in order to maximise benefits from economic growth and development to Zimbabweans as a whole. (*Ibid.*, 1)

As with 'Growth with Equity,' the emphasis was placed on adopting popular participation as the development process. Rather interestingly, the Plan states that 'any economic system that perpetuates past injustices cannot be tolerated nor, in the long term, sustained. If it were, the costly struggle for liberation would be meaningless and the cause of the revolution betrayed' (*Ibid.*, 1).

Interestingly, a section of the Plan devoted itself to the important governance issue, 'The People: The Motive Force For Change'. This section put the people as the driving force, arguing:

> It is therefore imperative that the people who constituted the revolutionary force which charted the course of our political history be fully liberated to chart once more the course of our economic history. It is they who must provide the essential motive force for change. The general strategy of the Transitional National Development Plan is to provide a solid framework and basis for participation by popular mass organizations and to create new socio-economic institutions capable of harnessing and utilising the resources of the people. (*Ibid.*,18)

Although the rhetoric proclaims the desire to involve people, they were not, however, consulted in the design of TNDP.

The overriding objective of TNDP was to achieve an average real annual rate of growth in GDP of 8 per cent during the Plan period. Other objectives were to increase employment at an annual rate of growth of over 3 per cent; increase investment (Gross Fixed Capital Formation) from 19 per cent of GDP in 1981/82 to 23 per cent by 1984/85; savings from 16 per cent in 1981/82 to over 20 per cent of GDP; raise imports and exports to an average 26 per cent and 23 per cent of GDP respectively during the Plan period. Large net inflows of foreign capital were expected to account for over 46 per cent of funds and inflation was projected at 15 per cent per annum over the same period. The Plan targeted to resettle 162 000 families during the Plan period.

Total debt was expected to increase from Z$2694 million in 1981 to Z$3864 million by 1985. Domestic debt was projected to rise from Z$2012 million to Z$2384 million, while external debt was anticipated to increase from Z$682 million to Z$1480 million over the same period. It was expected that the share of external debt in total debt would increase from 21 per cent in 1981 to 38 per cent by 1985.

Overall performance: TNDP period, 1982–85

As was discussed above, even during the period of boom (1980–81), the economy was already showing signs of overheating. The boom was cut short by three consecutive years of drought, the worst since 1911–14, the onset of world recession, the decline in the terms of trade and the deteriorating internal security situation as insurgency mounted in Matabeleland

Table 3.3 Economic performance, 1980–85[6], (selected indicators)

	1980	1981	1982	1983	1984	1985
GDP % (1980 prices)	10.7	9.7	1.5	−3.6	2.3	7.4
Employment (%)	2.6	2.8	0.8	−1.2	0.3	1.8
Money: M1 (%)	36.6	7.3	13.8	−3.9	18.8	10.3
M2 (%)	34.2	8.7	19.6	2.6	22.2	4.2
Current account ($m)	−156.7	−439.6	−532.9	−454.2	−101.9	−149.3
Capital account ($m)	−43.8	133.6	342.6	258.9	232.6	259.8
Overall BOP ($m)	−29.4	−202.1	−96.9	9.3	250.3	172.2
Inflation:						
Lower income group	5.4	13.1	10.7	23.1	20.2	8.5
Higher income group	9.2	14.6	18.4	16.4	12.5	9.9

Sources: Calculated from *Quarterly Digest of Statistics*, CSO; *Quarterly Economic and Statistical Review*, Reserve Bank of Zimbabwe.

and the Midlands. Under the weight of these forces, the economy flagged, as real GDP growth rate declined from 10 per cent in 1981 to 2 per cent in 1982. The current account balance worsened from a deficit of Z$440 million in 1981 to one of Z$533 million in 1982, partly owing to the liberalization of imports, failure of exports to cover increased import demand and rising domestic demand resulting from the liberal incomes policy.

The main causes of the macroeconomic imbalances were exogenous shocks (drought, world recession, high interest rates abroad, declining terms of trade) and internal policies (liberalization of dividend and profit remittances abroad, an overvalued exchange rate, relaxed import controls, overheating arising from an expansive incomes policy, and expansionary fiscal and monetary policies during the period 1980–81). The government had put faith in the US$2.2 billion that had been promised at the Zimbabwe Conference on Reconstruction and Development (ZIMCORD) donors' conference of March 1981. Unfortunately, by the end of 1984, only a fifth of the amount had been disbursed (World Bank 1985).

In response, the government borrowed indiscriminately, especially from non-concessionary commercial sources, with short maturity periods and high interest rates. Zimbabwe had been described as under-borrowed by third world standards by the IMF (Stoneman 1988b). As a result, total debt rose markedly from US$786 million in 1980 to US$2304 million by 1983 (World Bank 1993c). The debt service ratio, which represented 1.3 per cent of export earnings in 1979, had risen to 25 per cent by 1983, generating additional pressure on the balance of payments. Table 3.4 traces the operations of central government for the period 1981/82–84/85.

Table 3.4   Central government operations, 1980/81–1984/85 ($ million)

	1980/81	1981/82	1982/83	1983/84	1984/85
(a)					
Revenue & grants ($m)	949.1	1 364.5	1 789.2	1 997.2	2 212.2
Expenditure ($m)	1 283.9	1 681.1	2 247.8	2 627.2	2 923.0
Deficit ($m)	−334.8	−316.6	−458.6	−630.0	−710.8
Deficit/GDP (%)	8.5	6.6	8.0	9.9	10.6
Votes to (%):					
(b)					
Defence	16.1	15.3	13.5	14.5	12.2
Health	5.4	5.6	4.8	4.8	4.9
Education	15.2	16.6	15.8	16.5	16.2

Source: Calculated from *Quarterly Economic and Statistical Review*, Reserve Bank of Zimbabwe.

The budget deficit, which amounted to 8.5 per cent of GDP in 1980/81, improved to 6.6 per cent of GDP in 1981/82 before deteriorating further thereafter. The budget deficit for the TNDP period averaged 8.7 per cent. It remained high because of security commitments in Mozambique and at home, expenditure on drought relief, and because social services were sustained. By the end of 1982, it was clear that the crisis was not transitory and that the situation required intervention. In response to the balance of payments crisis, the government adopted a 'home grown' stabilization programme. The policy adjustments adopted were as follows:

(1)   devaluation of the Zimbabwean dollar by 20 per cent on 9 December 1982 and thereafter tying it to a trade weighted basket of undisclosed currencies;

(2)   introduction of new incentives for exports;

(3)   restrictions on new non-concessionary foreign borrowing from 23 March 1983;

(4)   balance of payments controls (27 March 1984) through (a) temporary suspension of remittances of dividends and profits; (b) temporary reduction of emigrants' settling allowances; (c) acquisition of blocked external securities pool; and d) sharp cutbacks in foreign exchange allocations each year until the second half of 1985;

(5)   price and wage controls through cuts in subsidies and increases in administered prices (from May 1982); wage freeze (January 1982) and thereafter the adoption of a contractionary wage policy;

(6) restriction on government credit expansion; restriction on new recruitment by the government (1983/84);
(7) contractionary monetary policies through increases in interest rates, restriction on domestic credit expansion and increased liquidity ratios (from February 1981);
(8) a major increase in central government revenues (they rose by about 10 per cent of GDP between 1979/80 and 1983/84) through both increases in taxes and a shift from quotas to tariffs; and
(9) increases in the controlled prices of key food items and utility and rail tariffs (see Davies and Sanders 1988; World Bank 1985).

From the range of instruments used, it is clear the programme had both stabilization and structural adjustment components. The export incentives and exchange rate depreciation were the structural adjustment measures, while the rest constituted stabilization ones.[7] Stabilization measures are aimed at reducing both external and internal imbalances, and are therefore deflationary. However, the use of the exchange rate as an instrument for stabilization was not accompanied by a liberalization of the trade regime and the removal of price controls as is the case with orthodox stabilization and adjustment programmes. The option of liberalizing trade and foreign exchange allocation was rejected by the Zimbabwean government.

More critically, an 18-month IMF standby agreement reached on 24 March 1983 initially supported the stabilization programme. This was subsequently suspended following the measures adopted (see the fourth measures in the stabilization package outlined above) in March 1984. The adoption of a stabilization programme produced angry reaction from civic society groups, and especially trade unions. These groups questioned the claims by the government that this was a 'home grown' programme. Probably the most poignant criticism came from an academic, Mkandawire (1985), whose article on '"Home Grown" Austerity Measures: The Case of Zimbabwe', drove the point home that the stabilization programme was strikingly similar to the IMF programmes administered elsewhere. This raises an important issue regarding (economic) governance. What became of the much proclaimed 'popular participation' of 'Growth with Equity' and TNDP?

Of importance to the survival of the ordinary Zimbabwean was the reduction and removal of consumer subsidies as part of the stabilization programme. Table 3.5 traces the trends in the allocation for consumer subsidies during the period 1979/80–84/85. The amount allocated to consumer subsidies was increased from as low as Z$6.3 million in fiscal year 1979/80 to Z$57.4 million by 1981/82. In addition, the range of

Table 3.5   Consumer subsidy payments, 1979/80–84/85 ($ million)

	1979/80	1980/81	1981/82	1982/83	1983/84	1984/85
Subsidy	6.3	33.6	57.4	51.1	28.0	14.4
Flour	3.1	6.7	5.7	1.9	–	–
Maize meal	1.9	20.1	41.4	49.2	28.0	14.4
Sugar	1.3	–	–	–	–	–
Edible oil	–	5.8	4.8	–	–	–
Opaque beer	–	1.0	0.5	–	–	–

Source: Government of Zimbabwe 1986b, 88, table 7.4.

subsidized items was extended in the fiscal period 1980/81 to include edible oils and opaque beer (largely consumed by the lower income group) and for those items already subsidized, the levels were increased. The most significant increase in subsidy went to maize meal, which was raised from only Z$1.9 million in 1979/80 to Z$41.4 million by 1981/82 (2179 per cent increase).

However, following the introduction of the stabilization programme, consumer subsidies were reduced from fiscal year 1982/83 so that by 1984/85, the only surviving consumer subsidy was that which applied to maize meal. Even this one was substantially slashed from Z$49.2 million in 1982/83 to only Z$14.4 million by 1984/85. This subsidy was later removed in 1986.

The impact of the removal of the subsidy can be traced from Table 3.4. Whereas the higher income group experienced a higher rate of inflation compared with the lower income group during the period 1980–82, the rate of inflation for the lower income group was higher thereafter (except for 1985). This is so because the lower income group spent 54.9 per cent of its income on foodstuffs, compared to only 20.5 per cent for the higher income group.

Following the adoption of the stabilization programme, the current account deficit improved from −Z$533 million in 1982 to −Z$101 million by 1984, before deteriorating again to −Z$149.3 million in 1985. The improvement emanated from the severe reductions in normal allocations of foreign exchange in 1982, 1983 and 1984 and domestic disabsorption, which curtailed the demand for imports. This was also facilitated by the improvement in exports arising from the depreciation of the exchange rate and the introduction of export incentives. The marked fall in the current account deficit recorded in 1984 was partly owing to the temporary suspension of remittances of dividends and profits and temporary reduction of emigrants' settling allowances (measures adopted in March 1984).

The worsening of the current account deficit in 1985 resulted from increased demand for imports arising from the return to favourable weather conditions. This also reflects increased global allocation of foreign exchange for importers.

With real GDP averaging only 1.9 per cent during the TNDP period, against the Plan target of 8 per cent per annum, and employment growing at an annual average of only 0.4 per cent during the Plan period, it is clear that the Plan targets were not met. Such performance compares unfavourably with the intercensal (1982–92) population growth rate of 3.1 per cent per annum. Gross Fixed Capital Formation, which had peaked at nearly 20 per cent of GDP in 1982, collapsed to around 12 per cent of GDP by 1985, against TNDP targets of 23 per cent by 1984/85. The planned resettlement of 162 000 families could not be achieved. In fact, by the early 1990s, only 52 000 families had been resettled. Table 3.6 summarizes the trends in nominal and real minimum wages during the period 1980–90.

Although real minimum wages were by 1990 still above their 1980 levels, they were well below their peak 1982 levels. However, on a more positive note, the Labour Relations Act was promulgated in 1985. It repealed the Industrial Conciliation Act of 1934 and incorporated the

Table 3.6 Nominal and real minimum wage trends, 1980–90

Period	*Domestic & agriculture*		*Commerce & industry*	
	Nominal wage $ per month	*Real minimum wage index*	*Nominal wage $ per month*	*Real minimum wage index*
1980	30.00	100.0	70.00	100.0
1981	30.00	88.4	85.00	107.4
1982	50.00	133.1	105.00	119.8
1983	55.00	119.0	115.00	106.6
1984	65.00	117.0	125.00	96.4
1985	75.00	124.4	143.00	101.7
1986	85.00	123.4	158.00	98.3
1987	85.00	109.7	158.00	87.4
1988	100.00	120.1	182.00	93.7
1989	116.00	123.4	226.00	103.1
1990	133.00	120.5	266.00	103.3

Note: For the index, 1980 = 100.
Source: Zimbabwe Congress of Trade Unions (ZCTU) Economics Department.

Minimum Wages Act and the Employment Act of 1980. For the first time, it outlined workers' fundamental rights and set up mechanisms for collective bargaining at the national, sectoral/industrial and shop-floor levels. It also established a comprehensive and elaborate dispute procedure.

The First Five Year National Development Plan period, 1986–90

In April 1986, the government launched its First Five Year National Development Plan covering the period 1986–90. The Plan was informed by the experiences of TNDP. This time, the planned rate of annual real growth was revised downwards from the 8 per cent of TNDP to 5.1 per cent. The planned investment to GDP ratio remained, as with TNDP, over 20 per cent. The planned number of families to be resettled was reduced from 162 000 under TNDP to 75 000 by the end of the Plan period. Table 3.7 examines the performance of the economy during the period of the First Five Year National Development Plan, 1986–90.

In terms of real GDP growth, the economy grew at close to the target growth rate of 5.1 per cent, averaging 4 per cent per annum for the period 1986–90. Employment grew at an annual average rate of 2.7 per cent during the same period. This average annual rate of growth is inadequate to deal with new entrants into the labour market, as reflected in the growth rate of the labour force of around 3 per cent per annum.

Table 3.7   Economic performance, 1986–90, (selected indicators)

	1986	1987	1988	1989	1990
(a)					
Current account ($m)	12.6	127.7	210.5	−0.3	−455.0
Capital account ($m)	166.8	115.5	89.9	99.7	348.6
Overall balance ($m)	11.4	103.9	64.3	−106.8	−255.6
(b)					
GDP (1990 prices) (%)	1.8	1.5	5.9	3.6	7.2
Employment (%)	2.5	0.2	5.5	3.2	2.2
Money: M1 (%)	9.2	13.4	30.5	18.9	26.9
M2 (%)	13.6	12.3	24.1	25.5	21.1
Inflation:					
Lower income group (%)	14.3	12.5	7.4	12.9	17.4
Higher income group (%)	14.1	11.3	6.7	10.3	13.6

Source: Calculated from *Quarterly Digest of Statistics*, CSO; *Quarterly Economic and Statistical Review*, Reserve Bank of Zimbabwe.

The current account improved markedly during the period 1986–88, before deteriorating in 1989 and 1990. At the beginning of 1986, factor payments abroad were resumed. The pressure exerted on the current account was largely absorbed through cuts in foreign currency allocations. It is estimated that the real value of the 1986 allocation amounted to about 35 per cent of its 1981 value. Further cuts in the foreign exchange allocations were made in 1987 such that the real value of the 1987 allocation was about 30 per cent of its 1981 level. These measures were taken up in view of the bunching up of debt repayments, which reached a peak with a debt service ratio of 33 per cent in 1987. There was pressure on the government to reschedule its debt obligations, but the desire to maintain creditworthiness ensured that the government honoured its obligations. Instead, the government introduced austerity measures by imposing a price and wage freeze. This measure was highly unpopular, resulting in workers in the leather and shoe sector going on strike to protest against the measures. ZCTU complained that while price controls were being flouted, the wage freeze held.

The crunch period was 1987. Thereafter, the debt service ratio declined to 23.5 per cent by 1990. Slight improvements in foreign exchange allocations occurred after 1987 so that the real value of the 1990 allocation was about 40 per cent of its 1981 value. The use of import compression to stabilize the balance of payments through exchange rate depreciation and severe cutbacks in foreign currency

Table 3.8 Central government operations, 1986–90 ($ million)

	1985/86	*1986/87*	*1987/88*	*1988/89*	*1989/90*
(a)					
Revenue & grants ($m)	2 616.1	3 036.5	3 784.9	4 356.9	5 307.1
Expenditure ($m)	3 307.8	4 053.3	4 680.9	5 467.4	6 444.9
Deficit ($m)	−691.7	−1 016.8	−896.0	−1 110.5	−1 137.8
Deficit/GDP (%)	9.0	11.6	9.2	9.6	9.5
Votes to (%):					
(b)					
Defence	16.1	15.3	13.5	14.5	12.2
Health	5.4	5.6	4.8	4.8	4.9
Education	15.2	16.6	15.8	16.5	16.2

Source: Calculated from *Quarterly Digest of Statistics*, CSO; *Quarterly Economic and Statistical Review*, Reserve Bank of Zimbabwe.

Table 3.9 Government expenditure, 1979/80–1989/90 ('000)

Period	Original estimate	Supplementary estimates
1979/80	1 082 516	143 418
1980/81	–	–
1981/82	2 013 484	108 239
1982/83	2 798 775	136 785
1983/84	2 709 410	343 279
1984/85	3 389 163	179 215
1985/86	3 644 627	230 662
1986/87	4 573 810	263 454
1987/88	5 173 630	216 610
1988/89	6 052 163	298 597
1989/90	6 937 717	304 145

Source: Moyo 2000, 34.

allocations took a heavy toll on imports and had a knock-on effect on investment and capacity utilization. Table 3.8 reports the performance of central government during the period 1986–90. The budget deficit for the period under review averaged 9.8 per cent of GDP, which is on the high side. Table 3.9 traces government expenditures for the period 1979/80–1989/90 and illustrates the lack of fiscal discipline.

Clearly, therefore, budgetary overruns have become a permanent feature of the budget. This promotes fiscal indiscipline among ministries since they are aware the supplementary vote is always there. This therefore implies the budget has no sanction for over-spending ministries, they always get away with it. In this context, it is not surprising that over-spending has developed into a culture among ministries. Table 3.10 examines the functional distribution of Gross Domestic Income during the period 1985–90. Whereas wages and salaries accounted for 47.7 per cent of gross domestic income in 1985, their share had declined to 47 per cent by 1990. The share of the surplus (profits) increased from

Table 3.10 Percentage distribution of gross domestic income, 1985–90

	1985	1986	1987	1988	1989	1990
Wages and salaries	47.7	49.1	53.7	49.1	47.2	47.0
Surplus	52.9	51.4	46.7	50.8	52.4	52.9
Rent	1.9	2.0	2.4	2.5	2.6	2.3

Note: Percentages do not add up to 100 owing to the omission of bank charges.
Source: Calculated from *Quarterly Digest of Statistics*, CSO December 1999.

52.9 per cent in 1985 to 52.9 per cent by 1990. This suggests that employees have lost out to capital in the distribution of income.

An analysis of economic performance and management during 1980–90

For the majority of Zimbabweans, independence provided an opportunity to transform the economy in a manner that would mainstream the hitherto deprived blacks. From the foregoing discussion, it is clear that earlier attempts at redressing the anomalies of the past were abandoned, following a period of drought (1982–84), the world recession during the same time, and the resultant balance of payments problems. Thereafter, the economy was managed on a reactive management-by-crisis basis. Throughout the first decade of independence, Zimbabwe did not pursue a comprehensive development strategy. The measures taken treated the symptoms and not the real causes of the problems that were of a structural nature. During this period, the civil society groups hardly participated in the design and implementation of policy.

The manner in which independence had been won, through compromise, to some extent mitigated against the adoption of a radical agenda, around which the people had been mobilized during the war for independence. The Lancaster House Agreement effectively protected the status quo. It was a dejected Mugabe who commented about Lancaster that 'even as I signed the document I was not a happy man at all. I felt we had been cheated to some extent . . . that we had agreed to a deal that would to some extent rob us of the victory that we had hoped to have achieved in the field' (quoted in Mandaza 1986b, 38). The Bill of Rights, which formed part of the agreement had a provision on 'Freedom From Deprivation of Property,' which provided for a ten-year guarantee on the inviolability of private property. Any future land redistribution exercise would be guided by market concepts of willing-buyer, willing-seller, with the British government providing 50 per cent of the cost of acquiring the land.

Furthermore, it was feared that a radical approach would result in an exodus of white skills, as had happened in Mozambique. The adoption of such an approach would also affect the flow of international aid and capital and influence the pattern of trade. The use of aid as a political weapon therefore made the radical option unattractive. For instance, it is estimated that Zimbabwe lost some US\$40 million in US aid for voting against the USA invasion of Grenada and for abstaining against voting on the Soviet shooting of a South Korean airliner (Sibanda 1988). At a farewell luncheon for the outgoing USA ambassador in April 1986, a speech read on behalf of the then Minister of Foreign Affairs attacked US policy on Angola and declared that Zimbabwe will not be controlled by any power. This precipitated a walkout by former US President Jimmy Carter and US officials attending the function. Consequently, the USA suspended its aid to Zimbabwe (Sibanda 1988). The IMF and World Bank continuously pressurized Zimbabwe to pursue more market-oriented policies (Stoneman 1989).

Yet another constraint to the adoption of a radical agenda was the presence of a hostile neighbour, South Africa. Hanlon (1988) chronicles the economic and military measures adopted by South Africa to desta- bilize the Zimbabwean economy. At the time of the ZIMCORD donors' conference in March 1981, South Africa gave Zimbabwe one month's notice that it would not renew the bilateral trade agreement, which had been in force since 1964. At the same time, South Africa stopped renew- ing contracts for Zimbabwean migrant workers and started sending them back home. An estimated 40 000 workers and remittances worth about Z$25 million per year were affected. It is estimated that by March 1981, 300 000 tonnes of Zimbabwean goods were stranded at South African ports. The technicians who had been seconded to Rhodesian Railways by South Africa were withdrawn and on 4 April 1981, 24 diesel locomotives that had been leased to Rhodesian Railways were also withdrawn. Since the Beira–Mutare oil pipeline was not yet operational, the slowing down of goods from and to Zimbabwe (locomotive diplo- macy) created fuel shortages in August 1981.[8]

When this approach failed, South Africa changed strategy, ending its railway embargo in November 1981, and even leased 26 locomotives to its neighbours. To maintain Zimbabwe's dependence on it, South Africa used RENAMO to attack the Beira–Mutare corridor. Faced with such destabilization, Zimbabwe sent its troops to Mozambique to guard its trade routes at high cost. Thus, under such constraints, Zimbabwe adopted a cautionary, reconciliatory strategy.

Tandon characterized the state as schizophrenic, 'a state torn apart between on the one hand the democratic forces of the people, and on the other hand the imperialist forces of international financial oligarchy' (1984, 3). The forces calling for change were weak and ill-organized, while those preferring the status quo were locally well-organized, with strong international ties. Socialism was still being debated in the ruling party, with those opposed to it predominant (Sibanda 1988; Mandaza 1986a).

There was no proper planning as the post-independence plans 'were more matters of elucidating the pleasant ends desired than setting out the means for getting to them' (Stoneman 1988b, 53). In addition, there was no attempt to synchronize the plan and the instrument for its implementation, the budget. Sadly, as observed by the government of Zimbabwe, 'the present budgetary system was neither designed, nor is it easily adaptable to meet the demands for planning, programming and budgeting required by government's commitment to comprehensive planning' (Government of Zimbabwe 1982a, 46). During the period under review, the budget was designed in a shroud of secrecy, Parliament was ineffective, reduced to rubber-stamping, and line ministries were marginalized in its preparation. The private sector and civil society were only 'consulted' through pre-budget meetings with Ministry of Finance officials. Their inputs were hardly taken seriously.

Within these limiting parameters, the government adopted a conservative programme. This involved continuing with the inherited structures, while adding a few state-owned corporations and providing social services. Thus, it became clear that radical rhetoric was being used to mobilize people. Thus, Lehman argued that 'while in public he has espoused the arguments and rhetoric of the radical group, in private Mugabe has favoured the implementation of more orthodox policies' (1990, 53). An official of a large US bank is reported as having observed that businessmen 'seem to be impressed by and satisfied with Mugabe's management and the increased level of understanding in government of commercial considerations . . . I feel it is a political pattern that Mugabe give radical, anti-business speeches before government makes major pro-business decisions or announcements' (quoted in Hanlon 1988, 35). Hence, Nyawata's caution that 'the rhetoric of politicians is a poor guide to a country's economic policy' (1988, 115) is well placed.

More fundamentally, the aspirations of the people were abandoned: 'as the African petit bourgeoisie (the ruling elite) began gradually to find access to the same economic and social status as their white counterparts so, too, did it become increasingly unable to respond effectively to the aspirations of the workers and peasants' (Mandaza 1986b, 51). These contradictions became particularly glaring with respect to the role of foreign investment. While on the one hand government was suspicious of foreign investment, at the same time it sought to attract it. In the words of Stoneman, 'the juxtaposition of socialist aims and the need for investment produces the bizarre implication that foreign capital may be attracted to help achieve such a revolution' (1988b, 55).

Meanwhile the World Bank and IMF continued to put pressure on the government to adopt trade liberalization. For instance, in 1987 it refused to sign an agreement for an extension of the export revolving fund until measures were taken to liberalize trade. The World Bank's position prevailed. The adoption of investment guidelines in April 1989 marked a major shift in government policy. This was followed by the establishment of the Zimbabwe Investment Centre in mid-1989, a move designed to create a 'one-stop' investment window. In addition, in a bid to reassure investors, the government signed the World Bank's Multi-lateral Investment Guarantee Agency Convention (MIGA) in September 1989, and in June 1990 signed the USA's Overseas Private Investment Corporation (OPIC) Agreement.

It is important to point out that there was general consensus that reforms were needed to boost depressed investment, streamline ineffi-cient labour regulations, restructure the economy by addressing the inefficiencies discussed earlier, promote exports and create employment. The sticking point was the direction (nature) of the reforms.

The reform period, 1991–2000[9]

At the behest of the IMF and World Bank, Zimbabwe adopted an orthodox Economic Structural Adjustment Programme (ESAP) in 1991. The adoption of an orthodox structural adjustment programme in Zimbabwe in 1991 entailed a fundamental shift from the comprehen-sive intervention system to one largely driven by market forces. The expectation was that ESAP would raise investment levels, thereby facil-itating higher growth rates and employment creation, and uplifting the standard of living of the majority of the people (Government of Zimbabwe 1991).

It needs to be pointed out that civil society was not consulted in the design of ESAP. Even within the government itself, the issue was not subjected to debate. The key targets of ESAP were to:

- achieve GDP growth of 5 per cent during 1991–95;
- raise savings to 25 per cent of GDP;
- raise investment to 25 per cent of GDP;
- achieve export growth of 9 per cent per annum;
- reduce the budget deficit from over 10 per cent of GDP to 5 per cent by 1995;
- reduce inflation from 17.7 per cent to 10 per cent by 1995.

To achieve these, the Economic Reform Programme (ERP) had as its main components competition enhancing measures including trade and exchange rate liberalization, domestic (including labour market) deregulation and financial sector reform and institutional reforms pertaining to fiscal reform. The fiscal reforms encompassed fiscal and parastatals deficit reduction, privatization and commercialization of public enterprises. It also included measures to mitigate the social costs of adjustment through the Social Dimension of Adjustment Programme. The question is: have these objectives been met and have the people benefited?

Reducing the budget deficit to 5 per cent of GDP

As part of measures designed to reduce the budget deficit, the civil service wage bill was targeted for reduction from 16.5 per cent of GDP in 1990/91 to 12.9 per cent by 1994/95, through reducing the number of civil servants (excluding health and education) by 25 per cent (23 000 posts) and implementing wage restraint. In view of Zimbabwe's high tax ratio, it was envisaged that most of the budget reducing measures would focus on cutting expenditures.[10]

Most importantly, it was resolved that with the re-emergence of external imbalances since 1988 and accelerating inflation, fiscal adjustment would be front-loaded. The front-loading of fiscal adjustment was intended to release resources early in the programme in order to support the restructuring of production in the private sector (Government of Zimbabwe 1991). It was also envisaged that ministries would be encouraged, through ministry-based efficiency units, to streamline their structures by identifying areas of redundancy and duplication. It was hoped that such reforms would deliver an efficient and effective, leaner and well-remunerated civil service. Cost recovery measures were also to be introduced as a way of reducing public sector expenditures. In addition, expenditures would be reduced through subcontracting and commercialising some government activities.

Public enterprise reform aimed at reducing the level of direct subsidies and transfer from around Z$629 million in 1990/91 to a maximum of Z$40 million by 1994/95. Much of this reduction was expected to occur during the first two years, when the subsidy was expected to fall to about Z$360 million in 1991/92 and Z$130 million in 1992/93. For the purpose of the reforms, all public enterprises were classified according to the action to be taken. Public service monopolies were to remain in government control, but these would be rehabilitated to run as commercially viable enterprises. Viable commercial entities were to be operated on a commercial basis, while non-viable commercial entities or industrial entities were targeted for liquidation. Those entities with a social role that duplicated that of another entity would be closed or merged. Entities with a valid social role were to be maintained under government, with any remaining sub-sidy to be small and transparent.

The objective of reducing the budget deficit from 10.4 per cent of GDP in 1990/91 to 5 per cent by 1994/95 was not achieved. On the contrary, the budget deficit had increased to 13.4 per cent of GDP by 1994/95. The lack of fiscal discipline on the part of the government, which had resulted in excessive use of the overdraft facility with the Reserve Bank, saw the budget deficit rise to 23 per cent of GDP by the end of 2000. The lack of fiscal discipline is exemplified in the fact that supplementary budgets rose from Z$181 million in 1990/91 to Z$4 billion in 1997/98 and Z$35.5 billion by 2000.

According to information from the Ministry of Finance, reforms in the civil service have led to the following changes:

Size of service before reform	192 000
Size of the service in 1994/95	171 472
Exempted posts in the Ministry of Education	10 000
Exempted posts in the Ministry of Health	90 000
Posts subject to the 25 per cent reduction	92 000
Target posts to be reduced	23 000
Cumulative abolished posts as at June 1995	21 547
Balance of posts to be abolished	1 453

A major criticism of civil service reform is that:

> budget cutting appears to have been an end in itself (with a focus on numerical targets, such as a 25 per cent reduction in the number of civil service posts), without a systematic assessment of the structural changes needed to improve efficiency and effectiveness. In the case of civil service reform, this has resulted in few efficiency gains and has encouraged the exodus of key civil servants, already disgruntled with severe salary compressions. The widely reported 'brain drain' of experienced teachers and health workers in the public sector, despite no official retrenchments in these areas, has been particularly worri-some. (World Bank 1995, 9)

Furthermore, the civil service reforms became an impediment to the implementation of the adjustment programme since 'insufficient atten-tion has been paid to skills requirements and too much reliance has been placed on overburdened staff and existing institutional structures to implement the reforms' (World Bank 1995).

As for public enterprise reforms:

> Progress until now has mainly consisted of the introduction of finan-
> cial measures, in the form of tariff increases and price adjustments,
> to reduce operating losses. However, the point is rapidly being
> reached where such increases are becoming a constraint on growth
> and affecting the competitive position of Zimbabwe's economy.
> Parastatals need to be weaned away from 'cost plus' pricing and
> forced to pursue greater internal efficiency in order to enable them to
> maintain a degree of price stability. (World Bank 1993b, 10)

During 1997/98, the eight largest parastatals had a combined deficit of
Z$11 billion. The major loss makers were the National Oil Company of
Zimbabwe (NOCZIM) (Z$5.5 billion), ZESA (Z$2.2 billion), Cold Storage
Company (Z$900.6 million), National Railways of Zimbabwe (NRZ)
(Z$703.1 million) and ZISCO (Z$688.4 million). According to the government, the reasons for the dismal performance include: 'management
inefficiencies, exchange rate depreciation, inadequate pricing policies,
inappropriate investments and generally the unfavourable macro-
economic environment' (*Government of Zimbabwe Ministry of Finance and
Economic Development Monthly Bulletin* 1999 3, 5). To which we should
add corruption. By the end of 1999, total parastatal debt was estimated
at over Z$45 billion, of which over 50 per cent was foreign.

As a result of extensive borrowings, Zimbabwe is in a debt trap. As at
end of 1998, the country's external debt amounted to Z$90 billion,
while the domestic debt stood at Z$43 billion, resulting in a total debt
of Z$133 billion (95 per cent of GDP). With an estimated 44 per cent of
total expenditure or 14 per cent of GDP in the 2001 national budget
going towards interest repayments alone, substantial resources are tied
up in servicing the debt. As at week-ending 2 March 2001, the domestic debt had reached Z$176 billion.[11] As a result of reduced foreign
funding since 1995, the government increased reliance on domestic
bank financing. Over time, there has been a marked shift in the composition of domestic debt as the government increasingly resorted to
short-term instruments. Whereas short-term Treasury bills accounted
for 3.9 per cent of the total debt in 1990, its share rose to 53.4 per cent
in 1995, 88.1 per cent in 1999 and 94.5 per cent by December 2000.

The combined effect of high budget deficits, a depreciating exchange
rate, the decontrol of prices, the removal of subsidies, and poor supply
response due to drought delivered high levels of inflation. Inflation rose
from 15.5 per cent in 1990, peaking at 42.1 per cent in 1992, before

falling to 22.3 per cent and 22.5 per cent in 1994 and 1995 respectively. These high levels of inflation have, in the face of loose fiscal policy, necessitated the maintenance of excessively high interest rates. Thus, the lack of progress on civil service and parastatal reforms remained a major area of weakness; as the IMF put it; 'a strengthening of fiscal policy, combined with an acceleration of public enterprise reforms were prerequisites for Zimbabwe's return to its targeted adjustment path and continuation of Fund support' (IMF 1993, 1). Interestingly therefore, following the lack of real progress in this area, the IMF suspended disbursement of funds under the Enhanced Structural Adjustment Facility (ESAF) in September 1995 and put Zimbabwe on a shadow programme for the next six months. Since then, the relationship between Zimbabwe and the IMF has been on-off, culminating in the withdrawal of the Fund in 1999.

Performance of the external sector

At the heart of adjustment programmes is the liberalization of trade. The share of trade (exports and imports) in GDP is often used as a measure of the extent of outward-orientation of an economy. Table 3.11 shows trade as a percentage of current price GDP for the period, 1980–98.

Clearly, following the opening up of the economy under economic reforms in 1991, trade has increased from 50.6 per cent of current price GDP in 1990 to 110.9 per cent by 1998.

Exchange rate depreciation, in conjunction with trade liberalization, is expected to reorient the economy towards exports. Apart from encouraging exports, the exchange rate is expected to dampen the demand for imports, which would have become more expensive in terms of the domestic currency. This, together with inflows of capital, are expected to improve the balance of payments position. Table 3.12 summarizes Zimbabwe's external performance during the reform period, 1991–98.

Export performance during the reform period has been dismal. In US$ terms, exports grew at an annual average rate of only 1 per cent during the period 1991–99, against a targeted rate of 9 per cent per annum. Imports rose at an annual average rate of 4.9 per cent during the period 1991–98. The Reserve Bank argued that the absence of a correlation between the 1997–98 currency fall and export performance is due to the heavy dependence on imported raw materials, intermediate and capital goods. The import content of the manufacturing sector lie between 10 and 65 per cent. Given an import content of 30 per cent, most firms are

Table 3.11 Trade (exports and imports) as a percentage of current price GDP

1980	1982	1984	1986	1988	1990	1991	1992	1993	1994	1995	1996	1997	1998
71.1	62.3	69.8	47.4	45.0	50.6	61.2	80.1	71.0	81.1	92.6	81.8	102.2	110.9

Source: Adapted from Bhalla *et al.* 1999, 19, Table 7.

Table 3.12 Performance of the external sector, 1991–98

	1991	1992	1993	1994	1995	1996	1997	1998
(a)								
US$ Export growth (%)	1.8	−14.3	5.2	20.9	13.8	12.6	−2.9	−20.6
US$ Import growth (%)	12.5	4.8	−15.1	17.6	19.7	5.6	18.1	−23.9
External debt/GDP(%)	43.6	60.9	66.7	65.4	60.4	58.1	57.3	80.0
Debt service ratio	23.5	30.0	30.0	25.0	19.8	17.6	18.0	28.0
(b)								
Current a/c balance (US$m)	−547	−842	−311	−318	−368	−179	−827	−359
Current a/c (% of GDP)	−5.3	−8.9	−2.1	−2.0	−5.2	−2.1	−9.4	−6.3
(c)								
Reserves (months of import cover)	2.1	2.0	4.1	3.3	4.2	3.9	1.0	1.2

Source: Reserve Bank of Zimbabwe (unpublished data).

adversely affected by the depreciation of the exchange rate, implying that exchange rate depreciation has double-edged effects.

The Reserve Bank argues that this is not helped by the lack of an export culture, as suggested by the fact that almost half of all manufacturing firms export only 10 per cent of their output, 30 per cent export 11–50 per cent of their output, while only 20 per cent have an export threshold in excess of 50 per cent. Even the provision of tax-based incentives in the 1999 budget (readjusted in the 2000 budget), the establishment of Export Processing Zones since 1995 and the recently established Export Credit Guarantee Company, which assists exporters in accessing pre- and post-shipment finance and export credit insurance cover, have failed to stimulate exports.

The overall balance of payments deteriorated from a surplus of US$210 million in 1995 to a projected deficit of US$596 million in 2000. As a result, the country failed to meet its external obligations for the first time in May 1999. Its arrears reached US$488.1 million in November 2000. Reserves, which represented 4.2 months of import cover in 1995, were down to one month by 1998. As the situation deteriorated, the Reserve Bank directed Foreign Currency Account (FCA) holders on 29 November 1999 to off-load half their balances on to the spot market. Such policy reversals undermine confidence, which ultimately holds back the required supply response.

External debt had risen from US$3.5 billion in 1991 to US$4.9 billion by 1997 before declining to US$4.5 billion in 1998. Such high indebtedness sacrifices future resources for development. In addition, it mortgages future generations. The debt service ratio, which had fallen from 30 per cent in 1993 to 17.6 per cent by 1996, had risen sharply to 28 per cent by 1998.

Table 3.13 compares the performance of the economy before the period of economic reforms (1985–90) with that during the economic reform period (1991–99) using selected indicators. For the economy as a whole, the rate of growth decelerated from an annual average of 4 per cent for the 1986–90 period to an annual average of 0.9 per cent during ESAP (1991–95) and improved slightly to an annual average rate of growth of 2.7 per cent for the period 1996–99. This real annual average rate of growth is way below the ESAP target of 5 per cent per annum. The rate of growth in employment decelerated from an annual average rate of 2.4 per cent during the period 1985–90 to 0.8 per cent during the period of ESAP (1991–95) and 1.5 per cent during the period 1996–99. The annual average rate of employment growth during the reform period is far below the rate of growth of the labour force of 3 per cent,

Table 3.13 Economic performance, 1985–99 (selected indicators)

%	1985–90	1991–95	1996–99
Real GDP growth	4.0	0.9	2.7
Real wage index (1980 = 100)	100.6	75.7	86.0
Employment growth	2.4	0.8	1.5
Investment (of GDP)	15.5	22.5	15.5
Savings (of GDP)	16.8	16.9	14.3
Inflation	11.6	27.6	32.6

Source: Calculated from the *Quarterly Digest of Statistics*, CSO (various years).

implying that new jobs are not being created fast enough to absorb new entrants into the labour market. A major cause for concern, especially for agriculture, is the increased 'casualization' of labour. Whereas 73 per cent of all employees on large-scale farms were employed on a permanent basis in 1981, the level had gone down to 47 per cent by 1998.

The lack of growth and employment expansion is not surprising given the collapse of savings from constituting on average 16.8 per cent of GDP in 1985–90, 16.9 per cent during 1991–95 and 14.3 per cent during 1996–99. Savings declined substantially from 20 per cent of GDP in 1995 to only 9 per cent by 1999. Consequently, the share of investment in GDP, which had risen from 15.5 per cent in 1985–90 to 22.5 per cent in 1991–95, declined to 15.5 per cent during 1996–99. Investment collapsed from 23.4 per cent of GDP in 1995 to 13 per cent by 1999.

The absence of an employment response during the period of reforms is particularly worrying, especially considering the collapse in real wages. Orthodox theory requires that in the context of unemployment, real wages be flexible. As the World Bank commented with respect to the collapse in real wages in Sub-Saharan Africa, such a trend represents, 'a brutal but necessary adjustment to reflect a labour force that has outstripped job creation and the need to become internationally competitive' (World Bank 1989, 29).

With respect to Zimbabwe, Collier contends that:

Certainly, inflation has been faster during the liberalisation than prior to it, and so it is reasonable to conclude that the liberalisation has contributed to the decline in real unskilled wages. Note that this is not a decline in the equilibrium real wage, but rather acceleration in what was already a gradual adjustment to the equilibrium. Such an adjustment raises employment. The transfer from wages to profits may also raise savings. (Collier 1995, 5)

In terms of which sector benefits most, Collier boldly predicts that 'both of these effects happen to benefit the import-substitute sector (which is largely coincident with manufacturing), because it is more intensive than other sectors in imported inputs, and because it is more subject to disequilibrium wages for unskilled workers than other sectors' (Collier 1995). The World Bank sees the fall in real wages in Zimbabwe in such a light, arguing that 'Zimbabwe's labour costs are now very competitive in international terms' (World Bank 1997, 3).

In virtually all sectors of our economy, real wages have collapsed. The average minimum wage in the private sector (excluding parastatals and domestic service) is around Z$2500. This amounts to only 30 per cent of the Poverty Datum Line of Z$8310 as at June 2000 prices.[11] This clearly shows that the current minimum wages are starvation wages, which cannot meet the basic needs of an average family of six, a father, mother and four children. In Zimbabwe, there is now a serious problem of the working poor.

Studies on low-wage policies have linked these to poor morale, shirking, moonlighting, multiple-jobbing, low productivity, high turnover and corruption, which undermine human development. The often quoted case in this respect is the extreme example from Uganda, where civil servants are reported as having spent only a third of or half their normal working time on government duty. The Public Salaries Review Commission of 1982 in Uganda established that 'the civil servant had either to survive by lowering his standard of ethics, performance and dutifulness, or remain upright and perish. He chose to survive' (quoted in Lindauer *et al.* 1988, 21).

In this regard, Singer contends that 'it does not follow that squeezing wages is the best way of getting labour out of non-tradables and low productivity sectors . . . exploitation wages must themselves be treated as a labour market "distortion" ' (Singer 1992, 34). A recent study of labour markets and adjustment by the World Bank came to a similar conclusion, observing that 'beyond a certain point the macro-economic consequences of real wage declines may lead to an additional cost of adjustment that relies too heavily on labour markets' (Horton, Kanbur and Mazumdar 1991, 5). Furthermore, falling purchasing power in countries such as Zimbabwe, where 80 per cent of products are for the domestic market, results in depressed demand, leading to a loss of jobs.

The share of wages and salaries in gross domestic income has declined, on average, from 49.2 per cent during the pre-reform period 1986–90 to an average of 41.1 per cent during the ESAP period 1991–95. On the other hand, the share of profits, on average, rose from 50.8 per cent during the period 1986–90 to, on average, 55.9 per cent during the ESAP period. This therefore suggests that the burden of adjustment has largely fallen on workers relative to owners of capital.

Poverty and the Social Dimensions of Adjustment Programme

A recent study by the Central Statistical Office (CSO 1998) suggests that the incidence of poverty in Zimbabwe has increased from 40.4 per cent in 1990/91 to 63.3 per cent by 1995/96.[13] The incidence of extreme poverty (households that cannot meet basic food requirements) increased from 16.7 per cent to 35.7 per cent during the respective periods. The results are similar to those found in the Poverty Assessment Study Survey (PASS) of the Ministry of Public Service, Labour and Social Welfare (1995).

The PASS study found that 61 per cent of households live in poverty and 45 per cent in extreme poverty. Levels of poverty are higher in rural areas (75 per cent of households) compared to urban areas (39 per cent of households). The incidence of poverty was found to be higher in female- as opposed to male-headed households with levels of poverty of 72 per cent and 58 per cent respectively.

The studies identified the causes of poverty as mainly structural. In particular, lack of access to land remains a major cause of poverty. The government had planned to resettle 162 000 families during the period 1982–84, and 75 000 families during 1986–90, but by the mid-1990s only 52 000 families had been resettled. Effectively, therefore, the land problem remains unresolved.

To protect the poor and assist the unemployed during the adjustment programme, the government created a Social Developments Fund (SDF) within the Social Dimensions of Adjustment Programme. According to the constitution of the Fund, women and youths, who constitute two-thirds of the disadvantaged social groups, were the main targets of the programme. The programme had the following components:

(1) An employment and training programme, including support for informal small-scale enterprises and public works;
(2) Targeting of food subsidies;
(3) Provision for exemption from cost recovery measures for vulnerable groups; and
(4) Monitoring and evaluation of developments.

The Social Dimensions of Adjustment Programme has failed to cushion vulnerable groups from the social costs of adjustment.[14] To begin with, whereas government had indicated that the programme would be given high priority and established urgently, a co-ordinator was only appointed in March 1993, well after the adjustment programme had started and its social costs were already being felt.

The employment and training component of SDF focused entirely on retraining retrenchees. These retrenchees were offered a five-day business course on 'how to start and run your own business', after which they were to apply for project funding through their training agency. By the end of the first phase of training in 1995, only 12,946 retrenchees had been retrained.[15] These represent about 28 per cent of retrenchees (using official statistics). However, considering that official statistics grossly underestimated actual retrenchments, the proportion of retrenchees re-trained is much lower.[16] A total of 2237 projects worth Z$205 million were approved by the end of 1996. These were expected to create 8744 jobs, implying that only about 16 per cent of retrenchees were redeployed (using official data).

The failure to mitigate the social costs of adjustment has been attributed to:

(1) The extremely slow progress arising from cumbersome procedures;
(2) Narrow focus of the training component on retrenchees to the exclusion of school-leavers; the existing unemployed; the existing poor, who are even worse off;
(3) Inadequacy of the five-day training (it is too short to be effective); not all retrenchees are suited to running businesses; it may have been better to provide more suitable skills re-training;
(4) Small coverage, considering the extent of the problem; furthermore, given the high failure rate of existing business, little employment may be created on a sustainable basis;
(5) Little knowledge about the programme; and
(6) Too centralized system (based in Harare) with a very small staff complement (see ILO 1993; Chisvo and Munro 1994).

The programme has suffered from under-funding and over-centralization. Although in practice the programme is only benefiting retrenched workers, the original programme was designed to assist the unemployed and poor. Given these weaknesses then, and the lack of proper funding, the programme was restructured in 1996. Training was reorganized so that trainees had to pay Z$500 for their training. This aspect only lasted until

December 1996. By the end of 1996, only 671 retrenchees had been trained under phase II of the programme, only 10 per cent of whom were women. A revised programme, the Poverty Alleviation Action Plan (PAAP) was unveiled.[17] The programme seeks to address the problem of poverty at all levels (rural, urban, etc.). A policy board, drawn from government ministries and civil society groups (including trade unions), oversees the activities of PAAP. Under the SDF board are the Loans Allocation Committee (LAC) and the Grants Allocation Committee (GAC).

A new programme, the Micro-enterprise Development Programme, which covers all sectors, was initiated. Through this programme, funds are now disbursed through micro-finance institutions (MFIs). The MFIs select beneficiaries on the basis of the new criteria, whereby the focus is on the urban and rural poor who can repay.

A Community Action Project (CAP) has been developed to assist local (mainly rural) communities with infrastructural development programme funding. Because it disburses funds to participating organizations in the form of grants, CAP operates under the Grants Allocation Committee. A major weakness of GAC is that it draws its membership from government ministries alone. Under CAP, communities are expected to identify their own programmes and obtain funding from the Ministry through local authorities. In view of its being a quick-dispensing fund, approval of projects under US$50 000 is delegated to the Rural District Councils, and beyond that amount, approval rests with GAC. Funding is from the World Bank.

Owing to the failure of the safety nets, the government has developed a new programme, the Enhanced Social Protection Programme (ESPP), which covers social protection policy, targeted education subsidies, labour-intensive public works, support for community childcare initiatives and public medical supplies. This programme, which was developed in 2000 in collaboration with the World Bank and civil society, has not yet taken off. Its funding by the World Bank is conditional on the government reducing its arrears on debt repayment. However, the government has started implementing the targeted educational support component on its own.

This programme comes at a time when the budget is in serious crisis. The budget deficit progressively deteriorated from 4.4 per cent of GDP in 1998 to 9.8 per cent in 1999 and an estimated 23 per cent by the end of the year. The deficit had been targeted to decline to 3.8 per cent of GDP by year end. The bulk of the allocation (69 per cent) is going to non-discretionary expenditures (wages, interest payments, constitutional and statutory obligations), leaving very little (31 per cent) for discretionary expenditures (capital investments, operations and for goods and services). Recurrent expenditures (consumption) rose from 120 per cent of total revenues in 1995/96 to 164 per cent as at November 2000. In addition, supplementary budgets have become the norm, with these accounting for 37 per cent of the original expenditures in the 2000 budget (Z$35.5 billion). Against this background, funding for the social sector in particular has declined from 10.3 per cent of GDP in 1997/98 to 8.7 per cent by 2000. In real terms, the social expenditure declined in real terms by nearly 30 per cent. Thus, the gains that had been achieved in the social sector during the 1980s were largely reversed during the period of economic reforms.

The deterioration in economic performance is particularly clear since 1997. This was caused by the payment of an unbudgeted-for Z$50 000 (in December 1997) and a monthly pension of Z$2000 (as from January 1998) to each of the 50 000 war veterans, massive depreciation of the exchange rate in 1997 and 1998, involvement in the DRC war, awarding of an unbudgeted-for wage increase of 69–90 per cent to all government employees in January 2000 (ahead of parliamentary elections), poor export performance, among others. The farm invasions and the general breakdown of law and order since the parliamentary elections of 2000 has adversely affected the economy, which has now been plunged into a serious crisis, the most challenging since independence.

Given the economic crisis Zimbabwe is facing, and the freezing of aid by donors, the resuscitation of the relationship with the donor community is crucial for economic recovery and development.

In a bid to arrest economic decline, the government launched an 18-month recovery programme, the Millennium Economic Recovery Plan (MERP), in 2000. Like its predecessor, Zimbabwe Programme for Economic and Social Transformation (ZIMPREST), it appears the programme is already off course and is not being followed, as the economy is now being managed on a crisis basis. A critical shortage of foreign currency resulted in a shortage of fuel.

Why economic reforms have failed

Although the severe drought of 1992 had a contractionary effect on the economy, it is generally agreed that drought alone cannot account for the lacklustre performance of the economy during the period of economic reforms (see World Bank 1995; 1996). The failure to create macroeconomic stability played a major part in holding back growth. The incidence of high inflation, resulting from excessive government borrowing to finance largely recurrent expenditure, delivered high

Table 3.14 Sectoral contribution to GDP and employment, 1980–97 (%)

Sector	% of GDP				% of employment			
	1980	*1985*	*1990*	*1997*	*1980*	*1985*	*1990*	*1997*
Agriculture	14.0	16.2	12.1	16.9	32.4	26.3	24.3	27.2
Mining	8.8	7.6	7.1	4.0	6.0	5.3	4.8	4.7
Manufacturing	24.9	23.7	24.9	18.2	14.7	16.0	16.7	14.4
Electricity	2.2	2.1	3.5	2.1	0.7	0.7	0.8	1.0
Construction	2.8	1.7	1.3	2.7	4.1	4.4	5.7	6.1
Finance	6.3	6.1	6.4	8.4	1.2	1.5	1.5	1.7
Distribution	14.0	10.2	11.4	18.9	6.9	7.7	7.9	8.0
Transport	6.6	6.2	5.9	7.9	4.4	4.8	4.4	3.9
Public administration	9.0	9.8	9.6	3.8	7.5	8.6	8.0	5.6
Education	5.2	9.4	9.7	7.0	3.4	8.1	8.9	10.0
Health	2.2	2.6	2.6	1.8	1.5	1.9	2.0	2.1
Domestic service	2.0	1.6	1.4	1.5	11.2	9.5	8.8	8.0
Other services	5.4	6.2	6.7	4.7	4.3	5.3	6.1	7.3

Source: Calculated from *Quarterly Digest of Statistics*, CSO (various issues).

interest rates, well in excess of 60 per cent. Such punitive interest rates discouraged borrowing, resulting in economic contraction. Macro-economic instability dampened manufacturing activity, and, following trade liberalization, a number of firms (especially in the textiles and clothing sectors) were forced to close down.

Table 3.14 captures the sectoral contribution to GDP and employment for the period 1980–97. Clearly, the role of agriculture, finance and real estate, distribution, hotels and restaurants in the economy has risen, while that of mining, public administration and especially manufacturing is waning.

Trade liberalization, together with high interest rates, has been blamed for much of the retrenchments. As a result, fears of de-industrialization have been raised with the Economist Intelligence Unit (EIU) observing that 'the situation is certainly worrying, and those analysts who saw liberalization as a solution to the industry's former problems now look very foolish' (EIU 1996). As Gunning and Mumbengegwi (1995) found, ESAP did not raise capacity utilization following the increased availability of imports. They found that firms operated at around 65 per cent of capacity. The situation was further exacerbated by the *impasse* in the bilateral trade agreement with South Africa following the expiry of the trade agreement in 1992. Besides, the removal of the export incentives which many analysts believed accounted for export growth prior to reforms further worsened the situation (see Muzulu 1993).

The adverse effects of trade liberalization have now raised calls for protection, especially with respect to South Africa. Conscious of the negative impact of the tariff reductions proposed by the Tariff Commission on revenues, the Ministry of Finance has recently rejected such recommendations.

This raises an important question with regard to the sequencing of reforms. Toye (1996) rightly observes that though economic theory does not offer an optimal sequencing path, the sequencing of reforms should encourage the complementarity of measures, which the 'big bang' approach adopted in Zimbabwe does not encourage. As he observes, 'to embark on a radical programme of economic liberalization and de-regulation before taking measures to stabilize macroeconomic imbalances is an incorrect sequence which will not produce the desired welfare results' (Toye 1996, 72). In fact, he suggests the importance of providing 'a clear advance warning before liberalising the trade current account. This gives a limited time to firms operating in protected industries either to improve their competitiveness, or to diversify their assets into other activities that will not be damaged by the removal of protection' (Toye 1996, 72–73).

More importantly, ESAP failed because it did not bring benefits to the majority of the people. According to the World Bank, 'unless the programme is seen to be generating benefits for everybody in Zimbabwe, it might not be possible to follow through with and maintain the momentum of many of the recent policy changes. This will require dealing more effectively with poverty and with the social dimensions of adjustment' (World Bank 1995, 18).[18] The failure of ESAP to redress the inequalities inherent in the Zimbabwean economy means the majority of the people cannot take advantage of the opportunities offered. This constitutes a major impediment to the success of reforms. 'Trickle down', often argued to be the route through which the majority would benefit from reforms, has not occurred in a manner that raises the welfare of Zimbabweans (see ZCTU 1995, chap. 1).

Interestingly, a recent World Bank 'performance audit' of ESAP concedes that:

> the concerns, however, go beyond the issues of pace and design: the comprehensiveness of the program seems a fundamental issue, especially given the objective of reducing poverty. Given the highly

dualistic nature of Zimbabwe's economy (where the white minority dominates formal sector economic activity and owns two-thirds of high potential land, and the black majority is concentrated in rural, communal areas and the urban informal sector), it would appear that some basic questions were not explicitly addressed at the outset. First, would ESAP, predicted on the formal sector acting as an engine of growth create sufficient jobs, quickly enough, to address the serious problems of employment? . . . Even realisation of the most optimistic scenarios for formal sector growth will not provide a quick solution to the unemployment problem. (World Bank 1995, 11)

On the structural bottlenecks that undermine development, Mhone (1999) argues that in the presence of allocative, distributive and microeconomic (technical) inefficiencies, development is stymied. Allocative inefficiencies imply the existence of under-utilized resources, especially with respect to unemployment and underemployment. A more inclusive growth path will unlock such structural bottlenecks in all markets and unleash a more dynamic and sustainable growth path. Distributive inefficiencies refer to the pervasive economic and social inequities that resulted in preferential access to resources.

The land issue is the most controversial with respect to inherited inequities. About 70 per cent of fertile arable land still lies in the hands of less than 1 per cent (about 4000 farmers) of the population, mainly whites, while 70 per cent of the black population eke out a living on two-fifths of the land in agro-ecological zones with poor soils and unreliable rain. On average, a large commercial farm is about 2200 hectares, while the average small-scale commercial farms (largely owned by black master farmers) average 125 hectares and the average communal farm is 4.5 hectares. The communal areas are overpopulated, overgrazed and ecologically degraded. Laws such as the Water Act that were passed during the colonial period ensured that large-scale farmers had a monopoly over water rights, resulting in the current situation where 85 per cent of irrigation schemes are in large-scale commercial farming areas. Government expenditures on research, infrastructure, marketing and storage were biased in favour of large-scale commercial farms.

Microeconomic inefficiencies refer to distortions at the enterprise level that militate against economic efficiency and international competitiveness. It is reflected in the low productivity of the communal, informal and parts of the formal sector. A very interesting example is the vertical, hierarchical structure of firms in Zimbabwe, which undermines efficiency and effectiveness. The issue is that the market on its own cannot resolve this triad of inefficiencies. Thus, in their presence, growth benefits only a few, and hence the phenomenon of 'jobless, rootless, ruthless, futureless' growth.

The failure of the supply response suggests that while getting prices right is necessary, however, it is insufficient. Studies on successful exporting point to the importance of non-price factors such as incentives, infrastructural development, building of technological capabilities, of which marketing and the development of human capital are central (Lall 1990). The removal of export incentives at a time when other regional economies are maintaining them contributed to the poor performance of exports. Furthermore, the emphasis on static comparative advantage inherent in World Bank advice that Zimbabwe should focus on being 'a supplier to industrialized economies, based on its resource base and low labour costs' (World Bank 1995, 133) is misplaced.

In fact, the expected switch from capital intensity to labour intensity may not occur due to the fact that firms had already adjusted to the absolute shortage of foreign exchange in Zimbabwe by employing an 'optimal' workforce. Any further shifts towards labour intensity would adversely affect the quality of products (see Muzulu 1993). In any event, promoting the extensive use of unskilled labour is no longer suitable in a world economy where competition is increasingly skill-driven (Lall 1990). Thus, sustained growth is increasingly associated with the building of technological capabilities, the provision of incentives especially for research and development, and the establishment of requisite institutions.[19] Within the current division of labour, the location of production is influenced much more by the level of technological capacity existing, and in particular the level of human resource development. In this context, 'labour tends to be seen as much as an innovatory resource whose potential has to be maximized than as a factor whose cost should be minimized' (Kaplinsky and Posthuma 1993, 1).

The experiences of successful exporters in South East Asia suggest that these completely ignored their areas of existing comparative advantage and developed output in areas where the world market was growing fastest (Amsden 1993). The state therefore has an important strategic role to play in building these technological capabilities.

The World Bank's 'Performance Audit Report' provides an interesting self-examination when it contends that:

> The Bank's overall performance was satisfactory, but its shortcomings were in focusing, almost exclusively, on policies and targets. In

retrospect, it is clear that the Government needed assistance in formulating specific action plans, as well as institutional strengthening to enable it to carry out, in particular successful fiscal and parastatal reform and an effective program to alleviate the burden of adjustment on the poor. (World Bank 1995, 10)

The lack of institutional capacity, and absence of strategic planning, with so much emphasis on meeting numerical (quantitative) targets, meant that the goal of achieving development was lost. Hawkins rightly observes that:

the arbitrary decision to retrench 25 per cent of the civil service is a meaningless exercise. The civil service – and the parastatals – need root-and-branch reform, not just number shedding. It means starting by asking what services do we want and what resources are needed to satisfy them. Then – and only then – can we say how many public servants are needed in each department. Cutting numbers is not the problem. It is a culture problem, an attitude problem – a matter of getting people to understand that they are there to provide a service, not to obscure and obstruct. Its a qualitative issue, not a quantitative one. (Hawkins 1995, 50)

Quantitative targets should therefore be a means to attaining a desired objective, and not the end themselves. In this regard, we may conclude with Kapoor that '[g]iven the weak implementation capacity in African economies . . . structural adjustment programs, in general, have unrealistic expectations about how fast adjustment can occur; consequently, the political costs of speedier implementation are also often underestimated' (Kapoor 1995a, 3).

This introduces an important dimension in the sequencing of reforms. Toye (1996) argues that for reforms to be sustainable, they must begin with those areas that promise the greatest benefits. Thus, before liberalizing the trade regime, the financial sector should be able to provide credit at affordable rates so as to broaden the economic base. Because this did not succeed in the case of Zimbabwe, the absence of an enabling macroeconomic environment meant that it was more profitable to 'park resources in the money market or engage in trading speculation, rather than manufacturing, resulting in a destruction over time of the productive sectors in the economy' (Kapoor 1995b). The speedy liberalization of the trade regime did not give local industries sufficient time to adjust, resulting in de-industrialization (Kapoor 1995b). Given then that issues of capacity, infrastractural development are medium-to long-term issues, the sequencing of reforms becomes of crucial importance.

The emphasis of ESAP was, as in other SAPs, on 'getting prices right' and hence over-reliance on 'free markets'. However, successful exporting requires 'the upgrading of export infrastructure, the provision of export finance, and the development of market intelligence' (Kapoor 1995a, 4). Industrial development, as the lessons from South East Asia suggest, requires a strategic role of the state in guiding and leading the market through the provision of incentives to those productive sectors offering the best returns (picking winners).

More importantly, the failure to consult other social partners hindered progress. In the words of the World Bank, 'the Zimbabwe case demonstrates the importance of popular ownership and participation throughout the process of adjustment. An open, transparent dialogue can help generate realistic expectations, reduce uncertainty, and contribute to a unified sense of national ownership for reforms' (World Bank 1995). Thus, as the World Bank (1996) found, ESAP is highly unpopular in Zimbabwe.

In recent years, the World Bank has openly admitted that ESAP failed. Addressing the First Forum of the Structural Adjustment Participatory Review Initiative (SAPRI), on 2 September 1999, Tom Allen, the Resident Representative of the World Bank, admitted that ESAP has been a failure. He attributed its failure to the following:

- growth needs to be inclusive – 'Partial deregulation *without* a restructuring of the dual economy creates social tensions and not enough jobs';
- social sector expenditures need to be protected and targeted measures to deal with poverty should not be seen as 'add ons' but as an integral part of the programme;
- state intervention is necessary – 'Getting the prices right and making markets work better are important, but these need to be complemented with measures to ensure that the "unequal" balance of power of those who can readily engage in the market and those who cannot, does not lead to dangerous levels of social tensions'; and
- national ownership is critical.[20]

Lastly, the nature of governance in Zimbabwe creates conditions for failure. The fact that the war of liberation was fought from external bases divided society into the liberators and the liberated. The liberators at the political level were referred to as the 'chefs', while the liberated were generally referred to in disempowering terms, as the 'povo'. Liberation credentials assumed an unassailable position in Zimbabwe's governance. This governance structure made the 'chefs' powerful, unaccountable and self-serving. Ultimately, no costs were imposed on failure.

In this context, political expediency has overshadowed economic rationale, with telling effects. Zimbabwe has developed very good policies (Government of Zimbabwe 1981, and more recently Government of Zimbabwe 1998b), but these have not been implemented. The implementation of ESAP has heightened the conflict between government and civil society. As the economic hardships associated with ESAP increased, civil society became increasingly outspoken, to the discomfort of leadership. Civil society demands resulted in the government agreeing to establish the National Economic Consultative Forum in 1997.

Conclusion: the way forward

This chapter has shown that since independence, the development strategies implemented have largely been top-down and have not resulted in (human) development. The economy has largely been managed on a 'fire-fighting' basis. As a result, whatever growth has been achieved has not benefited the majority. In fact, growth has been erratic and Zimbabwe is now in a deep crisis.

It is now widely accepted that ESAP and other market-driven reform programmes that have been implemented in Zimbabwe have largely failed. What appears also to be an emerging consensus is that there is a need for a new generation of development strategies that are developed through a stakeholder participatory approach.

If this then is the case, the way forward should involve the restructuring and consolidation of the institutions for consultations. The National Economic Consultative Forum (NECF) has become a 'talking shop' and even the most ardent participants are largely disenchanted by its lack of teeth. The NECF has failed because participants were invited in their individual capacities. In this case, it cannot engender national ownership. It is important to go back to the original idea of a forum where organized labour, organized business, NGOs, the academia and other stakeholders are represented at institutional level.

However, with the current economic crisis and descent to lawlessness, it is difficult to envisage much positive change in the foreseeable future. The situation will certainly get worse, before it gets better. Meanwhile, some positive developments are already taking place. Civil society is mobilizing itself within the SAPRI and the National Constitutional Assembly framework for participation in nation building, while the new culture of dialogue and consultations within the Ministry of Finance and Economic Development is encouraging.

Notes

1. An estimated 6000 white farmers held claim to 51 per cent of the land outside urban areas. Their farms ranged between 500 and 2000 hectares.
2. Drought cycles were expected to occur every two to three years (Stoneman 1988b).
3. Even the role and importance of the informal sector was acknowledged.
4. For urban areas, the PDL was fixed at Z$128, while that for rural areas was estimated at 60 per cent of the urban PDL (Z$77).
5. Furthermore, the opening up of the economy in 1980 resulted in cheaper trade arising from the removal of middleman premiums that had been necessitated by sanctions-busting during the Unilateral Declaration of Independence (UDI). Green and Kadhani (1986) suggest that by the late 1970s these premiums could have been as high as 15 per cent for imports and 20 per cent for exports.
6. The CSO cleaned up its data from 1985 onwards. Here, for the sake of comparison, we use the earlier data.
7. Exchange rate depreciation is an instrument for both adjustment and stabilization. An export revolving fund (ERF), designed to provide foreign exchange to import inputs required for the production of manufactured exports, was initially established with the assistance of a Z$70.6 million World Bank loan on 1 April 1983. Another scheme, the export incentive scheme, was established on 1 August 1984 to provide a 9 per cent tax-free cash payment in local currency to exporters (export performance based). The scheme was based on export performance and applied to 'qualifying export commodities' with a minimum of 25 per cent local content and a minimum value of Z$100 per consignment (for a detailed discussion, see CZI 1990). These incentives have been credited for the recovery of exports since 1983 (see Muzulu 1993).
8. The oil pipeline was opened on 19 June 1982.
9. The economic reform period can be divided into the period of the Economic Structural Adjustment Programme (ESAP), 1991–95, and the Zimbabwe Programme for Economic and Social Transformation (ZIMPREST), 1996–2000. However, the latter programme was launched belatedly on 9 April 1998 and was not implemented.
10. According to the Government of Zimbabwe (1991, 6), average salaries in the public sector were to be allowed to fall in real terms.
11. Government domestic debt amounted to only Z$6.7 billion in 1990.
12. The PDL used is for a family of six, two parents and four children.
13. Here, the incidence of poverty is measured in terms of the number of households (and not people) whose incomes cannot meet the basic requirements for living.

14. These social costs of adjustment were aggravated by the severe drought of 1991/92.
15. Of these, 8474 were from the private sector (66 per cent of total) while 4472 (34 per cent of total) were from the public sector. Of these, only 1923 (15 per cent) were females. There is no breakdown by age. However, given the focus of the programme on retrenchees, youths would only constitute a marginal proportion of these.
16. For instance, the official statistics suggest that only 59 workers were retrenched in the textiles industry in 1994, and yet the widely publicized closure of Cone Textiles alone affected 6000 workers.
17. The PAAP succeeded the SDF after the end of the first phase of ESAP in June 1995.
18. Already, the government has announced that laws pertaining to retrenchment will soon be further tightened, so that public sector employment may have to be, contrary to ESAP prescriptions, raised, and calls for protecting local firms are rising.
19. These involve human skills – entrepreneurial, managerial and technical – required to operate industries efficiently (Lall 1990).
20. Similar sentiments were echoed by the acting World Bank resident representative Rodgier van den Brink and his staff at the second forum of SAPRI held on 9–10 April 2001 in Harare.

4
Natural Resource Management in the Communal Areas: From Centralization to Decentralization and Back Again

Marja Spierenburg[1]

Introduction

The Communal Areas are a heritage from the Rhodesian white minority regime, which divided the country in to 'European Areas' and 'Tribal Trust Lands'. After independence the new government promised the return of the stolen lands to the African farmers and developed plans for an ambitious resettlement programme. The first post-independence development plan envisaged the resettlement of 162 000 families on to former European Land before 1986. By 1991 about 48 000 families had been resettled (von Blanckenburg 1994, 30) and by 1998 about 73 000 families, while almost 525 000 families were still awaiting resettlement (Government of Zimbabwe 2000a). Though quite an achievement, it was far less than the target set. During the first years after independence, the government had been able to acquire a substantial amount of land from farmers who had abandoned their farms during the war or who wanted to leave the country just after the war, uncertain of the new government's intentions. However, after a number of relatively stable years far less land became available for sale (Palmer 1990, 169–170). During the first decade after independence, confiscation seemed no option. The rights of property owners had been guaranteed for 10 years under the Lancaster House Agreement, and despite its Marxist orientation, the new government was keen to assuage the worries of international and local investors.[2]

In 1992, after the Lancaster House Agreement had expired, a Land Acquisition Act was adopted that facilitated the expropriation of land by the state. The Act allowed the government to acquire land compulsorily even when it is fully utilized at a 'fair price' instead of the ruling market prices – as had been specified in the Lancaster House Agreement. Nevertheless, not much happened in the period between 1992 and 1997; only about a hundred farms were designated for redistribution in this period.

The year 1997 was marked by violent protests from war veterans demanding compensation for their efforts during the struggle for independence, in the form of pensions and land for resettlement. In November that same year a list of 1471 large-scale commercial farms designated for resettlement was published in the *Government Gazette*. This was criticized by the commercial farmers' lobby, the private sector and the donor community who claimed that it was not clear how the government would use the designated farms and that the plan would seriously undermine the commercial farming sector and confidence of investors. Partly in response to this criticism, the government organized a donor conference in September 1998 at which a draft policy entitled 'Land Reform and Resettlement Programme Phase II' was presented (Hammar 1998, 21). During the conference, the government agreed with the other parties – donors, commercial farmers and representatives of the private sector – that the land reform programme should start with an Inception phase during which 118 farms would be used for resettlement. The donor community promised Z\$17 million to assist acquiring farms. Yet, in 1998 acquisition orders for over 800 farms were signed by the Minister for Lands and Agriculture. Around the same time several senior government leaders stated that more farms would be confiscated and that owners would receive compensation only for farm improvements, not for the land itself. However, again practice differed from rhetoric and in reality only a part of the designated farms was confiscated and fair market value compensation for the land was paid.

Twenty years after independence the land issue flared up again. In the run-up to the general elections in June 2000 a new constitution was drafted. Apart from further strengthening of the position of the ruling party, ZANU(PF), and the sitting president, the proposed constitution was also marked by far-reaching possibilities for confiscating land for resettlement, obliging the former colonial government to pay for the land while the government of Zimbabwe would pay for only land improvements. The draft constitution was the subject of a referendum in February and was rejected: government spokespersons argued for the radical land reform proposals, the opposition declaimed them. The rejection was followed by a spate of farm invasions, led by the Zimbabwe National Liberation War Veterans Association, which has a somewhat ambiguous relationship with the government. The invasions were accompanied by much violence against members of the opposition. The farm invasions[3] and the violence continued after the general elections in which the opposition won 58 of the 120 contested seats in Parliament.

Although the struggle for redistribution of land between the Large-Scale Commercial Farming Sector and the Communal Areas dominates the political scene, land reforms in the Communal Areas themselves are at least as significant for the ordinary Zimbabwean farmers. These areas make up 42 per cent of all land in Zimbabwe and harbour 57 per cent of Zimbabwe's population (Moyo *et al.* 1991, 58; Weiner *et al.* 1991, 147). They thus remain economically as well as politically important. Plans for the Communal Areas may seem to have been far less radical than the plans for land distribution; after all, the dual property regime and the principle of communal tenure have been maintained so far. Yet, they have been numerous, often contradictory and have had a great impact on the lives of people who inhabit them. Most policy contradictions revolve around three key issues that are intrinsically related: (1) ideas concerning the viability of the principle of communal tenure itself; (2) the form of local government: 'traditional' versus 'modern' local government structures; and (3) how much control should be devolved to local government structures: decentralization *vs* central government control.

Despite recent renewed calls for land redistribution, during the first twenty years of independence there had been a gradual shift in attention away from resettlement on European Lands to what is referred to as 'internal resettlement'. The viability of communal land tenureship was questioned and calls were made to implement land use reforms that would render land use in the Communal Areas more efficient so that they could 'carry' the large populations they were still harbouring. These reforms were also an attempt to reorient the settled social practices and social identities of rural people away from traditional forms of authority towards forms of political authority consistent with a modern nation state (Hammar 1998, 12). It is true that in the early days of independence 'traditional'[4] leadership was left out when a new local government structure was introduced, but over the years chiefs and headmen have gained influence again. Policy concerning traditional leadership has not been consistent over the last twenty years, as was the case with decentralization policies. Attempts to decentralize decision-making powers to newly established elected local government

structures were hindered by contradictions between and within legisla-
tions facilitating the reimposition of central control.

In the period between 1988 and 1995 I conducted research in Dande,
in the Zambezi valley in the north of the country.[5] This period was characterized by increasing tendencies to reassert central control over land
use patterns and resource use. Dande was one of the areas subjected to
internal resettlement and land reforms. Before looking at the contradictory tendencies in the post-independence government's policies concerning land use patterns, local government and traditional authorities
in Dande, it is good to overview the land tenure policies under the
Rhodesian state, since many of the contradictions in the policies have
their roots there.

Land tenure and allocation policies under the Rhodesian state

The management of land in the Rhodesian state was characterized by a
dual property regime. The Land Apportionment Act of 1930 divided
Rhodesia into European Areas and Tribal Trust Lands. Land in the
European areas was held under private property tenure. The tenure
system that was encouraged by the Rhodesian state in the Tribal Trust
Lands (TTLs) was essentially 'communal', although in effect the state
had taken over ownership of the TTLs (Ranger 1985a; Murombedzi
1990). A 'decentralized' system of local authorities became institutionalized from chiefs to headmen to kraalheads who were to manage the
land on behalf of the population in the TTLs.

Cheater (1990), Murombedzi (1990) and Ranger (1993a) argue that
the term 'communal', used to describe the tenure system practised by
African farmers before colonial intervention, was not only inappropriate but also the result of an ideologization of the land issue by colonial
authorities (and subsequently by post-colonial authorities as well).

Several myths form the basis of the notion of communal tenure. First,
it is based on the idea that chiefs and headmen were guardians of the
land and that no individual ownership of land existed. This implied
that land had no exchange value and therefore was not subject to
market forces (Cheater 1990; see also Mamdani 1996, 17). Nevertheless,
Cheater (1990) found historical evidence of forms of tenureship that
resembled private ownership as well as land sales and exchanges. A second myth is that communal tenure represented an egalitarian form of
land use. Ranger (1985a; 1993a), however, states that in fact it was the
colonial state, through its attempts to prevent the emergence of peasant

entrepreneurs in the TTLs, that diminished existing disparities in land holdings and other productive resources. A third assumption was that communal tenure was mainly geared towards subsistence farming, while the existence of peasant entrepreneurs as described by Ranger again indicates otherwise (1985a; 1993a).

The 1950s saw a – albeit temporary – break with the ideology of communal tenure and indirect rule through chiefs and kraalheads. As more and more land was alienated from the African population, the TTLs became increasingly overpopulated and the soils rapidly deteriorated. Since a total collapse of agriculture would have had harmful effects on the Rhodesian economy, the government introduced the Native Land Husbandry Act in 1951 (Ranger 1985a; Drinkwater 1991). Through it, the government sought to confer individual tenure rights on specific parcels of grazing or arable land presuming that individual tenure would lead to more efficient land use. The right to allocate land in the TTLs was taken away from chiefs and kraalheads. Because of a great deal of opposition and resentment among the population of the TTLs, the implementation of the Act failed.

Following the Unilateral Declaration of Independence in 1965, a 'community' approach to the development in the Tribal Trust Lands marked a return to the ideology of communal tenure. This approach relied heavily on the co-operation of the chiefs, headmen and kraalheads who had their rights to allocate land restored (Thomas 1992; Government of Zimbabwe 1994b). The underlying motive for this reversal of authority can be seen as an attempt to replace African nationalism with 'tribal government', which would be more controllable and act as a buffer against grass-roots opposition (Ranger 1985a). The government was also seeking to keep costs low by administering through the traditional institutions, including customary law (Thomas 1992). Although colonial administrators maintained that traditional election procedures were followed in nominating chiefs, a number of dynasties were affected by government interference. The government could veto any candidate for the chiefship in favour of a co-operative candidate, and the status of a chieftaincy could be lowered or raised (Bourdillon 1987a, 119).

There is a debate concerning the effects this development had on the legitimacy of chiefs and headmen. Quite a number of authors argue that the policy of indirect rule seriously damaged their legitimacy, that any co-operation with the Rhodesian government was interpreted as collaboration (see, e.g. Garbett 1966; Ranger 1982; Lan 1985; Thomas 1992). Lan even claims that many of the functions formerly performed by chiefs and headmen were transferred by their subjects to the spirit mediums, including the allocation of land. Bourdillon (1987a) and Alexander (1996) argue that the role of chiefs and headmen in the pre-independence period, especially during the war, has been oversimplified and misunderstood by many authors. First, not all collaboration served solely in the interests of the chiefs; there were many instances where they may have felt compelled to comply with the government's policy out of fear of loosing the government's support for infrastructural development and development projects (Bourdillon 1987a, 119). Furthermore, they claim that there were also many chiefs and headmen who supported the freedom fighters, assumed party positions and co-operated with the guerrillas, citing several examples from Masvingo and Chimanimani Districts.

Post-independence land policies in the communal areas and the introduction of a new local government structure

The observation made by Ranger (1993b, 106) that the Zimbabwean state 'simultaneously claims to be the heir of African tradition and of colonial modernity, the custodian of proletarian ceremonial (the invented May Day parades), of national glory and of rural customs' applies very well to the state's relation with traditional authorities as well as to land use and allocation policies in the Communal Areas, which have been fraught with ambiguities.

The land property regime became officially 'de-racialized', but not, as Mamdani (1996) would have it, 'de-tribalized'; the dual property regime continued. During the first twenty years of independence the former European Areas were left largely untouched and were renamed Large-Scale Commercial Farming Areas. For the majority of Zimbabwean farmers access to land remained dependent on their membership of a group, as inhabitants of a chiefdom. The Tribal Trust Lands were renamed Communal Lands.

The Communal Lands Act of 1982 stated that authority over land in Communal Areas is vested in the President who holds all Communal Lands in trust for the people. The Ministry of Local Government, Rural and Urban Development became responsible for administering Communal Land through the District Councils (Thomas 1992; Government of Zimbabwe 1994b, 22). The act stated that Councils shall 'have regard to customary law relating to the use and allocation of land' (Government of Zimbabwe 1994b, 23).

The installation of District Councils in the Communal Lands so soon after independence and before a new administrational structure had been officially introduced had caused quite some resentment among local residents (Alexander 1996, 181). Till then, local administration had been in the hands of either the former support committees that had helped the ZANU-related ZANLA forces during the war (Lan 1985, 209, 210) or local branches of the ZANU party, sometimes in co-operation with traditional leadership, sometimes in competition with them (Alexander 1996, 181). The establishment of District Councils indicated an attempt to re-establish a powerful state bureaucracy in the rural areas, mostly by the Ministry of Lands and the Ministry of Local Government. Decisions concerning development policy and land reform were taken at the national level, and the channelling of state resources to rural areas was controlled by the ministries, with little sensitivity to bottom-up demands, as noted by Alexander (1996, 183). Continuities from the past were evident and the presidential directive, which allowed the appointment of Africans to any section of the public service if the president on the advice of the prime minister deemed it necessary in order to redress past imbalances, did not bring a change to the prevalent modernizing and authoritarian ideology of the civil servants (Alexander 1996, 180; see also Drinkwater 1991).

In 1984 the Prime Minister issued a directive outlining the institutional framework for development in Zimbabwe which completely excluded chiefs and headmen. Democratically elected Village Development Committees (VIDCOs) were to be the basic planning unit in this new system of local government. Each VIDCO represented about 100 households. The VIDCO was to submit its development plans on an annual basis to the Ward Development Committee (WADCO), which represented about 600 households. The WADCO would co-ordinate the plans from all VIDCOs under its jurisdiction. It would then submit the ward plan to the District Development Committee (DDC). The DDC would then incorporate the ward plans into an integrated district plan for approval by the District Council. The DC comprised all Ward Councillors, who were the chairpersons of the WADCOs. In the DC the ward councillors were assisted by a district administrator (DA), who also served as the chief executive officer,[6] who was appointed by the Ministry of Local Government, Rural and Urban Development. The DDC, which was to develop the district development plan, was composed entirely of district heads of central government ministries and departments, together with representatives of the state security organizations and was chaired by the DA. It was therefore a committee of central government. Once the DC approved the district plan, it was to be submitted to the Provincial Development Committee (Murombedzi 1992; Thomas 1992).

The Prime Minister's directive officially constituted an attempt to decentralize government and promote community participation in developing development policies. But in practice, DCs tended to be dominated by the governmental officials serving on them. Furthermore, the fact that development plans had to be submitted to the District Development Committee before being submitted to the District Council did not help either (Thomas 1992, 10). However, many councils lacked both the expertise necessary to formulate development plans and the resources to implement them. DCs were almost entirely dependent on grants and on resources and the expertise of sectoral ministries (Alexander 1996, 183). Plans to train VIDCOs and WADCOs in administrative skills proved over-ambitious because of the lack of sufficient financial and human resources (Thomas 1992, 12). Where training was provided, the emphasis was on implementing central government policies rather than training VIDCOs and WADCOs to develop their own development policies.[7]

Although the operation and recognition of VIDCOs and WADCOs differ from area to area, there have been complaints about the lack of local support and participation within these structures.[8] Alexander (1996, 183) argues that the alleged weakness of VIDCOs and WADCOs can be attributed to the arbitrary nature of the units. VIDCOs and WADCOs were not built on previous communities and affiliations but simply on the figures of 100 and 600 households (see also Government of Zimbabwe 1994b, 25). However, in some instances local amendments have been made: figures were reduced or enlarged to create some overlap with existing communities.[9]

Apart from the lack of decentralization of authority and resources to VIDCOs and WADCOs, there were also problems with their representation. The Commission of Inquiry into Appropriate Agricultural Land Tenure Systems concluded: 'In practice, VIDCOs have no *modus operandi* allowing regular elections or other recognizable characteristics of democratic governance. Some, if not most, have had only one election since 1984. There was evidence of autocracy and manipulation' (Government of Zimbabwe 1994b, 24). Derman and Murombedzi discuss the domination of ZANU(PF) in local government institutions in the Zambezi Valley: 'The provincial governors and district administrators are political appointees and well-placed in the party. It is an unspoken assumption that to be on the District Council one has to be a member of ZANU(PF)' (Derman and Murombedzi 1994, 122).[10]

While after independence 'communal tenure' had been maintained in the Communal Areas, at the same time this form of tenure was considered inefficient. Plans to introduce land reforms in the Communal Areas further undermined local control over land issues. These plans re-surfaced in response to a period of serious droughts, which lasted from 1982 until 1984, and problems experienced with the acquisition of land from the large-scale commercial farming areas for resettlement. The assumption underlying the land reforms was that improvement of efficiency and intensification of land use could alleviate the pressures existing in most Communal Areas in Zimbabwe and would reduce the demand for land in the former European Areas. Many authors have pointed out the similarities between the land reforms and the Rhodesian Native Land Husbandry Act of 1951, among them Drinkwater (1991), Alexander (1996) and McGregor (1995).

The reforms were officially introduced in the First Five Year Development Plan of 1986. But in fact they had already been prepared when the Communal Land Amendment Act was passed in 1985 (Thomas 1992, 15). The amendments facilitated the intention of the government to introduce the demarcation of arable and grazing lands, and areas for rural housing construction. In contrast with the Prime Minister's 1984 directive, which appeared to seek to promote 'grassroots' development, the Communal Land Amendment Act authorized the non-elected governmental officials of the DDCs to prepare and adopt development plans of their own volition[11] (Thomas 1992, 15). No mention was made of consultation with local people, other than the fact that when a plan had been prepared and approved by the council, a copy should be sent to the chair of every VIDCO or council affected by the plan (Section 4 (5), cited in Thomas 1992, 15) who is given 30 days to consult local inhabitants and report back any objections to the plan to the council, together *with the identity of the objectors* (Section 4 (6), cited in Thomas 1992, 15, emphasis by Thomas).

In the end the Ministry of Local Government Rural and Urban Development took direct control over land allocation in those Communal Areas that were subject to internal land reforms. In these areas land allocation was carried out by its Department for Rural Development, and not by the District Councils (Government of Zimbabwe 1999a).

In 1988 the Rural District Councils (RDC) Act was adopted, though it was implemented only in 1993. In theory, this Act provided a deepening of the decentralization process, but in practice it firmly established the state's authority at the local level (Hammar 1998, 25, 26) The Act aimed at establishing a single type of rural local authority through amalgamating two previously separate types of council: the District Councils that served the Communal Lands, and the Rural Councils that served the Large Commercial Farming Areas. The RDCs were empowered by the Act as the land allocation and land conservation authority (Hammar 1998; Roe 1992). The act presupposed a considerable devolution of power and resources to elected local authorities. Nevertheless, as has been the case with the District Councils, the RDCs were far from autonomous in relation to the centre – neither in terms of resources nor in terms of decision-making powers – and served in fact to reassert the power of the central state over the rural areas.

In the second half of the 1990s, however, the objectives of decentralization changed. As part of the economic structural adjustment programme the government undertook a reform of the public sector. Decentralization and devolution were supposed to help reduce the role of the public sector as well as reduce the costs of government operations. More and more ministries started to decentralize funds and responsibilities to the local level. To better co-ordinate these efforts, a Committee of Ministers on Decentralization was set up. A lack of local resources and capacities, the latter especially among the elected RDC councillors, had been identified as the main obstacles to decentralization. In response, a nationwide RDC Capacity Building Programme was launched in 1996, with financial support from a number of European countries as well as the World Bank. Training and the deployment of resource persons were to foster institutional and human resource development. Furthermore, each RDC received a considerable development grant to develop projects and activities that could serve as test cases for newly developed skills, accountability and local democracy (Government of Zimbabwe 1999b). This programme was to continue in the year 2000, but with recent changes in government and the political upheavals that preceded and continued after the general elections in 2000, its future is unclear.

Meanwhile, significant changes in the position of 'traditional leadership' took place. Although the 1984 Directive excluded chiefs and headmen from the new institutional framework – they could only participate if elected in either VIDCOs or WADCOs – and although attacked by technical planning ministries as anachronisms that stood in the way of progress, there were also voices in the new government defending them. Immediately after independence, former employees of the Ministry of Internal Affairs lobbied for a continuing role for chiefs and headmen on the grounds that their exclusion from local government could lead to confusion, even anarchy in the communal areas (Alexander 1996,186). In many districts, chiefs were soon to be invited as ex officio members to the meetings of the District Council. Already in 1982, a Chiefs and Headmen Act was passed which recognized the institution of the chief, stating their right to a government stipend well in excess of that of ward councillors (Alexander 1996, 182, 187). The act however, did not, recognize the institution of the headmen, nor did it provide for a restoration of the chiefs' power over land allocation or court matters (Government of Zimbabwe 1994b, 25). Since independence the courts presided over by chiefs and headmen had been transformed into community courts, operating under the Ministry of Justice. In 1992 civil jurisdiction was restored to chiefs on all matters except land issues (Government of Zimbabwe 1994b, 26).

Alexander cites two reasons for the re-emergence of traditional leadership. Once the war ended '[b]acked by a strong pressure for a return to "normality" after the trauma of war, traditional leaders – and male elders in general – reasserted their power' (1996, 179). Another factor constitutes what she refers to as the authoritarian and modernizing ethic of the development bureaucracies. Especially the land reforms introduced in some of the Communal Areas and plans to introduce them eventually in all Communal Areas contributed to an increasing local respect for chiefs and headmen (Alexander 1996, 187). In the light of these developments and due to the structures in which they operate, VIDCOs and WADCOs became perceived as instruments of local administration, essentially implementation units for plans that continue to be developed in a 'top-down' fashion (Thomas 1992, 12). Alexander argues that by formulating an agenda based on a popular revival of 'tradition', traditional leaders were able to draw on a constituency that found itself threatened by the new agricultural policies. The traditional leaders certainly did not reject all aspects of 'modernization', but reacted to the authoritarian implementation policies and the further loss of local control over land. Traditional leaders invoked a version of the past in a bid to challenge the authority of the state and local development bodies. Spirit mediums played a supportive ideological role by providing a critique of the new land reform policies (Alexander 1996, 187; see also Spierenburg 1995 and 2000).

With all the contradicting acts and legislation, the situation with respect to land tenureship became increasingly unclear. In reaction to this, the government established a Commission of Inquiry into Appropriate Agricultural Land Tenure Systems. On the basis of extensive interviews and discussions the commission concluded that all local government institutions, from DCs to VIDCOs, claimed authority to deal with land issues (Government of Zimbabwe 1994b, 23). The commission added the fact that in practice chiefs and headmen were found to have illegally reassumed their former role in land allocation. The commission concluded that '[t]his profusion of overlapping and incongruent local organizational structures, each with its own boundaries and drawing on different sources of legitimacy, has thus created weak and disparate local institutions' (Government of Zimbabwe 1994b, 26). In its recommendations to the government, the Commission advised to restore the role and powers of both chiefs and headmen in matters of land: 'While traditional leaders are clearly not mentioned in the land laws, the requirement in the law that land administration is done with regard to customary law in itself implies some role of traditional leaders, given their status as executors of customary law.' (Government of Zimbabwe 1994b, 24). The problem, however, is that there exists a great deal of differentiation in the Communal Areas. Although the re-emergence of traditional leadership seems to be widespread, not everybody may feel that local chiefs and headmen represent their interests.

In September 1998, the Government of Zimbabwe organized the donor conference during which the draft policy concerning land reforms was presented. According to Hammar (1998, 21), this policy attempts to reconcile earlier contradictions concerning the role of traditional authorities in land allocation, but with limited success. The draft policy proposes to use local plans and involve chiefs, headmen, traditional assemblies, the Rural District Council and the district administrator without any articulation of how this would work in practice (Hammar 1998, 21). A new Act concerning traditional leadership that was presented in early 2000 did not provide much clarity on this either. The Act proposes the establishment of village and ward assemblies constituting all adult village and ward inhabitants. The assemblies are to be chaired by chiefs and headmen.[12] VIDCOs will become 'sub-committees' of the village assemblies and will be chaired by the village headmen as well. However, the position of the WADCOs *vis-à-vis* traditional leadership is less clear. WADCOs will continue to be chaired by the ward councillors, who will still represent the wards in the RDCs (Government of Zimbabwe 1999a). The draft policy presented at the donor conference in 1998 also proposed the establishment at the national level of a part-executive, part-advisory land board. Furthermore, it brought up the issue of a reorganization of the Communal Lands again (Government of Zimbabwe 1999a, 24). Hammar concludes that the draft policy 'retain[s] sufficient, and by-now familiar ambiguity with respect to land authority in Communal Lands ... to allow the state to play its cards in many possible ways' (Government of Zimbabwe 1999a, 21).

The implementation of land use policies in Dande: the Mid-Zambezi Rural Development Project

In 1993 the amalgamation of Rural Councils and District Councils took place, but its effect took some time to be felt in Dande. The first period of the amalgamation was especially devoted to solving problems such as the liquidation of the assets of the former Rural Councils. The Rural District Council Capacity Building Programme, which constituted a more genuine attempt at decentralization, had not yet started either. It was a period in which contradictions between and within land use policies, decentralization and the relations between the official local government structures and traditional authorities reigned.

Dande Communal Land

Dande Communal Land is situated in northern Zimbabwe, in the Zambezi Valley. In the north, Dande borders on Zambia and Mozambique. In the south, the boundary is formed by the Escarpment, in the west, by the Angwa River and in the east, by the Msengezi River (see also Lan 1985, 15). Dande falls under the jurisdiction of Guruve (Rural) District.

Conditions for agriculture in Dande are not all favourable. The climate is hostile, summers are hot and rainfall is unreliable. Close to the escarpment the soils are quite fertile, but further to the north the quality of the soils deteriorates (African Development Fund 1986). The majority of residents depend upon smallholder agriculture for a living, though often supplemented by income derived from temporary jobs in the major cities of Zimbabwe or on large-scale commercial farms on the plateau. The most important cash crops grown in Dande are cotton and maize; the latter is also used for household consumption.

Despite the difficult circumstances for agriculture, the area has attracted many immigrants. Especially between 1983 and 1985, the number of immigrants increased dramatically. In some villages in Dande recent immigrants constitute almost half of the population (see also Derman 1993). The majority of immigrants originate from the overpopulated Communal Lands surrounding Masvingo, though many came through commercial farms on the plateau where they were temporarily employed. A minority of the immigrants – about 13 per cent – is made up of people who, prior to migration, worked and lived on large-scale commercial farms on the plateau. Most of these people are of Mozambican, Malawian or Zambian origin but have lived all their working lives in Zimbabwe and have lost nearly all contact with their home area.

During the war for independence many guerrilla fighters entered the country from Zambia and Mozambique, through Dande. The importance of the area for the struggle for independence committed the post-independence government to develop it (Derman 1995, 14). Both government and donors assumed that virtually any development activity would be welcome.

The Mid-Zambezi Rural Development Project

The Mid-Zambezi Rural Development Project (MZRDP) was officially introduced in 1987, covering virtually all of Dande except the area west of the Manyame River. Its aim was to bring development to the area by rationalizing land use patterns and improving infrastructure and ser-vices. It was also one of the pilot projects for the internal land reforms. It was believed that with more efficient land use there would be room to bring in 3000 households from Communal Areas elsewhere in Zimbabwe that were experiencing acute land shortages. These were to be placed in 130 newly created villages (African Development Fund 1986).

The MZRDP was primarily funded by the African Development Fund. The actual implementation of the project was the responsibility of the Department of Rural Development (DERUDE, a department of the Ministry of Local Government and Rural and Urban Development of the Government of Zimbabwe) and AGRITEX (the national agricultural extension service).

Land was to be redistributed, with all households receiving new fields in a new or a reorganized village. In addition to the land reforms, the MZRDP was to provide improvements in infrastructure and services, that is construction and upgrading of roads, building of schools and clinics and the construction of water points (African Development Fund 1986).

Originally, the project was scheduled for completion in 1992. However, owing to technical and organizational problems, but, perhaps even more important, to increasing resistance by the local population, the project remained far behind schedule. In 1992 project funding was extended for another three years. In 1995 DERUDE ended its activities in Dande.

Most of the infrastructural development has been completed, with the (important) exception of the construction of water points. Access to health care and education facilities has improved and the upgrading and construction of roads has rendered the area less inaccessible. The reset-tlement/villagization exercise, however, has not been completed at all.

Though officially the District Council was responsible for the allocation of land in the area, this responsibility was taken over by DERUDE
when the MZRDP was introduced into Dande. During the first stage of
the project the DC was completely ignored. This led to a mistake that
generated much resistance later on: the gross underestimation of the
number of households already living in the project area. Based on the
1982 census, the Project Appraisal (African Development Fund 1986)
stated that approximately 19 000 people were already residing in the
project area prior to the implementation of the MZRDP. In 1985 Guruve
DC had census data available listing 24 000 people living in the project
area (Derman 1995, 15). However, even these figures were outdated by
the time the MZRDP was implemented, as spontaneous immigration
continued after 1985. When the MZRDP management finally discovered
that many more people were living in the area than the project catered
for, only the goal of moving new settlers to the area was abandoned. All
those already present were supposed to conform to the new land use
patterns. The project thus became an internal resettlement or villagiza-
tion project.

Land was to be redistributed, with households receiving twelve acres
of arable land and a one-acre residential stand in a reorganized village.
Households would not obtain a permanent title deed to the land, but be
given temporary user rights (African Development Fund 1986). Without
any consultation of local government structures, AGRITEX (Agricultural
and Technical Extension Services) conducted the designation of arable
fields, residential stands and grazing areas on the basis of aerial photographs and analysis of vegetation. Existing settlement patterns were not
taken into account. Once the maps were designed, teams of AGRITEX
officials moved into the project area and started demarcating fields and
stands with metal pegs.

When it came to allocating the fields and stands, at first the project
local authorities were bypassed again. DERUDE appointed a project
manager and support staff, and a number of resettlement officers who
were responsible for the actual allocation. Allocation of residential
stands and arable plots was carried out on the basis of a set of criteria
similar to those employed for selecting farmers for resettlement projects
on former European land. To qualify, one had to have Zimbabwean
nationality, have no other source of income than farming and be a
married male. Allegedly on the basis of customary law, women were
excluded.[13]

In the first wards where the MZRDP was implemented it soon
became clear to the population that the project would have disastrous

consequences, including rendering many people landless. DC councillors, who received many complaints, also about the allocation procedures, demanded to be involved in the process. Getting people to comply with project regulations turned out to be rather difficult, and as problems increased project management decided to implicate the DC. This led to some changes in the allocation criteria. The District Council demanded that, in order to qualify for land in the project area, farmers would have to be registered at Guruve District. This was to prevent recent immigrants from obtaining land at the expense of those who consider themselves autochthonous (from now on referred to as long-term residents). The District Council also decided that immigrants who had arrived after 1985 should not qualify. Furthermore, certain provisions for women were demanded. Project management gave in to the demands, with the important proviso that women could obtain land – be it not more than two-and-a-half acres – only if they were widowed and had minor dependants.

The process of moving farmers to their new fields proved to be a tremendous task. In some cases whole villages had to be moved according to the project plan. Transport was not provided for, nor did the project budget allow for financial compensation for houses or other immovable property that had to be left behind.[14]

When already existing villages were being reorganized, the procedure was as follows. Once fields and residential stands were demarcated, lists were compiled of those applying for plots, employing the official criteria. At first the lists were compiled by the resettlement officers; later this task was handed over to the VIDCO secretaries and ward councillors. The lists were then handed over to the resettlement officers, who did the actual allocation of plots and stands. Those who were not able to obtain land in their original village were told to apply in one of the new villages, or the less densely settled areas in the north. When existing villages were reorganized, the newly demarcated fields were sometimes already partly under cultivation. In such cases the 12-acre plots were allocated to the person who was cultivating most acres within the boundaries of the new plot, provided this person met the criteria for resettlement.

The project has created immense land insecurity. As already stated above, project planners had seriously underestimated the number of households already residing in the project area. Instead of bringing new families to Dande, the MZRDP now threatened to evict a large number of those already present when the project was introduced. Derman (1993) estimates that about a third of the present population, that is about 3800 households, would be rendered officially landless if the project were ever to be completed. Where these new landless would have to go to is absolutely unclear. The imminent landlessness has resulted in a scramble for 12-acre plots and increasing conflicts over land within the project area.

The designation of 'arables', residential stands and grazing areas did not conform to existing settlement patterns. Local farmers determine the quality of the soils on the basis of vegetation, in a similar way to the AGRITEX experts – though of course without aerial photographs. However, in choosing where to settle and cultivate they also take into account other factors, for example the availability of water as well as the presence of wildlife.

Most residents of Dande had settled along the banks of the many rivers which flow from the escarpment into the Zambezi river. The rivers provide water for drinking and the fertile riverbanks are very valuable resources, crucial for survival in an area where rainfall is highly irregular and unpredictable. Researchers from WWF have concluded that without riverine cultivation there will be no food security in the area (see Lynam *et al.* 1996). However, through the MZRDP AGRITEX wanted to enforce the old ban on riverine cultivation and move people away from the rivers.[15] By doing so people would not only be deprived of their most valuable resource for agriculture, but also of their main source of potable water. The MZRDP was supposed to solve this problem by constructing water points. Yet this part of the project was seriously behind schedule – not to mention the fact that the boreholes that had been drilled often broke down and were hardly ever repaired or maintained.

The MZRDP has resulted in massive deforestation (see also Derman 1995). Whole villages have been moved, new fields had to be cleared, while old fields were abandoned. The same applies when people had to change the location of their fields in the reorganized villages. Furthermore, competition between humans and wildlife has increased as quite a number of farmers have been moved by the MZRDP into areas hitherto occupied by wildlife.

Before the introduction of the MZRDP, chiefs and headmen, despite the new legislation, mainly dealt with land matters in the area. Headmen did the actual allocation of plots, reporting their decisions to the chiefs. Chiefs occasionally also allocated land, and decided upon the location of new villages. Contrary to Lan (1985) I have not come across spirit mediums allocating land, but the chiefs consulted them when locations for new villages were decided upon. The headmen had already, before independence, allocated most long-term residents' land.

The majority of immigrants also obtained land from chiefs and headmen, though after independence many also sought permission from the VIDCOs and ward councillors. Often headmen approached spirit mediums to ask permission on behalf of immigrants to settle in their villages.

The relations between traditional authorities on the one hand and VIDCOs and WADCOs differed from village to village. In many cases, headmen co-operated with VIDCOs and WADCOs. Traditional leaders themselves were rarely elected to the VIDCOs and WADCOs, but sometimes their close relatives were elected. There were villages, however, where some tension and competition existed between headmen and VIDCOs. Where immigrants formed the majority of the village population, they could dominate the VIDCOs. In such cases, immigrants, who felt the headmen did not adequately represent them, approached only the VIDCOs with their requests. Long-term residents who felt excluded from local government strove for the reassertion of traditional leadership. The existence of two structures of authority increased the possibilities for 'shopping'; depending on their background and position people approached one or the other and indeed, as the Commission of Inquiry into Appropriate Agricultural Tenure Systems concluded, the representatives of both structures felt they had the right to deal with land matters.

The local authorities that had been dealing with land matters had not been implicated either in the planning or in the early stages of the implementation of the MZRDP. But when it became clear that without them the implementation would certainly fail, they were given a small role in the project: the DC was given some influence over the selection criteria; and VIDCOs and ward councillors were mobilized to register land applications for land, all this in the hope they could obtain compliance with the selection criteria, which the resettlement officers had been unable to obtain.

Both traditional authorities and local government institutions have tried to get some grip on the situation and redress some of the problems arising from the MZRDP in their own ways. The VIDCO secretaries compiling lists of people requesting 12-acre plots did not always apply the official selection criteria, for example, by registering divorcees as widows. Furthermore, some VIDCO secretaries and ward councillors were known to discourage certain people from registering by giving them false information concerning the selection criteria. For example, many immigrants of Mozambican origin were told not to bother registering for a plot because, even if they had Zimbabwean citizenship and were officially registered at Guruve District, they would not qualify on the basis of their foreign origins.

In villages where resettlement had officially been completed, that is where all arable plots and residential stands had been distributed and allocated, it was not uncommon to find many people living in the village who had not been allocated land there. In some cases, people who were rendered landless by the project obtained permission from village headmen to settle in the grazing areas. In other cases, they 'borrowed' land from people who had not (yet) cleared all of their 12 acres. People who had access to riverine fields prior to the implementation of the project often still cultivated their 'mudimba'. This, however, is increasingly causing conflicts with farmers who own cattle but no streambank fields, and want to graze their livestock in those riverine areas now designated as communal grazing areas.

The MZRDP created a lot of tensions and conflicts. The struggles for control over land took place at two levels: there were conflicts between the residents of the project area and project management over the implementation of the project and fights amongst those subjected to the project over who would have the right to land under the project in case implementation could not be stopped.

The second level involved conflicts between long-term residents and recent immigrants, but also in some cases between traditional authorities and members of local government structures. The conflicts were related to the fact that the land reforms did not follow local land use patterns. As the number of immigrants expanded, it became increasingly difficult for them to gain access to riverine fields other than through borrowing or renting. The fields allocated by chiefs and headmen to the more recent newcomers were therefore generally situated further away from the riverbanks. When existing villages were reorganized, immigrants stood a better chance obtaining fields since they were often already farming in the upland areas demarcated by AGRITEX. Long-term residents had most of their fields near the rivers and hardly ever had demarcation pegs in their fields. Many immigrants had changed their registration certificate and obtained district citizenship in time to qualify for a 12-acre plot. Conflicts arose over the definition of 'immigrants' and 'long-term residents'.

Once AGRITEX had demarcated 12-acre plots in a certain area, this was often followed by a scramble for land within the new boundaries. Long-term residents suddenly claimed large parts of the newly demarcated fields, stating that long ago the chiefs had allocated land to them for future use. They transferred all their labour to the new plots, clearing as many acres as possible in order to stand a better chance of obtaining the land from the resettlement officers.

In those areas where immigrants dominated, the VIDCOs, tensions with headmen – who had no official role in the project – increased over the question which households qualified for plots.

Many councillors used DC meetings to vent the grievances of the population of Dande with respect to the MZRDP. Yet, the government officials serving on the DC were somewhat ambivalent about the project. On the one hand they agreed with the official line that land in the Communal Areas was used inefficiently and that land reforms were necessary. But over time they became aware of the problems created by the MZRDP and the difficulties to implement it. It was due to their insistence that the selection criteria were somewhat adapted.

Project management seriously underestimated the problems involved in moving large numbers of people, especially when this had to be done against their will. Project regulations were difficult to enforce in such a large area, particularly when local-level institutions were not co-operating.

As resistance to the MZRDP increased, project management decided upon a change of strategy that entailed the involvement of the hitherto ignored traditional leadership. In one of the wards where resistance had been quite strong it was decided to approach the chief. The idea behind the new strategy was that once the support of traditional leadership was obtained, its subjects would follow and implementation of the project would be facilitated. However, things did not work out the way the project management had envisaged. The chief, who may have felt caught between his subjects and his employer, referred the case to another 'traditional authority, the medium of a royal ancestral spirit'. Here we see a transferral of authority over land to a spirit medium as predicted by Lan (1985) when a chief's position *vis-à-vis* his subjects and the state becomes difficult, but this time the transfer was effected by the chief.

In 1992 Chief Matsiwo was approached by a delegation of the project staff. He was asked to give permission for the implementation of the resettlement exercise in Matsiwo A ward.[16] At first, the chief refused any co-operation with project staff on the grounds that a large part of his chiefdom had already been subjected to the implementation of the project without his prior consultation. He advised the project manager to approach the spirit medium of the area, the medium of Royal Ancestor (*Mhondoro*) Chidyamauyu. The chief argued that the *Mhondoro*[17] are the real owners of the land in Dande and therefore they are the only ones who can give permission for resettlement.

The project manager persuaded the chief to visit the medium of Chidyamauyu on behalf of DERUDE. The medium, however, refused to deal with the chief and ordered him to tell the project manager to come and talk to the spirit about the MZRDP himself. After some hesitation, the project manager decided to do so, but he still wanted the chief to accompany him. The chief and project manager were told that the spirit of Chidyamauyu had forbidden the implementation of the MZRDP in the Matsiwo A ward. By March 1993 the project manager decided he would not accept the verdict of Chidyamauyu and tried to negotiate with the medium. After mediation by the chief, another meeting was organized with the medium, the village headmen and about fifty villagers. During the meeting the medium was possessed. He asked the chief why he had called the spirit of Chidyamauyu. The chief answered that he might be the leader of the people, but that the *Mhondoro* was the owner of the land. When the project manager and the resettlement officer asked whether they could get permission to start the demarcation exercise, both the chief and the spirit medium told the village headmen to discuss the matter at a separate meeting. The village headmen withdrew from the meeting and discussed the matter among themselves. When they returned about half an hour later, they told the project manager and the resettlement officer that they did not want the resettlement project introduced in their area.

Faced with all village headmen and the spirit medium opposing the project and in the presence of the medium and the project manager, the chief also publicly objected to the project. However, the project manager refused a second time to accept the pronouncement of the spirit and started to organize meetings in the different villages in the Matsiwo A ward to promote the MZRDP. At these meetings the chief could be heard advocating the project.

The project manager sent the chief to the medium one more time. The chief returned highly upset. He claimed that he had suddenly felt sick during the meeting and had lost consciousness. He was revived again by the spirit medium who warned the chief never again to bring up the issue of the MZRDP.

The medium had joined the ZANLA guerrilla forces during the war for independence. When the medium continued to reject the MZRDP, some government officials appeared on the scene and promised that the government would reward him handsomely for his assistance during the war. Contrary to local expectations[18] the medium of Chidyamauyu did receive quite a herd of cattle and MZRDP staff built a house for him. The project management tried to make it look as if the medium had been bribed into accepting the project. Most people in the area then withdrew their support for the medium and rumours started to circulate that he had been abandoned by his spirit and was speaking with his own voice. These rumours continued until the medium publicly denounced the project again.

The propaganda meetings that had been organized by the project management did have some effect though. There, as well as in more informal contact with project staff, hints were dropped suggesting that if the people of the Matsiwo A ward continued to refuse the MZRDP, their area would never see the improvement of services nor infrastructure. Some people actually believed this and decided that even if the project was creating many conflicts, it would be better to give up resistance to it or otherwise the area would never see any government-sponsored development. The spokesman for this group was a young man who was a member of the Apostolic Church who later was to stand as candidate for the post of ward councillor. The issue of the project and its supposedly developmental aspects may have exacerbated an already existing opposition between elders and youth. The proponents of the project emphasized their affiliation with the Christian (mainly Independent) churches, rejecting 'the old people's backward traditions'. The old ward councillor had chosen the side of the opponents of the MZRDP and had publicly denounced the project. When in 1994 ward councillor elections took place, he lost his support from the ZANU(PF) district branch, which decided to back the new candidate who was pro-MZRDP. The pro-MZRDP candidate won.

The new ward councillor tried to persuade the management of the MZRDP several times to continue with the implementation of the project, despite the directives of the spirit medium. The management issued statements that the redistribution of land would finally take place, but nothing happened. Apart from the organizational problems of moving large numbers of people, most of them against their will, fear on the part of the project staff may have played a role. Quite a number of them were afraid that if they continued with their work the *Mhondoro* would punish them with illnesses, accidents and bad luck.

In 1995 project staff were withdrawn from Dande and DERUDE ended its activities. The remaining tasks were devolved to the District Development Fund. What would happen to the now officially illegal settlers is not yet clear. The project staff had referred the problem to the RDC, but neither the government officials nor the ward councillors serving in the DC so far have dared to deal with this problem.

Conclusion

The case of the MZRDP shows at once the disastrous consequences of a far-reaching re-centralization policy, as well as the difficulties of enforcing such a policy. Owing to the complicated logistics of the project it could not be implemented without the help of local government structures. Yet, it also became clear how difficult it was to obtain this co-operation in the face of resistance by a major part of the population. Even the strategy of enlisting the help of traditional authorities did not help. Relations between chiefs and his subjects were misunderstood, the 'conversion' of a chief is not automatically followed by his subjects. Caught between his subjects and the state the chief referred the case of the project to a *Mhondoro* spirit medium as the representative of the real owners of the land. Spirit mediums are not included in any legislation on local government or traditional authorities.[19] The involvement of the medium had unforeseen consequences for the project. *Mhondoro* have a strong ideological relation to the land. Mediums do not directly control access to land or land use patterns, but they offer possibilities for local communities to discuss land-related issues (see Spierenburg 2000) and if their pronouncements reflect local public opinion these can become very important.

The opponents of the MZRDP have successfully resisted the implementation of the project. However, not all has been gained. The people in the project still suffer from the negative impacts of the project. Insecurity over land has significantly increased, food insecurity as well. On top of that, the project has created much environmental damage.

The swings between a recourse to traditional authorities and attempts to establish a modern local government structure, which have taken place since the Rhodesian period, resulted in complications and confusion about who is responsible for the allocation of land and other resources. A simple return of authority over land to traditional leaders is no longer an option. Some groups may not feel they are represented by these local government structures. Over time they have built their own 'constituencies'. I agree with Alexander (1996) that most problems with local government structures stem from a lack of true decentralization. If cries for a return to 'tradition' are heard, these can be interpreted as serious demands for local control over land and other natural resources.

The new proposals for village and ward assemblies propose a mix of 'traditional' leadership and elected local government structures without a clear definition of the relation between the two. This is bound to create similar problems to those described in this chapter. Furthermore, the assemblies will only be effective if substantive decision-making powers and resources are decentralized to these bodies. The RDC Capacity Building Programme seemed to be a serious step in the direction of real decentralization. However, given recent developments in Zimbabwe the prospect of increasing local control seems rather gloomy.

Notes

1. Initial versions of this chapter have been presented at the following two conferences: the 1998 African Studies Association Meeting (Chiefs versus Councils: Local Accountability of Authority in Natural Resource Management, Chicago: November); and the 9th General Assembly of the Council for the Development of Social Science Research in Africa (CODESRIA), Dakar, December 1998. I wish to thank Jesse Ribot, Amanda Hammar, Bonno Thoden van Velzen and the editors of this volume for their helpful comments. The only person, however, responsible for conclusions drawn and mistakes made is myself. I thank the Centre for Applied Social Sciences, University of Zimbabwe, for granting me the status of Research Associate during my stay in Zimbabwe. In the Netherlands I was affiliated to the Amsterdam School of Social Science Research.
2. In 1988, the government even reduced its land acquisition budget by nearly two thirds (Moyo 1995, 116).
3. The former Governor of Matabeleland, Welshman Mabhena, has the honour of being the most prominent black commercial farmer to have his farm invaded, in early July, after the elections had taken place in 2000.
4. The term Traditional 'is put in' inverted commas to recognize the fact that the position and authority of chiefs, village headmen and spirit mediums has been and continues to be influenced by many aspects and is not and has never been static or unchanging.
5. Fieldwork was made possible by the support of the Netherlands Foundation for the Advancement of Tropical Research (WOTRO).
6. Although there are cases in which the two functions are executed by two different people.
7. A ward councillor in the area where I conducted my research showed me the training material he received and the notes he took during the training he received in 1994.
8. In 1989 the Minister of Local Government Rural and Urban Development made the following statement: 'What is however disturbing is that in some areas there is an unacceptable level of participation in the planning process by residents at the village and ward levels. Reports reaching my ministry suggest that people are not sufficiently involved or active in the village and ward development committees' (quoted in Murombedzi 1990, 22).
9. Quite a large number of VIDCOs and WADCOs in Dande did not contain the specified number of households, but were delineated in such a way that they overlapped more or less with existing villages or neighbourhoods.
10. In one district in the Zambezi Valley it was more than an unspoken assumption. In Nyaminyami, before the 1988 unification of ZANU and ZAPU, ward councillors who were elected but were members of the ZAPU were not permitted to serve on the council (Derman and Murombedzi 1994, 122).
11. Communal Land Amendment Act, section 4(1), cited in Thomas 1992, 15.
12. The office of village headman will be officially reinstated. Village headmen will be supposed to collect the development levies for the RDC and in return will be able to keep a certain percentage of the levies for themselves as salaries.
13. Alexander (1996, 187) argues that while the government attempted to put women on an equal footing, the re-emergence of traditional leadership,

including spirit mediums, put a stop to this development. In Dande, with respect to land allocation at least, the opposite appears to have happened. While the government excluded women in the MZRDP project, allegedly based on traditional criteria, headmen and spirit mediums argued strongly in favour of women – at least widows of all ages and divorcees – obtaining land in their own rights. Indeed, many of the women left out by the project had been allocated their own land by headmen prior to the implementation of the MZRDP. It should be noted, however, that the criterion relating to sources of income was never seriously applied. Several resettlement officers as well as the project manager obtained 12-acre plots and residential stands in the project area, and they certainly had sources of income other than from farming.

14. There had been plans to provide selected farmers with loans for constructing new houses, but these never materialized. Some assistance was provided, though. On each new 12-acre plot, one acre was stumped and ploughed by project personnel, and seed and fertilizer packages for one acre were distributed.

15. This is based on the assumption that riverine cultivation leads to siltation and erosion. However, Scoones and Cousins (1991) demonstrate that the technical evidence on which the continuation of the ban is based contains many inaccuracies and that the practice is far less damaging than is often assumed (see also Dambo Research Unit 1987). When research demonstrated the profitability of maize production on wetlands, this resulted in a legalization of wetlands cultivation in the European areas in the 1960s (see Murombedzi 1991). Farmers in the Communal Areas, on the other hand, remain bound to the old legislation.

16. The chiefdom of Matsiwo includes several other wards as well.

17. *Mhondoro* are the spirits of royal ancestors, the great rulers of the past. All present-day chiefs of Dande claim descendance from one of the *Mhondoro*. The spirits are believed to continue looking after the territories they once ruled when they were still alive, by providing rain and soil fertility. In Dande, these areas have relatively clear boundaries, which are known by most inhabitants; they are termed 'spirit provinces' by Garbett (1969; 1977). The land and all other natural resources in a spirit province ultimately belong to the *Mhondoro* of that province. The *Mhondoro* are thought to communicate with the living through a medium (see also Lan 1985). Individuals in cases of sickness and misfortune can consult the spirit mediums of the Mhondoro. More commonly, however, village elders in the event of droughts or other natural disasters consult them. The explanation of climatological mishaps offers scope for *Mhondoro* mediums to voice social comment. Mediums and spirits are believed to be completely separate: a medium cannot be held responsible for what the spirit utters when taking possession of the medium's body. However, as I have argued elsewhere (Spierenburg 1995; 2000), there is room for adherents to influence the pronouncements of *Mhondoro* mediums. Mediums who do not take public opinion into account run the risk of being accused of speaking with their own voice instead of the spirit's, thus being frauds (see also Bourdillon 1979).

18. This was long before 1997 when war veterans staged several demonstrations to demand compensation for their sacrifices made during the war. During the period of this case study many veterans complained that even those who were physically handicapped or suffered from mental problems because of the war did not receive any assistance from the government.
19. Their rights and duties are laid down in the Traditional Medical Practitioners Act of 1981, which attempts to assign them a medical role instead of a political one.

5
Zimbabwe's War Veterans and the Ruling Party: Continuities in Political Dynamics

Norma Kriger

Introduction

Zimbabwe's liberation war veterans emerged as critical allies of the ruling party in the June 2000 parliamentary election campaign. Faced with the most serious electoral threat in its 20-year rule, ZANU(PF) forged an alliance with the Zimbabwe National Liberation War Veterans' Association (ZNLWVA). War veterans spearheaded the invasion and occupation of white commercial farmers, led compulsory political education sessions in the rural areas and terrorized farm workers and others suspected of being opposition supporters. For their services, the ZNLWVA was supposed to pay them with party money. The party provided other types of assistance for the veterans and their supporters. It gave them access to army, intelligence and police logistical support (such as food and transport), and protection against the rule of law. Veterans and party leaders together invoked the liberation war to justify their land grabbing and presented the new opposition as a neocolonial party which threatened to turn back the gains of the liberation struggle. The partnership between veterans and the party has persisted since the election. Veterans continue to invade and build on farms, and collect fees for land allocation and building rights. In the government's new accelerated land reform programme, veterans are a preferential group – they will receive 20 per cent of resettlement plots. But cracks in the alliance are already evident. Some war veterans complain they never got paid for their services. In late September, police were instructed to evict war veterans and their supporters from illegally occupied urban land around Harare and to demolish their structures. Responding to police action, veterans marched to Mugabe's office to protest. If past experience is any basis for predicting the future, veterans will likely exact a price from the party before they adhere to any new party directives.

This chapter is an attempt to provide some historical perspective on the current visible power of veterans in Zimbabwean politics. It draws on my unpublished manuscript, 'Guerrilla Voices: Power and Privilege in Zimbabwe'.[1] Contrary to the view that veterans' power is new, I argue that veterans were born powerful in 1980 and exercised power throughout the post-independence period. Since independence, the political dynamics between war veterans and the ruling party have been remarkably consistent. Their relationship has been characterized by collaboration, conflict and accommodation. Veterans and the party have used each other to pursue their different, though often overlapping, objectives. The party has used veterans to build its power and legitimacy. It has sanctioned and encouraged veterans' violence against its opponents and rewarded them for work well done. It has invoked its role in the liberation struggle to justify its use of veterans and its objectives. Veterans have used their allegedly superior contribution to the liberation struggle to justify their claims for preferential access to state resources – jobs, promotions, pensions and land. In trying to enforce their demands, they have often used violence and intimidation against competitors for resources, as well as party leaders and bureaucrats whom they believed were blocking their progress. For 20 years they have also sought allies within both the party (members of parliament, Cabinet ministers, senior party officials) and state institutions (bureaucrats, the army, the police).

In making the case for continuities with the past, I am not suggesting that there have been no important changes affecting the relationship between war veterans and the party in the post-independence period. Veterans were once divided sharply according to their war-time political loyalties. ZANLA fighters supported Robert Mugabe's ZANU(PF), Zimbabwe People's Revolutionary Army (ZIPRA) gave its allegiance to Joshua Nkomo's ZAPU. After an agreement to merge the parties in 1987, these divisions lost some of their force. Other divisions, too, have marked veterans' struggles: war disability, gender, state *vs* other non-state employment or unemployment. At times, veterans have also worked together across all these internal differences. Veterans issues were not always part of public debate. They burst into the media and Parliament in 1988 when the party had eliminated its chief opponent, ZAPU/ZIPRA. In contrast, during the first seven years of independence, veterans were almost never heard. Their barely audible voices in this period should not be equated with their powerlessness. Veterans did not always have an organization. The party only agreed to their forming an organization, and then only if it were under party patronage, before the 1990 election. Their organization, which helped to empower them, only got off the ground in 1992. The invasion of land was the first time in which veterans joined forces with other social groups. Their previous struggles with the party have been for exclusive privileged access to state resources. Veterans have not always been cast as 'the bad guys' by the opposition. Until 1997, when veterans won enormous pension demands at the expense of the taxpayer, the independent media supported veterans' gripes against the leadership as an opportunity to condemn the rulers. The political and economic environment in Zimbabwe has changed, too, with the introduction of accountability for the violence inside and outside the army against suspected opponents. Asked in 1992 about the attempts by ZIPRA veterans who were illegally discharged from the army in this period to get back their jobs or their pension benefits, the ZANLA head of the army's legal directorate passed responsibility for these problems to the politicians, as though the army had been innocent.

Government critics have focused on the role of the army and police against civilians, demobilized ZIPRA members and ZAPU local leaders in Matabeland and the Midlands. This apportioning of blame largely protects the conduct of ZANLA guerrillas towards ZIPRA in the regular army units. ZANLA veterans' vanguard role in the consolidation of ZANU(PF) power is akin to the veterans' leadership role in the party's effort to preserve its power in the June 2000 parliamentary election. Rather than ZAPU, the new threat was the Movement for Democratic Change and its suspected supporters: farmworkers, and white businesspeople and farmers. In its power struggle with ZAPU, the party rewarded ZANLA veterans, who did its bidding using extra-legal means, with career promotions. During the 2000 election campaign, the party paid veterans for campaigning and condoned their illegal land occupations and violence. Veterans were also guaranteed priority in resettlement and a generous percentage of resettlement plots.

The work place

Especially after demobilization, the ruling party hoped to find jobs for unemployed ZANLA veterans who might otherwise constitute a security threat. Having exhausted opportunities in the state sector, it turned to the white-dominated private sector. Party officials intimidated private companies to employ ZANLA veterans, skilled and unskilled, often charging employees with racism when they resisted. At the same time, the ruling party introduced legislation providing for works committees to give workers more say in the work place. Veterans sought positions on works committees because they wanted power and supported revolutionary work place changes which would benefit them. Unlike most other workers, the veterans were fearless. Veterans often threatened their work superiors and reported 'counter-revolutionaries' to party headquarters which would often intervene on behalf of the veterans. At some point in the mid-1980s – precisely when is contested – the party withdrew its support of ZANLA veterans in the work place. With new legislation to regulate labour relations and more confident that it could rely on bureaucrats, the party no longer needed veterans' revolutionary leadership in the private sector.

Private sector employers and managers speak eloquently of the nexus between veterans and party headquarters as they pursued their overlapping interests during these tumultuous times. Both the following quotes are from an African manager at National Breweries:[9]

> There were requests from Ministers to take on these people . . . Most were polite just we were scared. The bad guys were Banana [ex-President] and the late Dr. Ushewokunze [a national hero] who called regularly for favours, including beer supplies. They [ex-combatants] were hired as general labour. They see me. I never fired a single bullet. I'm a manager. I have a company car. They feel resentment. Whites are still here and the economy is 90 per cent in their hands. Out of this feeling, they lost loyalty to the company. They were elected to works committees. People thought they'd fought the war, they'd know how to fight and they'd fight management. But they took it too far. Most works committees were run by ex-combatants. They enjoyed this sort of thing . . . They were very militant, uncompromising . . . They have contacts with government – Kangai, or they report you to CIO, ZANU(PF). They are virtually a wing of CIO. People have been called in and questioned about things at work. Ah! How do you know? From ex-combatants, they'd tell them . . . They thought they could influence events in the government but they find they are powerless like everyone else . . . Like government, they wanted to dictate to us about socialism . . . Way back they'd be proud and say I was an ex-combatant . . . They identified closely with ZANU(PF) and the government, but now very few people are proud to be associated with ZANU(PF) and the government . . . There's no more fear of them or hating them.

An ex-combatant in the accounts department – he had 'O' levels and was 'very bright' – refused to do overtime. I fired him for refusing to take instruction from his superior. He went to complain to Manyika (now the late)[Deputy Minister]. Manyika called me to his office. I was searched by his body guards. Then the ex-combatant greeted Manyika with party slogans. He was trying to intimidate me and show his closeness to Manyika and reveal me as an oppressor. Manyika spoke to me in Shona. I said I preferred English. I was from Matabeleland and my Shona wasn't very good. I refused the tea he offered me. I told Manyika: 'I don't take government tea.' It was just to break the ice. Manyika listened to the story and found me to be right.

The parallels between ZANU(PF)'s use of ZANLA veterans in the early 1980s and in 2000 are striking. In the 1980s, the party found employment for ZANLA veterans to keep them within the party and then used them to transform labour relations in the work place. In 2000, the party deployed veterans to transform the distribution of land and to ensure veterans and rural people stayed inside the party. In the 1980s, veterans and the party targeted white employers and managers, whether African or white. In 2000, the party-veteran coalition's target was the MDC and its potential support base in African farmworkers and white farmers. In both cases, the party used veterans to build or salvage power and legitimacy. Veterans and the party justified their transformative missions with appeals to war promises – to remove racism in the 1980s and to return the land stolen by whites to the people in 2000. For the party, the veterans' dual image as revolutionaries and people of violence was valuable in eliciting compliance, both in the 1980s and in 2000.

Pensions

The idea that veterans should be compensated for their war services has been in the public domain since independence. A major locus of the struggle for war service recognition was in the context of retirement pensions. At independence, guerrilla veterans became aware that Rhodesian veterans counted their war service years towards their years of service when calculating retirement pensions. How could the ruling party reward the enemy oppressors, and not them, the liberators? Because there were no war service records, veterans' age groups were made the proxy for determining war service years. First to benefit in March 1989 were the veterans in the uniformed services (the police and the army). Less generous recognition of war service was quickly extended to veterans in the civil service. But this provision did not cater for veterans in the private sector or the unemployed. The urgency of closing this inequity among veterans was recognized both by the veterans' association and by at least some in the party. The Deputy Minister of Labour and Social Welfare remarked during the debate on the Veterans Bill in 1992 that the issue of retirement pensions for the unemployed was a more urgent issue than veterans' land grievances. Another arena in which the issue of war service compensation arose was the War Victims (Compensation) Act.

The War Victims (Compensation) Act of 1980 provides for disability pensions for civilians and guerrillas injured in the war, death pensions for the surviving spouse and dependants of the war dead, and medical and vocational rehabilitation for the war-disabled (Kriger 2000a; 2000b). The legislation grows out of the Victims of Terrorism (Compensation) Act of 1972. Whereas the colonial legislation was introduced to provide loyalists with state-disability pensions and state compensation for property damages arising from 'acts of terrorism', the new legislation acknowledges guerrilla veterans' power, legitimates their special status and legitimates the war. For calculating pensions, veterans' earnings are assessed by equating their guerrilla ranks at the time of death or injury with national army ranks and corresponding pay. Even though guerrillas performed unpaid combatant duties, their earnings are not assessed on the basis of minimum wages, as is the case for unemployed civilians. Guerrillas, the regime was saying, deserved to be treated like Rhodesian soldiers rather than unemployed civilians. The party also removed the slur of terrorism and defined 'the war' as 'the armed conflict . . . in connexion with the bringing about of, or resistance to, political and social change in Zimbabwe' (Government of Zimbabwe 1980, section 2(1)).

From the outset, many veterans were angry with the small size of their pensions which they saw as an insult to their war services. Because of ZIPRA insecurity in the 1980s, ZANLA veterans, especially those at Ruwa Rehabilitation Centre, were in the forefront of battles to increase disability pensions. Welfare bureaucrats in the Harare pensions office were routinely threatened for not processing applications fast enough and for paying too little. In 1981, veterans rejected their first pension payments as too small and took hostage a senior welfare bureaucrat and his veteran companion. In October 1986, veterans at Ruwa Rehabilitation Centre took hostage two rehabilitation officers, the pensions officer they had seized in 1981, the permanent secretary in the Welfare Ministry and the Director of Social Services, all of whom had come to explain the legislation to them. War veterans' pressures led to repeated concessions through administrative changes (for example using European rather than African soldiers' earnings to assess veterans' pensions) and legislative amendments (for example legally recognizing war marriages to enable surviving partners to claim death pensions). Veterans also benefited from sympathetic army colleagues, supportive medical practitioners (whether wittingly or unwittingly), and the cabinet minister himself, all of whom had discretionary power in the implementation of the legislation. Medical doctors could inflate or even fabricate disabilities. Army personnel could inflate ranks or authorize pensions at a higher rate by certifying that a veteran's war disabilities were so severe as to prevent him or her from joining the army and thus continuing their chosen profession. [The court's ruling in 1992 against treating guerrillas as having intended to make the structural adjustment in 1990 representing a major divide. Important as these changes in veterans' unity, public prominence, organization, social alliances, public image, and political and economic environment are, they do not interfere with the remarkably consistent dynamics of the relationship between veterans and the party.

The term 'war veteran' requires clarification. With the introduction of structural adjustment and free-market capitalism in 1990, influential ex-guerrillas recognized that continuing to call themselves 'comrades' was anachronistic. They also rejected the use of 'ex-combatants', widely used in Parliament, official documents and the media, because they thought it had contributed to society stigmatizing them. They chose to call themselves war veterans. Hence in 1992 their organization was inaugurated as the Zimbabwe National Liberation War Veterans' Association and legislation which was introduced to benefit them was called the War Veterans Act. This legislation defined war veterans as 'any person who underwent military training and participated, consistently and persistently, in the liberation struggle which occurred in Zimbabwe and in neighbouring countries between the 1st January, 1962, and the 29th February, 1980, in connection with the bringing about of Zimbabwe's independence on the 18th April, 1980' (Government of Zimbabwe 1992, No. 4, Section 2). Some ex-guerrillas thought the terminology of war veterans was inappropriate because many, and arguably most, guerrillas had remained in training camps and never participated in battle during the war. Also, civilian war participants objected to their exclusion from the definition of war veterans. In the year 2000, the term war veterans has become embroiled in fresh controversy. The media and the Commercial Farmers' Union (CFU) often refer to those who invade and occupy white commercial farms as war veterans even when it is apparent that many are too young to have fought in the liberation war. This loose use of the label of war veterans is evidently a CFU attempt to appease youthful invaders who insist on being identified as war veterans. It is important to acknowledge that ex-guerrillas are not the only land invaders, that a group of veterans formed the Zimbabwe Liberators' Platform in May 2000 to distance themselves from the ZNLWVA and its participation in land invasions,[2] and that there are many within the ZNLWVA who reject Chenjerai Hitler Hunzvi and his executive and that there is a competing national executive.[3] Nonetheless, the evidence seems strong that war veterans play a critical role in organizing and occupying farms, whether on their own initiative or following party officials' dictates.[4] War veterans now carry registration cards, so that identification is possible. Reports on court cases, where information about actors may be presumed to be reasonably accurate, also often identify the accused as war veterans.

The rest of the chapter gives examples of the recurring patterns in the relationship of veterans and the ruling party, both over time and across diverse arenas – the military, welfare, the work place and property rights. In particular, I examine veterans' politics in the assembly camps in 1980–81, in the army during the violent conflict in Matabeleland and the Midlands from 1982–87, in the private sector work place from 1981 to about the mid-1980s, and in the welfare sector over pensions from 1980 to 1997. In each case, I draw parallels between past and present political dynamics: the mutual dependence of the party and the veterans on one another to fulfil their particular objectives – for the party, the pursuit of power; for veterans, the quest for privileged access to state resources; their engagement in often simultaneous conflict, collaboration, and accommodation; and their appeals to their war contributions and their use of intimidation and violence.

The assembly camps

The 1979 peace settlement left the two guerrilla armies, ZIPRA and ZANLA, and the Rhodesian security forces mobilized, armed and concentrated under their respective leaders.[5] The guerrilla armies were in separate assembly camps, the Rhodesian forces in their barracks. The existence of multiple sovereignty cast a huge threatening shadow over the newly elected ZANU(PF) rulers. At the end of a war, all they had was control of Parliament, historically a much weaker institution than the executive. The bureaucracy, the army and the police, the power bases of the former Rhodesian regime, remained intact. The constitution protected former regime personnel by requiring that the new government pay their pensions if it removed them from their posts. In this precarious environment, the ruling party saw ZANLA guerrillas as its only reliable power-base. The ruling party also had to appear to be treating ZIPRA guerrillas as equals; discrimination would hasten a civil war between the two armies which the ruling party wanted to delay at that time.

The ruling party's response to the inauspicious legacy of the settlement thus guaranteed that guerrillas in post-independence Zimbabwe were born powerful. They self-administered their assembly camps – the police and the army were prohibited from entering without the permission of the assembly commander – and they had the status of soldiers-in-waiting until they were absorbed into the army. They were paid the monthly salary of a Rhodesian private (on the African pay scale) and provided with soldiers' rations. To legitimate itself and the guerrillas, the ruling party drew on their war contribution and glorified the war and those who had fought and died in it. Heroes' Day, the annual August official commemoration of the war, was introduced almost immediately after independence.

Empowered by their parties' dependence on them, the guerrillas made demands. They rejected the white Rhodesians on military call-up duty who were sent to preside over pay parades in the camps. They demanded that they themselves administer the pay. Having won the right to pay their forces, the assembly commanders abused their power, inflating the numbers of guerrillas under their command. Many netted big windfalls, often at the expense of their rank and file. Their guerrilla superiors' efforts to impose accountability met with threats and hostage-taking. Meanwhile, the guerrilla parties protected their forces from criticism, and themselves benefited from the corrupt administration of pay. Guerrillas also demanded decent housing as a reward for their war services. They were moved from their rural camps to new housing in Chitungwiza (outside Harare) and Bulawayo until new barracks were completed. The ruling party did not request the housing from the still white-run urban councils but essentially appropriated it. After violent fighting in this housing between ZIPRA and ZANLA in February 1981, the urban councils rather than the party or the guerrillas were saddled with financing the repairs. Just prior to the outbreak of this round of fighting, all but the lowest-ranking guerrillas won pay increases after successfully demanding their monthly pay take into account their rank.

While guerrillas belonging to both parties had equal access to pay and housing, ZANU(PF)'s intention to build power on its ZANLA guerrilla base was evident. Civil service posts went to ZANU(PF) guerrillas rather than ZAPU guerrillas. Military integration rules were changed to protect ZANLA from merit-based competition for officer positions. ZIPRA guerrillas' violence against civilians, especially in Matabeleland and the Midlands, was punished by army and police actions; ZANLA violence against white farmers, labourers and the police was handled in-house. The ruling party belittled ZIPRA and ZAPU war contributions and lionized the role of ZANLA/ZANU(PF). When fighting broke out between ZANLA and ZIPRA in November 1980 and again in February 1981, the ruling party blamed ZIPRA and ZAPU. The report of the official commission investigating this violence has never been released, leading one to believe that ZANLA/ZANU(PF) was no innocent bystander. Importantly, the Rhodesian security forces who were called on to restore peace in the township fighting in February 1981 attacked only ZIPRA guerrillas. Though born powerful, ZANLA guerrillas were born more powerful than ZIPRA.

The fighting between the two guerrilla armies in a Bulawayo township and in several military units in which ZANLA and ZIPRA had been merged was a turning point for guerrillas still in the camps. Bolstered by the Rhodesian military's attacks on only ZIPRA guerrillas during the township fighting, the party felt it had a new reliable ally. It thus chose to disarm the remaining guerrillas in camps and soon after announced its intention to demobilize them. Demobilization was made more palatable by a two-year monthly salary which was set, as before, at a private's monthly salary (on the African pay scale) plus the estimated value of rations. For the first time, there was a major split between guerrilla and ruling party interests. The guerrillas had been promised that they would not be disarmed till they were integrated in the army, and that every guerrilla had the right to choose a military career. Predictably, many guerrillas resisted disarmament and demobilization. Sensitive to the power of guerrillas, the party did not begin demobilization till the bulk of ZIPRA and ZANLA guerrillas had been brought into the army and the problem of multiple sovereignty was resolved. More secure *vis-à-vis* the Rhodesians and with ZIPRA partly in the new army and partly demobilized, the ruling party turned its attention to consolidating its ZANLA power-base.

The relationship between guerrillas and the ruling party in the assembly introduced dynamics which have persisted. The party depended on the guerrillas (and especially ZANLA) to build its power and legitimacy; the guerrillas needed party support to get access to state resources. Both appealed to their war contributions. The party drew repeatedly on state resources to meet guerrilla demands. Neither guerrillas nor ruling party upheld accountability or transparency. Guerrilla violence was often condoned. The authority of the constitutional police and army was challenged by guerrillas with party support. When the party had no further use for guerrillas still in assembly camps, it demobilized them with *big pay-offs*.[6] During and after the 2000 election campaign, the party and its veteran supporters inside and outside the army and police showed contempt for the constitution, the rule of law and the electorate. The constitution required state compensation for land which was appropriated. The party inserted a clause in the draft constitution to provide for land appropriation without state compensation but voters rejected the draft constitution in a referendum in February 2000. Nonetheless, the party hastily changed the constitution during the campaign to legalize land appropriations without state compensation. Having run down state resources, the party grabbed land to dole out to its patrons. During the campaign, the party undermined court orders to Police Commissioner Augustine Chihuri and to ZNLWVA leader Hitler Hunzvi (both veterans) to stop land invasions and supported veterans' violence against party opponents. In 1980 and 1981, ZANLA challenges to the army, police and local authorities were easy to confuse with revolutionary politics. After all, central and local state institutions were Rhodesian legacies. However, the persistence of a politics of violence, corruption, privileged access to state resources, and power accumulation make it easier to interpret early motivations and practices through different lenses.

The military

What happened in the military after the completion of merging the two guerrilla armies in late 1981 is a largely suppressed part of post-independence history. ZANLA guerrillas were used by the ruling party to consolidate its power against ZIPRA within the army. While the British and the Zimbabwean governments, along with academics, were celebrating the success of their integration programme, ZANLA guerrillas in the military were refusing to obey the orders of their ZIPRA superiors, locking them up without due process simply because they were ZIPRA, rejecting ZIPRA subordinates in their units and illegally discharging even ZIPRA superiors.[7] These activities took place against the background of a small group of ZIPRA dissidents in Matabeleland and the Midlands. The ruling party and its ZANLA guerrillas chose to portray all ZIPRA as dissidents.

One example of the abuses heaped on ZIPRA by their ZANLA colleagues will suffice. A founding member of the Mechanized Battalion spoke bitterly of his illegal discharge in May 1982, ZANLA's use of intimidation and violence and ZIPRA's lack of any legal recourse.

> I was illegally discharged from the army without any signal. I was never found guilty. I violated no regulations . . . I was only discharged verbally . . . I was just told to pack my bags and go home. It was not just me. It happened to many ZIPRAs. ZANLA could tell you to do something unreasonable and just kill you if you disobey. I said: 'Tell me the reason I'm being discharged.' The reply I got was: 'If you want to save your life, go home to Bulawayo.' . . . That man who gave me the order was the acting commander in place of Acting Battalion Commander Hickman. Hickman liked me for my performance but he could do nothing. If you're not a ZANLA, then you're not a com-mander . . . Many ZIPRAs were discharged from different battalions. We couldn't pursue these cases.[8]

The ruling party sanctioned and condoned this violence which served to strengthen its loyal power-base in the military and drove many ZIPRA members out of the army. At the same time, the Fifth Brigade, a unit trained by the North Koreans outside the integration pro-gramme, and later the regular army and police, engaged in party-authorized violence against demobilized ZIPRA members, civilians and ZAPU loyalists in Matabeleland and the Midlands (CCJP/LRF 1997; Alexander and McGregor 1999; Werbner 1991; Alexander, McGregor and Ranger 2000). ZIPRA's allegedly traitorous behaviour was presented as a continuation of its minimal war contribution; the party's right-eousness to its more significant war contribution. An official com-mission investigated violence in Matabeleland and the Midlands in 1985 but its report, too, has never been made public. After party unity between ZAPU and ZANU(PF), the political elite blamed Rhodesian intelligence for deliberately fanning ethnic and political violence and began to restore a heroic liberation war role to ZIPRA. At Joshua Nkomo's funeral in 1999, Mugabe finally apologized for the violence in Matabeleland between 1982 and 1987. But this had no real significant effect, largely because the pensions office fell under an ex-combatant (ZANLA) in 1992 who supported increasing ZANLA veterans' pensions by any means. From 1988, the Minister used his discretion to dele-gate his authority to approve the commutation of all war disability pensions which did not fulfil legislative criteria. The struggles of veterans for improvements in war victims' compensation illustrate a process of conflict usually followed by accommodation of veterans' demands.

Beginning in 1992, but especially from 1995, the war victims' compensation scheme became the vehicle for veterans to extract from the state the compensation for their war service which they felt was owed to them. Veterans had pushed hard for, and won, parliamentary approval of the War Veterans Act in 1992. But the legislation was merely enabling. To introduce schemes for veterans and their dependants required the Treasury's approval for funding. Year after year there was no funding and veterans grew angry. In 1995 Hitler Hunzvi, a government medical doctor, was elected to lead the veterans' association, despite belonging to the minority guerrilla party/army. Later, top guns in the guerrilla army to which he claimed to have belonged, denied he had ever even undergone military training. What Hunzvi offered his members was the (ab)use of his medical clout to get them compensation for invisible injuries, and more particularly post-war traumatic stress disorder – a type of disability claim not previously used. The War Victims Compensation Fund did not require Treasury approval because it was guaranteed money from the Consolidated Revenue Account. If there were compensation claims, the government had to fund them. Already beginning to grow slowly from 1992, new claims shot up (in rounded-off figures) from 800 in 1993 to 1000 in 1994, 6000 in 1995, 9000 in 1996, and 9500 in the first nine months of 1997 (Government of Zimbabwe 1998a, chap. 11.16). Almost all new claimants were ex-combatants. In March 1997, the private media blew the whistle on the looting of the fund, and the government stopped further payments on the commuted pensions, which involved thousands of dollars, and allegedly also other pension payments, pending investigations. In July 1997, Mugabe appointed a commission to investigate the War Victims Compensation Act's general administration, from its inception in 1980 to April 1997, to recommend reforms and to propose measures to recover state money which had been improperly paid (Government of Zimbabwe 1998a).

As events unfolded, it was often confusing as to whom the friends and enemies of the veterans were. Veterans responded with organized protests (including hostage-taking of party/government leaders) to the suspension of pension payments. They claimed that impoverished veterans had been denied pensions, despite their superior war contributions, while top government and political leaders had looted the fund. When the commission began public hearings, the protests continued. To demonstrate it was not going to protect prominent public figures, the commission interviewed 79 successful claimants solely because they were prominent – members of parliament, ministers, top-ranking army and police officials (including Army Commander Zvinavashe and Police Commissioner Augustine Chihuri), veterans' association officials (including Hunzvi) and senior bureaucrats. It also questioned another 43 recent recipients of war victims' compensation because their claims looked suspicious. Almost all 112 people called to appear before the commission were veterans. Veterans continued to attack, verbally and occasionally physically, top party and government officials. They now escalated their long-standing demand for monetary recognition for their war services. They demanded war service pensions. Even when granted a Z$50 000 gratuity (one-tenth of their actual demand) and a Z$2000 monthly pension in August 1997, veterans (mainly women) went on a rampage in the courtroom where the commission had just interviewed their leader about his alleged fraud. Throughout the hearings, they attacked the right of the commission to question veterans, on the grounds that many of the commissioners were 'sell-outs' and had served colonial governments. They worried aloud that the public hearings would embarrass the party and the veterans, and begged Mugabe to dissolve the commission. During this period of often violent protest, the police stood on the side-lines, intervening only when the small group destroyed property in the courtroom.

What exactly was the relationship between party and veterans over the looting of the compensation fund and the struggle for war service pensions? The private media, today hostile to veterans, portrayed a simple battle between good (veterans) and evil (the leadership). The 'real' fighters had been denied the recognition they deserved while the leadership ('not real' fighters) had greedily and uncaringly appropriated the fruits of independence. The independent press excused veterans' violence as the inevitable product of frustration from neglect of their legitimate grievances, and often pointed to more egregious instances of the leaders' breaches of the law. The story is more layered, though. In looting the fund, the veterans' leader Hitler Hunzvi had invited political heavyweights, invariably veterans themselves, to apply for disability pensions with his assistance. An intricate network existed between Hunzvi, the War Victims Compensation Fund Commissioner, Amen Sithole, himself a veteran, street-level bureaucrats in the pensions office (some but not all were veterans) and at least some medical doctors. All these people played crucial roles in inflating and fabricating claims, and most received handsome kickbacks for their services. The government must have known that the fund was being looted. It was open knowledge that if you wanted money, you should seek access to the war victims compensation fund. Hitler Hunzvi was a good leader who honoured his promises. He visited centres across the country and helped people to fill out application forms (for which they often had to pay him). Ensuring that the forms got priority attention was where those with connections were lucky. Thousands of applications were still pending when media attention forced the government to turn off the tap. Those whose claims had not yet been approved protested that the chiefs had benefited at their expense. But all the veterans' claims were bogus in the sense that they were cynical attempts to use invisible war injuries to obtain state money. The police, many of them ex-combatants, were not going to take action against veterans who were protesting against the commission because the police leadership was itself being investigated by the commission and openly challenging its legitimacy.

The commissioners, except for an ex-combatant lawyer, included to appease veterans, were timid and cowed before the aggressive veterans who defended their claims and said they deserved more for their war sacrifices and suffering. For some, these were sore toes and disturbed sleep at night. Chaired by staunch ZANU(PF) supporter Judge Chidyausiku, the commission defended the legitimacy of the veterans' claims for invisible injuries, and sympathized with their grievance that they had never been rewarded for their war services and their initiative to reward themselves through the war victims compensation fund. The commission's proposal that the state seek to prosecute and recover money where individuals had lied (for example, claiming a war disability when none actually existed which it believed to be rare) were pursued selectively. Though the case against Hunzvi for signing medical forms without requiring claimants to undergo a medical examination went to court, it remains stalled there. The looting of the fund and its investigation, despite the appearance of pitting the chiefs against poor veterans, was an almost entirely ex-combatant affair in which those with clout and connections benefited first. The unconnected veteran lost out only because the government, fully aware of how the fund was being used, was forced by public exposure to cut off the source of the gravy. Those who had already been paid kept their money. The commission's findings were in any event made almost irrelevant when the veterans forced the leadership to pay them gratuities and pensions. The party essentially legitimated, as did the commission of inquiry's subsequent report, the veterans' claims that their war service had never been adequately recognized and paid for.

Why did the leadership agree to such large payments which would hurt the economy? The veterans closed ranks with their colleagues in state employment, notably the army and police. Especially at the lower ranks, veterans (like most ordinary Zimbabweans) were hurting economically. The veterans' association, which in theory represented only veterans outside the security sector, resisted government efforts to divide the veterans. It spoke for all veterans on the issue of compensation for war sacrifices. Already thrown together in the looting of the compensation fund, the implicit bargain was that the association fight for the benefit of all veterans, and their colleagues in the police and army would not interfere with their protests. Moreover, there was the threat of united action against the party should it not meet veterans' demands. This alliance between veterans inside and outside the security sector in 1996–97 presented the party with a potential security threat. The contrast with Ruwa veterans' protests over the party's failure to recognize and reward their war services in 1986 could not be greater. Ruwa veterans had no such alliances. Army commander Rex Nhongo had no trouble fielding a force to evict ZANLA veterans at Ruwa Rehabilitation Centre. In 1997, fearing trouble in the police and army, where economic grievances were building up, the leadership – at least Mugabe – caved in. In doing so, he alienated urban workers, themselves suffering economic decline, who were told to fund the veterans' benefits through tax increases. It was the first occasion on which the leadership had explicitly asked taxpayers to fund veterans' benefits. Previously, it simply drew down state funds. But international financial institutions' pressure in 1997 forced the government to turn to the people for finance.

The alliances, formed when pensions were granted, between the leadership, the veterans' association, and veterans in the security sector surfaced in the election campaign and its aftermath. The split between workers and veterans, apparent in the work place in the early 1980s, was also a major fault-line during and after the campaign as workers supported the new opposition, the Movement for Democratic Change (MDC). The cynical use of war service to justify access to resources in 1997 was replayed again during and after the 2000 campaign. Whereas previously veterans had turned to state resources, these were so low in 2000 that it was necessary to expropriate private land to distribute as state patronage. Police and army tolerance for veterans' violence against the leadership and government and party property in 1997 was re-enacted as they stood by and condoned or supported land invasions and attacks on farmworkers and white farmers.

Conclusion

It would be absurd to portray the relationship between veterans and the party as an unbroken continuity. Indeed, many of the incidents of conflict and collaboration demonstrate fluid alliances. There have been continuities, though. The dependence of veterans and the party on each other is a well-established pattern. Veterans have used their power in the party to fight for more state resources, and most recently the conversion of private land into state land to which they claim privileged access. They have pursued narrow group gain. They have abandoned their war-time aides, rural youth and elders, and shunned political prisoners' and detainees' efforts to have similar privileged access to state resources. Their legitimate struggle for redistribution has been justified in terms of their superior war contribution, and backed by violence and intimidation. The contemporary land issue is the first time veterans have been engaged in a redistributive struggle alongside social allies. However, redistribution is no more a central party objective in and of itself than the party's earlier transformative efforts in the work place or in the military. The party's quest for power through destabilization recurs from 1980 to 2000.

How can the past 20 years inform expectations about the future relationship between veterans and the party, now focused on land redistribution and countering the MDC opposition? The party might reduce its reliance on veterans if it can find a new ally, perhaps even the MDC leadership, and attempt to return to land redistribution through bureaucratic and legal procedures. Such dramatic shifts have precedents. The party dropped its reliance on ZANLA veterans in the work place and relied on bureaucrats and legislation. Its use for ZANLA veterans in the army as allies against ZIPRA/ZAPU diminished after it formed an alliance with the leaders of its former enemy. The party came to trust the Rhodesians in the security forces in the 1980s when they directed their violence against ZIPRA rather than ZANLA who were fighting each other in assembly camps. For any side-lining of their current central role, the veterans will extract pay-offs. It is worth remembering that they considered the war service pensions of 1997 as merely a Z$50 000 down-payment on their demand for a Z$500 000 gratuity. It is possible, too, that the dynamics of the past 20 years may themselves change. Rather than colluding with and struggling against the party and its security organs, veterans outside the army might become an independent source of power and build up their own weapons supply. Veterans in the army and police might team up with their colleagues should they see the ruling party as a loser in the presidential elections scheduled for 2002. For two decades analysts have examined politics in Zimbabwe through the lenses of democratization, reconciliation, peace and stability. The past and present aspirations and practices of veterans and ruling elites suggest such frameworks have been misguided and misleading.

Notes

1. Kriger (forthcoming). Primary sources are cited only when quoted.
2. Background to Zimbabwe Liberators' Platform is contained in an invitation to the editor of the *Daily News* from Richard Chiwara, Interim Chairman, Northern Region, Zimbabwe Liberators' Platform, 25 August 2000. This correspondence was obtained courtesy of David Moore.
3. On competing executives, see Gwinyayi (2000); Holtzclaw (2000, 22). White farmers told Holtzclaw that local war lords in Mashonaland Central refused to acknowledge the national war veterans' leadership.
4. In reporting white farmers' understandings of farm invasions, Holtzclaw (2000, 23) describes how war veterans work with ZANU(PF) headquarters and/or provincial and local ZANU(PF) officials.
5. Most writings on the settlement have celebrated the settlement and/or its implementation. See Davidow (1984); Stedman (1991); Rice (1990); Tamarkin (1990); MacKinlay (1990); Soames (1980). Critics of the settlement have focused on how it stymied the revolution's objectives or failed to take into account 'tribal' identities but have missed its dire security implications for the new government. On how the settlement undermined the revolution, see Mandaza (1986b); Nzuwah (1980). On the settlement's failure to take into account 'tribal' politics, see Burton (1986).
6. Musemwa (1995) argues that demobilization payments were inadequate. In contrast, the World Bank (1993a) asserts the payments were extravagant. My interviews with ex-combatants in 1992 indicated that most saw the payments as attractive in the early 1980s. Importantly, the payments were not arbitrary but were made equivalent to what African soldiers in the army were receiving.
7. Most studies acknowledge that the new army was politicized from independence but are oblivious of how politicization undermined the military chain of command. Seegers (1986, 157) refers to the ZANA's 'cohesion and discipline under difficult conditions'. Evans (1988; 1992, 231–253) vacillates on whether military professionalism and politicization are contradictory or complementary but does not address how politicization undermines the military chain of command.
8. Interview, 19 May 1992, Bulawayo.
9. Interview, 10 June 1992, Harare.

6
Regional Voting and Cabinet Formation

Liisa Laakso[1]

Introduction

Zimbabwe is one of the very few African countries which never introduced a formal one-party system. Against the aspirations of ZANU(PF)
the Lancaster House agreement provided a multi-party system for a
period of at least ten years, and after 1990 the one-party state was
strongly opposed by most Zimbabweans. President Mugabe himself
argued in 1993 that opposition parties are a stabilising factor in political systems in Africa (*The Sunday Mail*, 9 May 1993). However, it has
been difficult for the opposition to get organized and to mobilize voters.
In 2000 harassment and intimidation of the new and popular opposition party, the MDC, were rampant.

In spite of the domination of one party, the multi-party elections in
Zimbabwe have not been insignificant. They have attracted a lot of attention among the ruling elite, those willing to enter that elite and those
criticizing it. It is interesting to see how electoral politics are reflected in
cabinet formation, as this relates to one of the basic mechanisms of liberal
democracies, the accountability of the government to ordinary voters.

The formation of cabinets in Zimbabwe was initially one of the
powers of the Prime Minister, but since 1987 has been a duty of the
executive President. Robert Mugabe has been the only person who
has held these posts. This chapter examines the importance of regionality in his policy of cabinet nomination. Regionality is related to the
notion of ethnicity (or 'tribalism'), which has been almost a taboo in
the political science literature on Zimbabwe, known as a case of
invented ethnicity (see Ranger 1985b; 1989). It is true that only in
very general terms and with regard to the rural population (that constitutes the majority of the voters) can it be said that Mashonaland
provinces are the regions of the Zezuru; Manicaland is the region of

the Manyika; Matabeleland North and South are the regions of the Ndebele; and Masvingo and the Midlands are the regions of the Karanga ethnic group, while the Midlands also includes a considerable Ndebele population. But even these ethnic groups can be divided into subgroups. (Sithole 1988, 222–3.) Definitions of ethnic identities in Zimbabwe, as elsewhere in the world, are fluid and contested. Furthermore, the language of regions is no more 'neutral' than these ethnic identities are. Indeed, both among government circles and critical intellectuals, there have been claims that the names of the provinces of Zimbabwe (that is Matabeleland, Mashonaland and Manicaland) reflect the colonial divide-and-rule strategy. It has been suggested that more neutral names based on the points of the compass should be adopted. This, however, would perhaps not render the regions apolitical. The political significance of regionality goes far beyond identities.

It has been argued that '[e]thnicity matters far less in Zimbabwe's wider society than it does in the alliances of personalities and interests that wrestle for power within ZANU(PF): the alliances are based on who can deliver which constituencies' (*Africa Confidential*, 15 July 1994, 3). If this is true, it is not surprising that the more regional leaders have to be included in the political elite, the bigger the governments tend to be. Indeed large cabinets are typical all over Africa (Bratton and van de Walle 1997, 75). This is often interpreted as creating a neopatrimonial political system or as power-sharing for the sake of peace (see Rothchild 1999). But as the Zimbabwean case shows, the question is about a much more complex political space than suggested by such models. As much as balancing regional representation in the cabinet is the policy of the leadership, regional politics itself stems from voters rationally promoting their regionally based interests in a difficult environment of government coercion and persuasion which represses political dissent (see Cowen and Laakso 2002).

Cabinet posts and regional politics

In considering regional politics in Zimbabwe it is useful to start with cabinet formation and regional voting. Table 6.1 shows the share of each region in ministerial posts as percentages of the total. The fact that individual ministries have different political status makes percentages somewhat arbitrary, but they still give an idea of the inclusiveness of the cabinet. The mere size of the cabinets, often including about forty ministers, suggests that inclusion has been Mugabe's first

Table 6.1   Regional distribution of cabinet posts, (%)

Region	1980	1984	1985	1988	1990	1992	1995	1996	1997	2000
Mashonaland Central	13	13	16	14	16	18	11	13	11	20
Mashonaland West	3	9	10	14	13	11	14	11	11	16
Mashonaland East	16	17	24	5	13	14	16	21	21	16
Manicaland	26	26	24	22	18	18	11	11	8	12
Masvingo	10	13	13	16	13	11	11	11	13	12
Midlands	19	11	13	11	8	11	11	8	11	8
Matabeleland South	10	9	–	14	16	18	16	16	16	16
Matabeleland North	3	2	3	5	3	–	11	11	11	–

Source: Calculated from tables presenting the regional distribution of seats in Laakso 1999.

consideration. Besides, even the most important ministers, such as Foreign Affairs and Finance, are crucially dependent on him. The deputy ministers and the so-called ministers of state are also included in the table. Because it is difficult to understand the rationale underlying these nominations from a governance point of view, they are likely to be particularly significant for regional balance and recruitment of new people to the elite.

The Zimbabwean constitution requires that all cabinet ministers be members of parliament. The executive President has, since 1987, had the right to appoint 12 MPs of his own choice. Thus the cabinets also include non-constituency MPs. This does not preclude the significance of regionalism in their nomination. Non-constituency MPs might not have popular support but the President can use them to indicate the inclusion of a particular region

The definition of the regional background of individual ministers is based on official election results if the ministers have contested the elections, printed sources and inquiries put to Zimbabwean nationals. If the candidates have been imposed on the electorate, in principle it is possible that they are not contesting their home region. This might cause some anomalies and adds to the necessity to look at the figures with a certain caution. Furthermore, representatives of the minorities are not included. Whites have had 1–3 ministers in each cabinet, while the nominations of coloureds and Asians have been too occasional to suggest that their representation would have been regarded as politically essential.[2]

Table 6.1 shows that dramatic changes have usually occurred after elections, 1988 being a significant exception. Furthermore, all the provinces have tended to have at least minimal presentation in the government. The only exceptions are the two Matabeleland provinces. However, one of them has always been represented. It is likely that the leadership treats them more or less as one region, which is also reflected in the popular conceptions. The second immediate observation is that the shifts over time in the percentages are very uneven between regions. Matabeleland, the Midlands and Manicaland have experienced great fluctuation, while Masvingo has been stable. The Mashonaland provinces have experienced occasional highs and lows. It is also revealing to look at their combined representation, which has been relatively stable, usually between 32 and 45 per cent, the only exceptions being 1985 and 2000, when the representation of Mashonaland was 50 and 52 per cent.

Regional voting power

The most obvious comparison is to look at the sizes of the electorate in different regions. Table 6.2 presents the regional shares of valid votes in 1980 and 2000 when all seats were contested. Valid votes are the most reliable figures available. There are errors in the electoral rolls and invalid votes have not been calculated reliably in all constituencies. Thus we are looking at the shares of 'effective' votes, those that directly

Table 6.2 Regional shares of votes for the whole country, (%)

Region	1980	2000
Mashonaland Central	7	10
Mashonaland West	11	11
Mashonaland East	24	10
Harare		16
Manicaland	12	11
Masvingo	12	11
Midlands	13	14
Matabeleland South	6	6
Matabeleland North	15	6
Bulawayo	–	7

Sources: Election Commissioner, *Results of Common Roll Election* 1980; *Daily News*, 28 June 2000.

affect the composition of the parliament and can be assumed to be relevant for cabinet formation. There have been relatively few changes over the 20-year period, notwithstanding the fact that by 1995 Harare was separated from the province of Mashonaland East and Bulawayo from Matabeland North.

Taken together, the Mashonaland provinces have the biggest voting power, but significantly their overrepresentation in the cabinet has been exceptional. Excluding 1985 and 2000, the average representation of the Mashonaland provinces is probably quite close to their actual voting power. Until 1995, Manicaland was clearly overrepresented, having at most 26 per cent of the cabinet posts. However, if there is a single group that has been arithmetically overrepresented in all the cabinets, it is the whites who, with about 2 per cent of the whole population, have had at least one seat in all cabinets.

The power-base of the ruling party

If the cabinet posts were distributed among the elite of the ruling party exactly according to its regional support, they should reflect the proportions shown in Table 6.3. As a matter of fact, this should also be the case if regional factors were not considered at all, and if the elite by definition were composed of those in the ruling party who have strongest support from the voters. The regional background of a random selection of the ministers from that elite should be quite close to the regional support of the ruling party.

Table 6.3 shows the regional power-base of ZANU(PF) in the parliamentary elections. 1995 is not included, as 55 of the 120 seats were

Table 6.3   The votes of the ruling party by region, (%)

Region	1980	1985	1990	2000
Mashonaland Central	9	9	5	16
Mashonaland West	12	11	14	13
Mashonaland East	30	28	21	16
Harare				7
Manicaland	16	15	11	10
Masvingo	17	17	11	14
Midlands	13	17	18	16
Matabeleland South	1	1	7	5
Matabeleland North	2	2	13	3
Bulawayo	–	–	–	2

Sources: Election Commissioner, *Results of Common Roll Election* 1980; *The Sunday Mail*, 7 July 1985; Jonathan Moyo (1992); *Daily News*, 28 June 2000.

uncontested, making it impossible to evaluate the support of ZANU(PF) by the number of votes. The percentages in the table show the regional share of the votes for the ruling party of the total it received across the country. For instance, in 1990 18 per cent of all votes for the ruling party came from the Midlands.

The shifts between different elections are again astonishing. The *de facto* one-partyism in Zimbabwe seems anything but firm from the point of view of the regional vote. The Matabeleland provinces have recorded the strongest fluctuation and the lowest share of ZANU(PF) support, especially in 1980 and 1985. In 1980, Matabeleland was very well represented in the government, but in 1985 and 2000 the government responded to the voting behaviour of the region by reducing its representation. Its support for the ruling party in 1990 was preceded by its inclusion in the cabinet in 1988. Manicaland's support dropped in 1990, and even further in 2000. Yet, as Table 6.1 shows, the most drastic reduction of its cabinet posts occurred in 1995. It is hardly surprising that the Mashonaland provinces have been the strongholds of the ruling party, comprising half its voters. However, only twice, in 1985 and 2000, has the representation of these provinces in the cabinet reached the level of their 'fair share' as far as their actual support for the ruling party is concerned.The regional support for the ruling party seems to correlate with the cabinet representation even less than the voting power of the regions. This suggests that persuasion plays a role when the regions outside Mashonaland are included.

Regional support for the opposition

Persuasion of voters can be further elaborated by looking at the strength of the opposition in each province. Table 6.4 shows the percentage of all valid regional votes given to the nationally strongest opposition party. These proportions are perhaps the most crucial message to the government, since they indicate the voters' eagerness to vote against the ruling party. For instance in 1990, 28 per cent of the voters in Manicaland voted for the then strongest opposition party. Opposition has not been institutionalized, as four different parties have held the position of the second biggest party. Furthermore, the strongest national opposition party has not always been the strongest opposition in all regions, and in 1980 and 1985 it would have been more accurate to speak about junior party in the government than opposition. The year 1995 is included, but it needs to be noted that a large share of the seats went to ZANU(PF) uncontested.

Table 6.4   Support for the main opposition party of regional votes, (%)

Region	1980	1985	1990	1995	2000
	ZAPU	ZAPU	ZUM	ZANU(Ndonga)	MDC
Mashonaland Central	2	1	6	4	20
Mashonaland West	13	3	12	3	33
Mashonaland East	5	3	26		24
Harare	–	–	–	10	76
Manicaland	2	1	28	25	47
Masvingo	2	2	8	6	33
Midlands	27	14	13	–	37
Matabeleland South	86	87	11	–	59
Matabeleland North	79	83	18	5	74
Bulawayo	–	–	–	4	84
Total	24	19	18	7	47

Sources: Election Commissioner, *Results of Common Roll Election* 1980; *The Sunday Mail*, 7 July 1985; Jonathan Moyo (1992); *Daily News*, 28 June 2000.

The support of the opposition has been minuscule only in the Mashonaland provinces. But even there in 1990 Mashonaland East (which still included Harare) and the elections in 2000 are exceptional. The biggest fluctuation is recorded in Matabeleland. Opposition has been considerable in Manicaland. Masvingo is more secure for the ruling party, but people also voted against the ruling party there in 2000.

The differences between Matabeleland and Manicaland are revealing. The opposition in the first two elections was popular in Matabeleland but not in Manicaland. In 1990 and 1995 the situation was reversed, a significant section of voters in Manicaland voting for the then most important opposition, while in Matabeleland they did not. In 2000, in addition to its urban popularity, the opposition received both overwhelming support in Matabeleland and very strong support in Manicaland. For the first time, Manicaland was quite close to the voting pattern of Matabeleland. Perhaps in order to prevent a possible alliance between these two regions, Mugabe turned to the divide-and-rule strategy, persuading one region and punishing the other. Manicaland's representation in the cabinet was increased by half while Matabeleland's representation was reduced almost as much (Table 6.1). The relative difference between Matabeleland South and North is also noteworthy. Matabeleland North's strong support for the opposition perhaps explains its complete exclusion from the cabinet in 2000.

Analysing the fluctuation in regional representation

The fluctuation in the cabinet's regional representation reflects the regional vote but does not follow it in an unambiguous pattern. In order to understand this better, we have to look at the sequence of political events as well.

In 1980, majority rule meant that the ruling elite was no longer an alien minority that had been associated with the rural majority through the state bureaucracy or the chiefs against which the young guerrillas had rebelled (see Kriger 1992), but an elite that linked to the people by their regional background. Consequently, regional interests became the substance of political competition at the national level. For the government, in turn, all competition was a potential threat to its position. Therefore, it wanted to control or suppress regionality.

Because regions are entities that are easily recognized by the state administration, they can be punished, which, however, is never a long-term solution as it soon leads to resistance. The government can then impose its own candidates to 'represent' the regions and make it difficult for others to campaign. Often the peaceful solution of this dilemma involves co-option and corruption. The more uncertain the government is about its support among the regional voters, the more certain it needs to be about the loyalties of the regional leaders. In the end, however, the failure of the government to foster development puts it under enormous pressure. Within a multi-party framework, voters can always vote against parties and leaders with whom they are not happy.

By learning how to bargain with the leadership, the regional leaders and the regional voters have powers *vis-à-vis* the leader. A further dynamic is created by the fact that the relationship between the regional voters and regional leaders is not given. There are obvious cleavages within the ruling party, and new political and civil actors can join the bargaining. What follows from this is that there are no unambiguous strategies available for the leadership to safeguard its position and to respond to regional grievances.

The founding elections

In 1980, Mugabe's decision that ZANU would not contest the elections with ZAPU, with which it had united as the Patriotic Front for the peace negotiations, was a disappointment for Joshua Nkomo, a more senior leader of the liberation movement. Both ZANU and ZAPU (under the name PF) contested seats across the country. However, the mobilization of Matabeleland behind Nkomo, who comes from that region, and other provinces behind Mugabe, who comes from Mashonaland West, cannot be regarded as the result of intense competition between the leaders alone – elites are supposed to compete in multi-party systems but was much more because of the result of local-level pressures to unite behind one party. This in turn needs to be understood in the context of the local power structures, which were affected not only by the Rhodesian indirect rule, but also by the two liberation armies, ZANLA (of ZANU) and ZIPRA (of ZAPU).

Because the parliamentary seats were allocated proportionally,[3] the results reflected some pluralism. Nkomo's PF got one seat in Mashonaland West and ZANU got one seat in Matabeleland North. Altogether ZANU got 57, ZAPU 20 and Abel Muzorewa's UANC 3 seats in the Parliament.[4] When Mugabe formed the cabinet as leader of the winning party, it was hardly surprising that a majority of the ZANU Central Committee members was nominated. As his deputy and Minister of Foreign Affairs, Mugabe nominated Simon Muzenda, who comes from Masvingo. Mugabe gave ZAPU 5 of the 36 cabinet posts. Nkomo was appointed as the Minister of Home Affairs. The president of the National Farmer's Union, Dennis Norman, became Minister of Agriculture and the former Minister of Finance, David Smith, Minister for Commerce and Industry. The distribution of the cabinet posts was a clear message to the whole nation that all regions and all groups were included.

The first cabinet reshuffle took place at the beginning of 1981. Nkomo was transferred from Home Affairs to Minister without Port-folio. In exchange, ZAPU got the Transport Ministry. Minister of State Emmerson Mnangagwa from ZANU(PF) became chairman of the Joint Command in charge of integrating the armed forces. The disciplinary actions did not concern ZAPU only. In October 1981, Mugabe sacked Minister of Health Herbert Ushewokunze, because of his criticism of the government's promotion policies among public employees. More than anything else, these moves showed how dependent the ministers were on the Prime Minister.

The next reshuffle followed in April 1982. Mugabe appointed two former members of the Rhodesian Front and three ZAPU members to the cabinet, saying that this was 'necessary to accommodate our friends and allies' (*The Herald*, 18 April 1982). At that time there were already 35 ministers and 24 deputy ministers, which was said to be 'a large and formidable team quite justified for some time by the size and gravity of the tasks ahead and the demands of national unity' (*The Herald*, 21 April 1982). Mugabe justified the size of his cabinet in no uncertain terms: it had the whole country as its area of responsibility, unlike the Rhodesian government 'that had only been indirectly related to parts of the country through native commissioners and their like' (*The Herald*, 30 September 1983). In reality, this was a sign rather of increasing tension and problems than co-operation among the elite.

The tense relationship between ZANU and ZAPU deteriorated into civil war in Matabeleland and parts of the Midlands, where the government troops committed serious atrocities against the civilian population. Mugabe accused ZAPU of trying to seize power by military means. In January 1984, he announced that economic restraints made it necessary to cut the number of ministries by four. The real motivation was to punish Matabeleland and the Midlands by reducing their representation. In this major reshuffle, the representation of Mashonaland and Masvingo increased (Table 6.1).

Nkomo returned from his self-imposed exile in Britain in August 1984. In November, the remaining ZAPU ministers were sacked. *The Herald* commented that this was bound to happen, because ZAPU had not stopped the murderous acts by the so-called 'dissidents' (3 November 1984). The message sent to Matabeleland voters was clear: if you want to be represented in the government vote for ZANU not ZAPU at the next election.

The 1985 elections and unity

The 1985 parliamentary elections were initially scheduled for March, but were postponed until July. Matabeleland voted for ZAPU again. After all the intimidation, voting for ZANU would have been tantamount to betrayal of the ZAPU leaders, who apparently were not eager to give up. ZANU won 63 seats against ZAPU's 15. Ndabadangi Sithole's ZANU(Ndonga) captured one seat in the eastern part of Manicaland. When compared to 1980, ZANU's better performance was mainly owing to the first-past-the post system that was implemented for the first time. By the same token, the regional polarization in the parliamentary seats became even more striking: ZAPU did not win seats outside Matabeleland, and ZANU did not win seats in Matabeleland. After the results of the elections were released, Mugabe invited all the opposition leaders to join ZANU(PF) (*The Herald*, 6 July 1985).

When the new cabinet was nominated, it became clear to the ZAPU leaders that the support they had received in Matabeleland helped them little. The only non-ZANU(PF) minister in the new cabinet was a representative of the whites. The number of ministers remained at 26, but the number of the deputies was reduced by 4, making it 11. This was explained by the trend to reduce the size of the cabinet. The strategic choice to punish Matabeleland made such a reduction possible. By the same token, the representation of Mashonaland increased drastically. Thus, Mashonaland's exceptional representation in 1985 was a function of Matabeleland's exclusion. It is important, however, to note that Matabeleland had representation in the cabinet through ZANU. Complete exclusion of the region was impossible for a government that claimed legitimacy in the whole country.

The only option available to the popular leaders from Matabeleland was to join the ruling party, if they wanted to share power. This was also the only option for Mugabe, if he really wanted to include the region under his regime. The focus was then on merging ZAPU into ZANU, which took place in 1987. The idea of uniting the two parties was not a new one, but had been on the agenda since the liberation movement had initially split in 1963. But the terms (especially the leadership and party symbols) under which the parties could unite had not been easy to negotiate.

The Unity Accord effectively increased the representation of Matabeleland in the cabinet, which now included five ZAPU leaders: Joshua Nkomo, John Nkomo, Edward Ndlovu, Lot Senda and Joseph Msika. A new feature was the appointment of senior ministers. This created a third category of ministers to accompany 'ordinary' ministers and deputy ministers. The new senior ministers were Joshua Nkomo, Maurice Nyagumbo and Bernard Chidzero. Mugabe noted that new posts were necessary to accommodate ZANU's 'counterparts' from ZAPU. A peace deal between the leaders was probably the most important outcome of the Unity Accord for people in Matabeleland. According to *The Herald*, 'a snap survey' before a joint rally of the parties in January 1988 revealed that people knew nothing about the Unity Accord, but when they were told that ZAPU leaders had been appointed ministers, the crowd cheered (11 January 1988). In 1988, Matabeleland representation was better than it had been even in the first 1980 government. This increase in Matabeleland representation meant a decrease in the representation of Mashonaland.

A completely new Ministry for Political Affairs was established under Nyagumbo. Political (that is party) affairs became important because of the need to integrate ZANU and ZAPU. The distinction between the party and the state became even more unclear than before, and the government stated that all civil servants should be or become party members. In October, the Parliament had amended the constitution by creating an executive president. By December, Mugabe had no difficulty in becoming the first executive president with the support of the united ZANU(PF). A subsequent amendment of the constitution created the office of vice-president, to which Mugabe appointed Muzenda. A *de facto* one-party state with a strong president was created.

The 1990 elections

In 1988 Edgar Tekere, member of the 'old guard' party elite, criticized the idea of a one-party state. The ZANU(PF) Central Committee expelled him. At the same time, the revelation of a corruption scandal led to the resignation of six cabinet ministers. Tekere formed a new party, the Zimbabwe Unity Movement (ZUM) in 1989 to contest the Parliament seats vacated by these ministers. Facing the threat of ZUM's anti-corruption rhetoric, ZANU(PF) tried to get Tekere back, but without success (Jonathan Moyo 1992, 38). In spite of ZANU's long endeavour to the contrary, there was thus party competition in the 1990 elections.

ZUM was able to mobilize people, especially in the urban areas, and the government's repressive response made the campaign period 'one of the most viciously contested' in the country (Makumbe 1991a, 1). These elections again exposed great regional differences. Mashonaland Central achieved a relatively high participation rate; even so, more than half its electorate was, in practice, disenfranchised owing to the large number of uncontested seats. At the other extreme, Matabeleland recorded very low participation and an exceptionally high number of spoilt votes. It seems that all former ZAPU supporters were dissatisfied with the way the two parties had been merged. Although ZUM was able to get 18 per cent of the votes, most from the big cities, it managed to win only two seats in Manicaland, which was Tekere's 'home region'. Thus, Mugabe proclaimed that his party had achieved a 'landslide victory' in the elections. One of the 120 seats went to ZANU(Ndonga).

The new cabinet was again big. It included 26 ministers and 12 deputies. Nkomo, Chidzero and Didymus Mutasa were appointed senior ministers. Mashonaland's position was strengthened again after the inclusion of ex-ZAPU members had reduced it in 1988. This was the first time this happened by reducing the representation of Midlands, Masvingo and Manicaland. The latter was clearly a message to the supporters of Tekere there. On balance, it needs to be noted that Manicaland was still very well represented, which was probably to compensate for the fact that Masvingo (Muzenda) held the second-highest post in the state hierarchy. To the disappointment of the ex-ZAPU leaders, Mugabe nominated only three former ZAPU representatives to the new cabinet (Chan with Chingambo 1992, 186). However, some of the expectations of the ex-ZAPU members were fulfilled in August with a constitutional amendment, which introduced a dual vice-presidency. Joshua Nkomo was sworn in as vice-president to accompany Muzenda.

At the end of 1991, the president once again announced that the cabinet was too large and expensive (*Sunday Mail*, 15 December 1991). But the next reshuffle did not take place until July 1992. Seven ministers and four deputies were dropped from the government (*The Herald*, 4 July 1992). Soon after that, the governor of Masvingo resigned because he had not been given a portfolio in the reshuffle (*The Herald*, 17 September 1992). His resignation reflected a more general dissatisfaction on the part of the people in Masvingo and the Midlands. Although their relative representation was not reduced, it was now lower than ever before in numbers. The same applied to the representation of the people from Manicaland. Paradoxically, after Matabeleland had been well accommodated, new inter- and intra-regional tensions seemed to be emerging. Speculation on 'tribalism' in the cabinet nominations became rampant, especially after a car accident in which one minister died and which was widely regarded as 'mysterious' (see *Sunday Gazette*, 13 March 1994).

The 1995 elections

The deteriorating economy eroded the popularity of the ruling party, but did not strengthen the opposition parties. ZUM disintegrated and several new small opposition groups were mushrooming, but none of them was able to mobilize voters massively. Key civil society organizations, such as the labour unions, were explicitly not involved in party politics. The opposition was too divided and weak to contest a sufficient number of seats to win the elections even in principle. Because ZANU(PF) got 55 seats uncontested and the President had the right to appoint 12 MPs and 8 governors, who also became MPs, as well as 10 chiefs who in practice were all supporters of ZANU(PF), it had secured 85 seats out of 150 seats in the Parliament even before the polling started. Apathy was widespread in most constituencies.

However, ZANU(PF)'s secure position was reflected in its very hotly contested primaries. Largely as a result of the way the primaries were conducted, a 'group' of independent candidates emerged. This revealed deep cleavages within the party at regional level. A special case was Masvingo province, where the independents got 18 per cent of the votes. According to official results released after the elections, the independents did not win any seats. Later, however, the polling in Harare South constituency was nullified owing to irregularities. In the subsequent re-election, the independent candidate Margaret Dongo was elected. Sithole's small ZANU(Ndonga) appeared to be the most significant opposition party in the 1995 elections. It got two Manicaland seats in the Parliament.

Among the cabinet nominations, the most important was the appointment of Ariston Chambati as the Minister of Finance because Chidzero had been ill for over two years. The business community and the World Bank welcomed this. Mugabe appointed Stan Mudenge to Foreign Affairs, side-lining Nathan Sahmuyarira, who got the portfolio of Public Service, Labour and Social Welfare. In this way, the President supported Muzenda's camp in the intra-regional fighting in Masvingo. Mudenge had already lost the contest for the ZANU(PF) provincial chair to the section supported by Eddison Zvobgo, a party intellectual with strong regional support and presidential ambitions.

The cabinet was enlarged, this time from 18 to 21 ministers, despite calls to cut it and reduce public spending (*The Herald*, 21 April 1995). Quite against the logic of the IMF and the World Bank trying to impose conditions on their aid and press the government in this regard, the more difficult the economic situation was the more important it became for Mugabe to buy the loyalty of the regional elite with cabinet posts. This time the exceptional strengthening of the Matabeleland representation suggested that the President wanted to ensure the loyalty of that region when he faced increasing problems with Masvingo and Manicaland. Manicaland lost two ministers and gained only one deputy minister.

The next cabinet reshuffle followed the presidential elections of 1996. Zvobgo, who had health problems, was demoted from Minister of Mines to Minister without Portfolio. An important nomination was again the Minister of Finance. Chambati had died soon after his appointment. The new minister was former Minister of Industry and Trade, Herbert Murerwa. A couple of other ministers were also reshuffled, while the deputy ministers were retained. The again increased size of the cabinet did not bring significant changes to the regional balance, Mashonaland's representation being slightly strengthened while the Midlands lost one ministerial post.

The next cabinet reshuffle in July 1997 reflected the deepening economic and political crisis. Mugabe explained that he had cut the number of ministries to reduce the budget deficit. In reality, he ended up with a larger cabinet. This time the President also described the appointment of five female politicians as affirmative action (*The Financial Gazette*, 31 July 1997). Most importantly, Zvobgo remained in the cabinet but without portfolio. He was among the nine ministers who had served in every cabinet since independence. The other ministers were Shamuyarira from Mashonaland West, Sydney Sekeramayi, Enos Chikowore and Witness Mangwende from Mashonaland East; Mnangagwa and Richard Hove from the Midlands; as well as Moven Mahachi and Kumbirai Kangai from Manicaland – all long-time members of the ZANU(PF) Politburo. When added to the former ZAPU leaders, John Nkomo and Dumiso Dabengwa from Matabeleland South and Msika from Mashonaland Central, the list of those politicians whose appointment to the cabinet seemed to be automatic was extensive. Thus the definition of their portfolios played a role. In this regard, leaving Zvobgo without portfolio and leaving Foreign Affairs with Mudenge was perhaps all the President could do, if he wanted to send a message to Masvingo.

The elections in 2000

By 1997, the pressure to check the powers of the President and to draft a more democratic constitution culminated in the formation of the National Constitutional Assembly (NCA) by many civil society groups. The secretary-general of the Zimbabwe Congress of Trade Unions (ZCTU), Morgan Tsvangirai, chaired the NCA. The government did not want to co-operate with the NCA, but it was not able to ignore it either. It formed its own commission to draft a new constitution to be put to a public referendum. The NCA in turn boycotted the government's commission on the grounds that it was dependent on the president, who had the power to amend its proposal. Both the NCA and the commission arranged civic education campaigns and were very visible all over the country.

In September 1999, a new party, the Movement for Democratic Change, was formed under the leadership of Tsvangirai, with the result that the whole society was much more politicized than ever before. When the government finally put the proposed constitution to a referendum, the NCA and MDC launched a campaign explaining to the public that the changes reducing the powers of the President were merely cosmetic and much more radical changes were needed. To Mugabe's surprise the voters rejected the proposal. Thus, the ruling party was worried about the upcoming parliamentary elections and a violent campaign, led by the War Veterans' Association, against the opposition was launched. Finally, ZANU(PF) won 62 seats against the MDC's 57, introducing a strong opposition into the Parliament. ZANU(Ndonga) got its traditional seat in Manicaland.

Participation in the elections was strong in the urban areas, while intimidation probably reduced participation in some rural areas. The most striking feature of the regional vote was not the overwhelming support the MDC got from the big cities, but the fact that ZANU(PF) got only two seats from the Matabeleland provinces. Voters in Matabeleland did not feel they were tied to the Unity Accord. Joshua Nkomo's death a year before had probably provided some elbow-room for the opposition in rural Matabeleland. In addition the MDC got seven against ZANU(PF)'s six seats in Manicaland.

The election results and the catastrophic economic situation did not make the formation of the new cabinet easy. That Matabeleland had voted against ZANU(PF) justified the reduction of its representation and the size of the whole cabinet. On the other hand the very difficult campaigning period had apparently made the leadership, especially Muzenda, promise cabinet nomination to several regional leaders. It took almost three weeks for the new cabinet was announced. Even after that one minister was changed because of the demands of the regional leadership of Mashonaland West (*Daily News*, 17 July 2000).

The new government included new faces and was soon characterized as technocratic, 11 ministers having a doctoral degree. Eight ministers were not elected MPs but were nominated by Mugabe. Only a few ministers from the old cabinet remained: Mahachi, Mudenge, Murerwa, Sekeramayi, John Nkomo, Joyce Mujuru, Ignatius Chombo, Nicholas Goche and Timothy Stamps (representing the whites). For the first time there was nobody from the first 1980 cabinet. Only Vice-Presidents Muzenda and newly nominated Msika came from that 'founding' cabinet. Several leaders, whose appointment to the previous cabinets had been more or less assured, were left outside, including Zvobgo, Shamuyarira, Hove, Dabengwa, Chikowore, Kangai, Mnangagwa and Mangwende. At least Zvobgo's and Kangai's exclusion from cabinet was widely regarded as punishment for their being 'sympathetic' to the opposition (*Zimbabwe Independent*, 21 July 2000).

If the nomination of ministers was at least partially guided by Mugabe's interest in getting 'professionals' into the government, regionality was perhaps even more important than usual in the nomination of the deputies. Mugabe announced his plans to appoint 13 deputy ministers and presented the list to the ZANU(PF) Central Committee. Most of these names were published in the newspapers. But perhaps the positions of the deputies were not regarded as satisfactory by the regional leaders, because finally only seven deputies were appointed. This reduced the overall size of the government by about ten. When the President, two Vice-Presidents, the Attorney-General and the eight governors are taken into account, the size of the new cabinet was 'only' 40. (*The Herald*, 26 July 2000.)

As could have been anticipated from the election results, Matabeleland was punished most severely. The ex-ZAPU leaders were reduced to their traditional Ministry of Home Affairs, which provoked immediate criticism (see *The Daily News*, 17 July 2000). In addition, Mugabe sacked the Governor of Matabeleland North, Welshman Mabhena, who had been third in command in the old ZAPU after Nkomo and Msika (*The Daily News*, 24 July 2000). Still, it is important to note that Matabeleland was not left without representation, although it might be that the people there do not regard Mugabe's choices as their own leaders. Manicaland had been punished in the previous reshuffles but improved its representation now.

Many sections of the ZANU(PF) elite were not happy with the nominations, which might mean that the regional power-base of the government was weaker than ever before. While this could imply relative independence of the government from the regions, enabling it to take drastic measures to enhance the economic development of the country, the government was even more dependent on the President than the previous ones had been.

Concluding notes

Mugabe's cabinet reshuffles have demonstrated his power over the nomination of ministers, yet he has also been dependent on the co-operation of the regional leaders. A particularly obvious characteristic is that Mugabe has used inclusion to try to persuade different regions under his leadership. In this regard, 1985 and 2000 are exceptional years and the only cases in which the Mashonaland representation in the cabinet has been concomitant with the Mashonaland power-base of the ruling party. Significantly, both years mark situations of crisis, in which opposition parties mobilized voters in spite of rampant state-sponsored violence. It seems possible to conclude that peaceful political order has been based on inclusion of the regions outside Mashonaland much beyond the popularity of the ruling party in those regions, and that exclusion has been implemented only in the event of crisis. Yet the 'overrepresentation' of the regional elite has not ensured popular support for the ruling party in that particular region. The elections in 2000 showed that the deteriorating economic situation and increasing corruption in the government provided fertile ground for the opposition, particularly in the regions outside Mashonaland. In a context of more favourable economic development the situation might have developed in another direction: perhaps the regional ZANU(PF) leaders would have been able to bring development to their constituencies and perhaps they could have earned and maintained popular support all over the country.

It is evident that an element of accountability exists in the Zimbabwean electoral system. Cabinet formation has reflected its limitation to the one-party framework and to the level of the regional party elite. When the position of the party has been threatened, the consequence has been not only exclusion but also coercion.

Urbanization is one factor that has potential to change the significance of regionality in Zimbabwean politics by bringing new class-based interests to the political agenda. It is also possible that the political influence of the cities is spilling over into the regions. Civic groups, trade unions, professionals and students have penetrated into the rural areas with their notions of electoral democracy, which is challenging the local mechanisms of the *de facto* one-party rule. However, for any new party aspiring to get into power, the regional dynamics of political participation remains an important factor. Thus the question is, are there any ways other than one-partyism and corruption to involve the regions, and their genuine need to foster development, in a government struggling with inflation, de-industrialization and a serious budget deficit.

Notes

1. An earlier version of this chapter was presented at the 43rd Annual African Studies Association Meeting, Nashville, 16–19 November 2000. The author is grateful for comments by Norma Kriger, Brian Raftopoulos and Staffan Darnolf.
2. These are textual definitions (as the sources of this research are texts). Only when, for instance, the President has stated that somebody has been nominated to the government as a representative of the coloured community can he or she be considered so. In principle, the tables are colour-blind.
3. There was no time to compile the electoral roll in order to divide the country into the first-past-the-poll constituencies.
4. Twenty seats were reserved for the whites until 1987.

7
Education in Zimbabwe:
A Matter of Success?

Anders Närman

Education for all

At the time of independence most African countries, including Zimbabwe, came out of a period plagued by serious colonial neglect in the provision of social service facilities. So, for example, in the case of formal schooling, factors such as racial segregation, low enrolment rates and quality problems were common. Consequently, in drawing up the guidelines for an educational policy, the quantitative expansion of education for integration of the majority of the population, was a main priority for Zimbabwe, just as it was for most other new African governments. Popular demand for increased access to education for all was followed by a strong community commitment to the building of schools, teacher accommodation, and so on. Donors were generally in favour of contributing towards the educational sector. Education was a key instrument for achieving development and thereby building the newly independent African nations.

In actual terms, a substantial increase in primary and secondary school enrolments, just after independence in most African countries, could be observed. At the same time, this often resulted in a serious deterioration in school quality and after a period of fast quantitative educational expansion, stagnation or even decline followed. As a result of this, it is evident that education in Africa today is in a dilemma, with a net enrolment well below 50 per cent as one of the most significant indicators.

With its comparatively late independence, Zimbabwe had an opportunity to learn from the lessons of educational experiences in other parts of Africa. Still the educational planners seem to have fallen into the kind of traps that were so well known from ten to twenty years of attempts to bring education to all people in a minimum of time. Equality was also a basic ideal for a Zimbabwe that was initially strongly connected to a left-leaning radical development strategy. Partly, the educational development in Zimbabwe had its roots in the particular circumstances existing during the struggle for independence.

The intention in this chapter will be to outline both the quantitative and qualitative trends in Zimbabwean education, since independence – but against a backdrop of the colonial past. Education will be examined in the light of its overall national and global development trends, and the chapter will also focus on the interrelationship between education and work – both industrial activities and agriculture.

The legacy of colonial education in Zimbabwe

The colonial experience in Zimbabwe differs to a certain extent from that of other African nations. A settler economy had its specific educational demands for a white minority regime. A primary objective for African education was to create a subservient agricultural working class, and to provide a few staff for the lower administrative sector. To achieve this, some kind of fragile coalition was constituted between the colonial government and the missionary churches. The interest to promote divinity was here coupled with the need to provide basic skills in reading, writing, arithmetic and simple vocational subjects. As educational philosophies differed between churches this meant that not only was a gap found on racial lines, but also stratification was based on the membership of different religious communities (Zvogbo 1994).

Educational content in the colonial schools was to a very high extent biased against basic African interests. The European conquest of the country was glorified, with the hailing of Rhodes as a hero, while at the same time the Ndebele King Lobengula was dismissed as of minor significance. As elsewhere on the continent, the African pre-colonial past was grossly ignored in the teaching of history (Mlambo 1997).

For the needs of the white-settler population a separate educational set-up of superior quality had been established from an early stage. According to a World Bank report of 1990 (as quoted by Lind 1995), the cost of education for each European child was twenty times that of the African one. A gap was also found in relation to the Asian and coloured population, even if it was smaller. At independence some part of the high-quality educational system was opened up to the Africans, including a variety of agricultural training centres. In addition to this, an African university education was now open to successful candidates from secondary schools. Previously, the only way open to bright African students had been to look for a higher level education outside the country.

A counter-effect towards the colonial legacy can also be found in the resistance towards the settler strategy for supremacy, particularly under the period of UDI rule, 1965–80. New radical alternatives in education were developed in the 'bush', largely built on the principles of 'Education with Production'. Chung and Ngara (1985) have described how education in camp schools in Mozambique and Zambia was organized, as a combination of study and productive work. As an example science could be studied both within its agricultural and industrial context:

> This system enabled the pupils to link learning directly to practice, and was particularly useful because pupils had to provide their own accommodation, furniture and fresh foods. This worthwhile experience planted the first seeds of the new ideology of education for Zimbabwe. (Chung and Ngara 1985, 106)

Below we will discuss how this educational philosophy in reality has affected actual policies. In addition to the effects on the ideology of education, the war also led to an interruption of education for numerous soldiers who were directly involved in war activities. Therefore, many of the men and women who were actively taking part in the fight for independence were educationally disadvantaged compared to those in school on colonial terms. This in itself was a further consequence of colonial rule, which in itself was a bone of contention after the end of the war. Partly, this can be connected to the sensitive overall issue with regard to the situation among the war veterans.

Educational expansion 1980–90

At independence, educational policies were giving priority to the following three points:

- Elimination of racial discrimination;
- Expansion of educational opportunity;
- Curricular changes to increase the relevancy of content.

As a consequence of the two first points, the Education Act of the newly independent country stated that every child in Zimbabwe had a right to school education. A direct result of this was that primary education should be free and a compulsory primary education would be a desirable objective (Government of Zimbabwe 1987).

Primary education

Already at the time immediately after independence, school attendance was comparatively high, showing a gross primary education enrolment rate of 88 per cent (1980). This represented a primary school population of more than 1.2 million. However, these kinds of statistics must be treated with caution as many pupils (of various ages) now returned to schooling after being restricted from going to school during the intensive war in the last part of the 1970s. In fact, the enrolment in 1980 indicates a 50 per cent increase in relation to the average figures for the period 1976–79, after which the enrolment figures expanded continuously up to the middle of the 1980s (see Figure 7.1).

With this expansion, girls were also brought into the primary schools to a large extent, reaching close to half of the pupils at the end of the 1980s (Mlambo 1997). Even so, the transition rate from primary to secondary schools was lower among females compared to males, and the share of females drops further at higher levels. This was particularly so in certain subjects such as science and technology.

Like so many other African countries, Zimbabwe reached an early estimated gross enrolment of well above 100 per cent. Pakkiri (1989, 280) pointed out that by this the objective of Universal Primary Education (UPE), that is free and compulsory education for all children, had been reached, 'but critics have questioned the efficiency of the system'. As a matter of fact, talking about gross enrolment of well over 100 per cent points to an obvious dilemma of a high repetition rate, and consequently a low internal efficiency.

Some additional data on school attendance can be taken from the 1992 population census. From Figure 7.1 it seems that the impacts of the ESAP programme on education had not been shown in the reduction of primary schooling at that time. From this source it is obvious that children at school are normally at least 7 years of age. Only 40 per cent of 6-year-olds are found in school, with a higher share in urban areas. In the 7–13 age group the net enrolment rate reaches slightly above 90 per cent. Among this cohort we are also finding that female participation is slightly above that for boys. Another comparison made is that enrolment is highest in the urban areas (Government of Zimbabwe 1994a).

One impact of the educational expansion was seen on the recorded literacy rates. According to the 1982 population census, the total

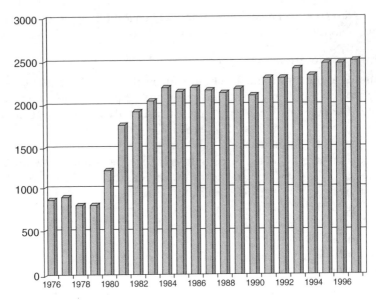

Figure 7.1 Primary school enrolment, 1976–1997

Source: Ministry of Education and Culture.

literacy rate for people above 15 years of age was measured at 62 per cent, with only 56 per cent among females. Ten years later the rate had increased to 80 per cent, with females standing at 75 per cent. Among the age group of 15–19-year-olds, that is the ones that had benefited from the educational expansion in the 1980s, not less than 96 per cent were given as literate, with males and females almost on a par. Still, some regional variations in connection with literacy are obvious. The highest literacy rate is found in the two major cities of Harare and Bulawayo, with females being only slightly behind the men. However, there is a distinct difference in the rural areas between men and females as regards literacy (Government of Zimbabwe 1994a). The high literacy figures for the two major urban areas can be explained by not only, possibly not even primarily, educational facilities, but rather in-migration following upon the completion of a certain educational level.

With a strong emphasis on education, a substantial share of the national budget was allocated to education, but in a country torn apart by a prolonged war of independence, some of this money was needed just to rebuild what had been damaged. At this stage, the government commitment was supplemented by a strong community contribution. Parents were assisting both financially and by providing manpower to construct new schools. In theory these contributions were voluntary, but on the other hand, as pointed out by Graham-Brown (1991), it was a matter of having or not having a school at all. At the same time, the government assured payment for teachers. However, as Dorsey (1989, 48) has described, pupils often met with buildings that were far from ready, or constructed for temporary use, or even classes that 'were held in the open under a tree'. Books and other materials were also in short supply at this time.

To provide primary teachers was another predicament in the years just after independence. In 1979 the number of teachers was well below 20 000, but reached almost three times as many a decade later. This was done through the recruitment of a high proportion of unqualified teachers, plus a four-year training programme: Zimbabwe National Teacher Education Course (ZINTEC). During this course, student teachers were posted in schools for two years to teach with a salary (Graham-Brown 1991). At the time of independence, less than 10 per cent were professionally qualified, while ten years later almost half were to be found in that category. This expansion also created an additional problem in that it would be impossible to pay the total salary bill for all teachers if they were qualified (Dorsey 1989, 40). In fact, Zimbabwe had been criticized by the World Bank for its high allocation, not less than 80 per cent, to teacher salaries as part of the total education budget (Johnson 1990).

Secondary education

Noting the fast primary school expansion, this is still overshadowed by what occurred at the same time on the secondary level. This is illustrated in Figure 7.2. Between 1980 and 1981 the total enrolment was doubled (up to 150 000 pupils) and that increase continued, to reach more than 900 000 pupils in 1990. In this way, Zimbabwe achieved one of the highest gross enrolment rates of any African country. This enrolment was largely built on direct community and private investments, including the continuously expanding access to private schools. As at the primary level, many unqualified teachers had to be employed to cope with the secondary school expansion. Even an intensive teacher-training scheme was not able to produce enough qualified and dedicated teachers to overcome the gap (Chivore 1990). It was common that a kind of double shift, that is so-called hot seating, had to be used to cope with the increased number of pupils. One dilemma faced at the

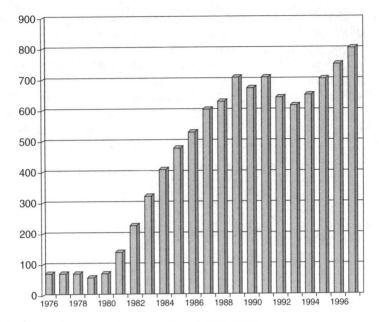

Figure 7.2   Secondary school enrolment, 1976–1997

Source: Ministry of Education and Culture.

secondary school level was that only a small minority (less than 20 per cent) were able to pass the O-level examination (Ordinary level) with the five required passes during most of the 1980s (Berridge 1993). For a long period of time, the Form IV examination was conducted by the British, and was awarded as an English degree. Even if this is no longer the general practice, it seems to be popular to enter a private school that still offers such a degree, which makes the exam much more competitive.

One very specific problem was the fact that knowledge of science was particularly neglected in secondary schools. Partly, this was remedied by the introduction of a science kit programme, but even this was hampered by a lack of well-trained teachers in the relevant subjects. To achieve a planned industrial growth this is a serious issue that Zimbabwe has in common with most other African states.

It has been argued by Colclough and Lewin (1993) that the mistake made by Zimbabwe, during the first decade since independence, was to expand education at all levels too fast. This could not possibly be achieved with effective and equitable management. Especially it seems that it had been reasonable to slow down the pace with which secondary education was expanded for a continuous improvement of primary school quality. One possible outcome of such a policy could have been that eventually the secondary school intake would have been of better academic standards, which in turn would have been a quality boost for that level – presumably ending up with a substantially higher percentage of O-level passes.

Tertiary sector

Up until the early 1990s Zimbabwe had only one university, the University of Zimbabwe in Harare. Initially, it was opened in 1955 as the University College of Rhodesia and Nyasaland, before it became the University of Rhodesia in 1971. In 1980 the total number of university students was approximately 2000, which increased to above 8000 in a decade. During the same period, the number of academic staff went from 322 to 739. Still, this seems to be far from sufficient in relation to the actual needs, as it has been observed that at the end of the 1980s no less than 25 per cent of all existing posts were held vacant (Närman 1991). During the 1990s the number of universities grew, with a technical university in Bulawayo (National University for Science and Technology – NUST) and a private (Methodist) university in Mutare (the African University). At the same time a number of constituent colleges allied to the main University of Zimbabwe were established, as well as an Open University. In addition to the universities, other post-secondary courses included agricultural colleges and institutes, teacher-training colleges, and technical colleges (including a polytechnic in Harare) with well over 25 000 students at the end of the 1990s, compared to some 6000 on independence.

The relative allocation to the various levels of education has been a matter of criticism. Out of the educational budget in the mid-1980s, no less than 24 per cent was allocated for the tertiary sector, with only 6 per cent of the total school population. In fact the annual cost of a university student was more than twenty times, and thirty times, in relation to a secondary, and primary school, pupil respectively (Johnson 1990).

Towards the end of the first decade of independence

In short, Zimbabwe had made an impressive impact in educational expansion during the first decade of independence. This followed the previous example of many other African nations, such as Kenya, Tanzania and Botswana. However, on the secondary level Zimbabwe was soon ahead of any other comparable African country.

Unfortunately, as elsewhere on the continent, this expansion could not be upheld with maintained standards of quality. In itself this created a new form of inequality among the African population, as expressed by Colclough and Lewin (1993, 109), 'a system of bad schools for the poor majority and good schools for the rich'. Furthermore, it has to be noted that even if the primary enrolment rates are well above capacity, that does not necessarily mean that all children are actually having access to education. Most importantly, the labour market had no possibility of absorbing that many new job seekers. The reaction to this state of affairs was to be found early on in the 1990s.

It is noticeable that even against the background of an impressive educational expansion during the first decade since independence, a low proportion of the total population has been educated above Form IV. In 1992 only some 4 per cent had acquired any form of tertiary education. Most of these had attained some kind of diploma, while the number of university graduates was just above 35 000 (0.6 per cent). A low proportion of the graduates were females (Government of Zimbabwe 1994a).

Educational stagnation in the early 1990s

Since Economic Structural Adjustment Programme (ESAP), the kind of pronouncements that were uttered were clearly conforming to a general educational policy for Africa, as 'advised' by the World Bank. The two trademarks for this were increased cost-sharing in primary education, and a sceptical approach to pre-vocational diversification at all levels. At the same time, Zimbabwe received much praise internationally for its 'Social Dimension Fund' that, among other things, should assist parents in paying for educational costs.

The new trend was expressed concisely in the 1990 budget speech, which was also the introduction of ESAP:

> Although education represents a long-term investment in human resources, its provision needs to be balanced with investment in immediately productive areas if the economy is to sustain the costs implied. The trend so far has been for social sectors such as education to grow at the expense of the productive sectors. (Government of Zimbabwe 1990a, 9)

This was partly an answer to a situation with erratic growth and a low rate of employment creation, with less than 10 000 new jobs annually for the first decade since independence. At the same time, the number of school leavers was estimated at 200 000 per year, therefore 'unemployment has become one of the most critical problems facing the economy' (Government of Zimbabwe 1990a). In addition, it was claimed that a primary school education without tuition fees would 'compromise the quality of education'. Both these points might in themselves be valid, even if the policy chosen to get out of the situation might not have been the correct one. In a new Education Act the principle of the reintroduction of fees came up. The lowest fee level in 1993 was set at Z$75 per semester for each pupil in high-density urban areas, while the rural schools were still exempted. At the same time, other unofficial fees were estimated at a total of Z$150 annually per pupil. It was the task of the headmaster to identify pupils of poor families who could get refunds from a 'social development fund' on their school fees. However, this system seemed to function only to a very limited extent (Gibbon 1995b). Undoubtedly, with comparatively low levels of salaries any kind of subjective evaluation of economic status among individual households opens the potential for various forms of corruption.

During the early 1990s it was common to find headlines, such as this one from *The Parade* (June 1992, 41): 'Nyanga school loses pupils due to high fees'. The general situation was described by *The New African* (April 1993, 32) in the following way:

> Educational provision has also suffered. Although the government has suspended a planned increase in fees because of the difficulties associated with the drought a rise in costs of school books, uniforms, exam fees etc. has meant the removal of many children from school. Families are now being forced to choose between children as to who should receive education or not, claimed one headmaster who indicated that it was usually girls who suffered as a result.

Many of us visiting Zimbabwean educational institutions during the early 1990s could notice this kind of decline in the number of pupils in classrooms. In another manner it can be illustrated as in Figures 7.1 and 7.2 for primary and secondary schools respectively. This also seems to be a clear tendency from some reports referred to by Ødegaard (1998). Even if the general policy has been to stress the lower levels of education, below the tertiary sector it seems that there has been a decline in expenditure per pupil in both primary and secondary schools, while there is an increase for university students on average from 1988/89 to 1993/94. The share of educational expenditures as a percentage of the national budget and GDP has decreased slightly between the same years. This led to an increase in pupils per teacher, coupled with a decrease in salary levels. The latter factor can be very negative from the point of view of teacher morale. At the same time, funds for teaching materials dwindled further (Gibbon 1995b).

In a study from Mbare in Harare and some rural schools in the vicinity, it seems as if virtually all are willing to pay to keep the children in school, even if some doubts were raised on account of the value of schooling owing to the perceived low quality. However, the actual ability to pay is more in doubt. A more sporadic attendance, coupled with an increased drop-out rate, can be related to various reasons directly or indirectly affected by ESAP, such as the fees themselves and declining economic conditions, in which the children are themselves increasingly needed as labour (Ødegaard 1998).

In studies referred to by Gibbon (1995b), no clear deductions can be made on the effects on enrolment figures that can be directly linked to ESAP. Some indications are mentioned, such as increased drop-out rates, mostly found among boys in large-scale commercial farming areas. The explanation for this would be that boys are needed as labour during certain parts of the year. Withdrawal was often temporary, and not as a definite dropping out of school. A further point brought forward was that the number of candidates for the O-level examination was dwindling especially in the number of subjects taken. In an evaluation report Mudzi (1998) points out that parents have been unable to pay fees and other educational costs due to increasing unemployment and retrenchments. It is even pointed out that in some urban areas the charges for schooling are substantial, in a deliberate attempt actually to exclude children from low-income groups.

A strong variation between urban and rural areas, as well as within the rural areas, has been evident. The situation is worst on large-scale commercial farms, where the school-age children of farmworkers are frequently missing out on education. Peasant children, on the other hand, are often given a chance in school, but few of them are completing a full cycle of primary education. In urban areas an absolute majority were at least entering primary school in the first part of the 1990s. Because of fees, coupled with increased economic hardships, even this might have changed slightly towards the end of the decade, as shown by Ødegaard (1998).

In short, during the two decades since independence Zimbabwe has experienced a quantitative expansion for the first ten years, but a simultaneous decrease in quality, while enrolment stagnated or declined in the second period – with continued problems concerning quality. Even if the unplanned expansion in the 1980s had a number of flaws, it is definitely very wrong to claim that the changes taking place in the 1990s were able to rectify the wrongs done. We are here back to the old saying that two wrongs do not constitute the right solution. Furthermore, it is noticeable that the actors in educational policy making have changed drastically. During the 1980s, strategies on education were largely in the hands of the social scientists/educationalists. These were largely replaced in the next decade by educational economists with a very superficial understanding of what education actually means in a process of development and nation building. In fact, this has been a general tendency all over the African continent for a long period of time, paving the way for something of a new lost generation in terms of educational, as well as general development trends.

Access and quality of schooling in Zimbabwe towards the end of the millennium

In an evaluation of education in Zimbabwe towards the end of the 1990s some important points are focused on (Mudzi 1998). It is simply noticed that, in spite of some very important achievements in education since independence, the major problems of equity, access and quality in schooling remain on the agenda to be solved.

On the equity side we can note that this is a matter of gender, region and class. Sometimes these factors also reinforce each other. Even if the primary school enrolment for girls has gone up considerably we can only find a limited number of girls at the higher levels of education, as well as in certain strategic combinations of subjects. In addition to this, girls seem to have a higher incidence of drop out.

It is obvious, furthermore, that access to education is lower among working families on the large farms. In some cases this can be put down to long distance from school or to the fact that the families are not able to afford schooling. In addition to this, many of the children might be needed to carry out work within the households. A decline in enrolment and participation in connection with ESAP has been noted. After a survey carried out in rural schools, the government newspaper *The Herald* (29 May 1999) referred to the situation as simply shocking.

The quality of schooling can be measured in various ways. Factors that show certain limitations have been classroom space, libraries, rooms for practical work and textbooks. In addition to this, the problem of many unqualified teachers remains. Performance in school can be measured by examination results, which show a fairly positive picture on the primary level. In secondary school, however, the O-and A-level results are regarded as very poor. This is also a matter of the socio-economic background of the pupils. *The Sunday Mail* (1 January 1999) compares a well-funded secondary school, with a 100 per cent pass rate, with most rural schools, in which it happens that not a single pupil will achieve five good O-level passes. It was noted that the good school could choose their pupils and would provide the best resources. On the other hand, the rural school is in a situation where there are scarce resources and unqualified teachers, which makes a pass something of a miracle.

Consequently, even if some successes have been noted within the educational sector in Zimbabwe, many of the original problems are still present and it does not seem as if there are any definite solutions in sight so far. Mudzi (1998) concludes that with ESAP the gap within Zimbabwean society between various sectors has tended to increase in terms of access to quality education.

The Zimbabwe Independent (13 February 1998) has described the Zimbabwe educational system as close to collapse. As a reason for this it quotes the tendency since independence to provide for a quantitative expansion of an academic education, without due regard to the actual needs of the labour market. So, for example, pupils leaving schools are in no way prepared for employment in the industrial sector.

Education for work

So far, a number of aspects devoted to the internal efficiency (to use an economist's vocabulary) of education in Zimbabwe have been discussed. It is essential to give some additional points as they relate to external efficiency. Partly, this is a matter of how well certain key subjects are being taught. One serious concern often raised in relation to secondary education is the issue of science education. Professor Chetsanga, for example, has focused on the issue of a limited number of science teachers (*The Sunday Mail*, 7 October 1990). To some extent it might have been eased by the establishment of a National University of Science and Technology (NUST) in Bulawayo, plus the upgrading of some teacher-training colleges.

A more controversial aspect is the one related to the more directly vocational subjects in the formal school structure. Mackenzie (1988, 350) has expressed the need for an emphasis on the development of subjects imparting:

skills that will be of practical value to school leavers, life skills that pupils can utilise outside the education system whether it is, for example, in subsistence farming or in small business enterprises or on factory assembly lines.

To follow up on this we will touch briefly upon some of the trends in vocational(ized) education, as it concerns both industrial and agricultural development.

Technical/practical education

Zimbabwe seems to have had a consistent policy in relation to vocationalized schooling. One expression of this was stated in the Development Plan 1986–90:

> the secondary school curriculum will be broadened to include a wide range of technical and vocational subjects which are oriented towards the manpower requirements of the productive sector. (Government of Zimbabwe 1986a, 57)

It has to be noted that this stand was to a large extent contrary to the official view of the World Bank in numerous policy declarations (World Bank 1991). In this case, most of the donors tended to follow a similar line of argument, going back to the concept of a 'Vocational School Fallacy' (Foster 1965) and later on emphasized in various World Bank publications (Psacharopoulos and Loxley 1985; Psacharopoulos and Woodhall 1985). Consequently, the World Bank (1991) in a sector policy paper advised strongly against having a vocationalized curriculum in the general school system. In spite of this Zimbabwe, like some other African nations, has continued to promote a vocationalized school structure, even well into the 1990s.

Arguments against vocationalization, with reference to cost-efficiency, do not seem to be valid taken from a broader perspective. On the one hand, we can observe that there is a considerable unemployment rate all over Africa. However, on the other hand there is a lack of skilled manpower in certain sectors – not least the technical/practical sector. To a large extent, industrial expansion and development is strongly connected with the availability of foreign experts and volunteers. From the point of view of the SAPs it would, then, seem a bit odd not to invest more fully in the creation of a cadre of technically skilled and semi-skilled people. It is hardly enough to think that this can be left solely to the private sector.

From the above it can be assumed that the official Zimbabwean stand on vocationalization of the secondary school curriculum is a challenge to the World Bank thinking on the issue, but at the same time a response to a highly felt need to take part in some form of modern development process. In the Education Plan of 1986 two models for vocationalization are suggested. One of them is to introduce technical/ practical subjects, as part of the general academic curriculum, as a part of the normal O-levels examination. In addition to this, a crafts certificate, that is the Zimbabwe National Craft Certificate (ZNCC), was introduced to pave the way for direct employment. Later on, because of unsatisfactory examination results in the ZNCC, the National Foundation Certificate (NFC) replaced this programme (Nherera 1998).

Nherera (1998) opposes the view that the vocational school is a fallacy for the situation in Zimbabwe. He regards the introduction of vocationalized education as an important part of the transformation of the society to consolidate independence in the country. He argues that this is an education not only for employment, but also for self-empowerment – to become job creators.

Like other countries in the region, Zimbabwe has been adopting a form of Education with Production (EwP) system. Partly, this has been linked closely with the thinking of Fay Chung, the previous Minister of Education and Culture, linking this specific form of education to the war of liberation – as mentioned above. At the same time, we can see that the EwP system has been introduced in many countries in the region which have a different background from the Zimbabwean one. The concept can be tied closely to the work done by Patrick van Rensburg in Botswana and his brigade concept, which originally was supposed to be a kind of local vocational training – a second-hand chance for those who could not afford continuous schooling. However, it went beyond that in an approach to link education closer to productive work (van Rensburg 1974).

Officially the Zimbabwe Foundation for Education with Production (ZIMFEP) was given the status of a trust under the Ministry of Education in 1981. It established eight secondary and four primary schools, which were supposed to be used as a model for the rest of the school system. Initially, the ZIMFEP schools were opened to cater for the refugees returning home from neighbouring countries. For financing, combined with training, the ZIMFEP schools were also provided with large farms (Gustafsson 1985; 1987). In addition to the farm income, it is noticeable that ZIMFEP has also been well provided for by development assistance.

Initially, it seems that the ZIMFEP concept was to influence the intro-duction of practical/vocational education in the entire school system. In spite of some initial success it seems that the ZIMFEP experiment did not achieve what it was originally intended to. Not even its own schools were able to promote the EwP philosophy properly, but were turned into a distinct part of the overall conventional formal structures. Theoretical subjects and the examination orientation were key issues also at the ZIMFEP schools. This particularly became evident as the for-mer refugee students were gradually replaced by new students (Nherera 1998).

To a large extent, it seems that the ZIMFEP schools in Zimbabwe have been faced with the same kind of dilemma as similar education in other parts of the world, as well as in neighbouring countries. The basic ideology of creating a schooling built on a combination of work and education normally leads to a conflict of interests. On the one hand, the task to establish a self-reliant independent schooling through EwP, and simultaneously making work an integral part of the whole learning exercise, is crucial. At the same time, external financing, in combination with outside influences from a conventional educational thinking, erode the original concept of EwP. Normally, then, we would end up with a string of rather conventional educational institutions. This issue can also be tied to the general development strategy of a country, for example to follow a general modernistic trend or to search for some kind of alternative development. After all, schools are not only pro-viding knowledge and skills for a modern world but they are also the main mechanism for the selections of individuals to realize their aspirations in this respect.

Agricultural education

In a country like Zimbabwe, with high dependence on agriculture for its survival, agriculture is also playing an important role in education. On the one hand there is the agriculture as offered in the secondary school curriculum. In the Chavanduka Report the importance of this, and specifically the need for well-qualified teachers, was stressed (Government of Zimbabwe 1982c). At the primary level, attempts have been made to integrate various aspects of agricultural knowledge into the science curricula – even to include local farmers in specific projects (Government of Zimbabwe 1990b). At the secondary level, agriculture has been introduced into many schools, but at an early stage the dilemma has been that the subject is mainly taught in a theoretical manner. In addition to this, the subject was not regarded in a very positive way as it was not a requirement for entry to higher education (Government of Zimbabwe 1989).

Of much more directly relevant value to the development of agriculture, the extension services can be mentioned. In the late 1980s, Zimbabwe was cited as having the best agricultural extension services in tropical Africa (Raikes 1988). Extension officers are trained in one of the two agricultural colleges (Gwebi and Chibero) to obtain a diploma, or in any of the four institutions (Mlezu, Esigodini, Kushinga Phikelela and Rio Tinto) for a certificate. Initially after independence, most of the graduates from any of these institutions were enrolled for work with AGRITEX – the official extension organization. However, since the early 1990s it has been difficult for AGRITEX to employ all the newly trained extension officers. Housing, transport, increased salaries and increased cost of in-service training have limited the potential to employ more staff in the extension services (Närman 1991).

Interestingly enough, in the plans to expand the extension services to reach more communal farmers an attempt was made to train more qualified staff in the colleges and institutes. Therefore, the courses were cut down in length and some parts of the extension techniques were handed over to AGRITEX. This in itself made it more expensive to employ anyone, as the cost of in-service training at AGRITEX increased, the end result being that agricultural colleges and institutes have increasingly trained potential agricultural teachers for primary and secondary schools, while the work that they are originally trained for is open to only a minority of the graduates. Consequently, the planned expansion of the extension services has not been met (Närman 1991).

Another dilemma with the extension services has been that training has mostly been geared towards the export sector in agriculture. It has been claimed by Chipika (1990) that the extension services are of little importance (or none at all) to an absolute majority of the poor smallholder producers. In other words, the priority has been on modern commercial agriculture, rather than on food security.

Modernization or alternative development

Although there has been a strong emphasis to provide for an education that will promote a better acceptability to the prevailing labour market – largely against advice given by the World Bank and major donors – the outcome of this has been rather limited. Attempts to diversify the curriculum have been more present in rhetoric than in reality, mostly owing the strong impact of diploma disease. To be successful in a modern development process a certificate is more essential than acquiring some kind of more relevant education.

In addition to this, it is rather obvious that education (formal and non-formal) is primarily meant as a preparation for a modern way of life. The basic ideology behind a concept such as Education with Production is watered down into a mere slogan, through the influence of donors and internal planners. Within agriculture, it seems that training provided is far from being an instrument to foster alternative thinking in the sector. As in the case of so many African countries, the initial concepts, such as education for self-reliance, have been replaced by an adjustment into a modernistic main stream.

Education – for what?

During the first decade of independence we can see how the Zimbabwe educational system was yielding to a popular pressure for expansion, on all levels. This can easily be connected with a concurrent radical ideological stand, which strongly promotes attempts towards equality. On the other hand, we cannot find any substantial adoptions in the educational content in line with the left-leaning political/strategic thinking. In short, a fast-expanding educational structure will educate the Zimbabwean children to fit in to the old society, with its prevailing colonial demands and ideals. There is nothing to suggest that education would be a crucial instrument in an attempt to create a new society. Furthermore, the trend following from quantitative expansion is eventually an even stronger stratification within the schools themselves.

During the second decade of independence the official development ideology has shifted considerably, towards the World Bank – inspired neoliberalism. However, during this period the quantitative expansion in primary and secondary education has levelled out, owing to increased costs and a general economic decline. This goes against the experiences from other parts of the world, which indicate that primary education is a crucial factor in achieving economic growth. Furthermore, the World Bank and official development agencies are taking a firm stand against attempts to make the formal school curriculum more relevant through various diversifications; this at a time when Zimbabwe is in great need of a skilled workforce to push forward towards an industrial society – at least according to the development model pursued by the donor community.

Irrespective of the general policy adhered to, the modernistic approach to education seems evident. The policy in terms of vocationalization in a technical direction is clear, against the advice of donors. In agricultural education/training the general tendency has been to encourage the export sector, rather than food security. Various attempts to establish a more alternative educational thinking, such as Education with Production, have been followed by popular aspirations in a modern society.

Obviously, the educational set-up in Zimbabwe has been exposing numerous contradictions. What could initially be seen as a commitment towards an educational system for all, has turned into its negation. The formal school has lost much of its credibility, as it is of very low quality and seriously stratified – favouring the emerging elites. Education in Zimbabwe has moved away from the humane aspirations of two decades ago, to become an instrument for reproducing an unequal modernistic society.

8
Vacillations Around Women: The Overlapping Meanings of 'Women' in the Zimbabwean Context

Christine Sylvester

Introduction

During Zimbabwe's first twenty years, the term 'women' has been an equivocation, an ambiguity, and a vacillation – at least in high places. The new state promised power and esteem to women as 'proletarians' and 'peasants,' while making liberal claims of gender equality in a pluralist society, and doling out authoritarian punishments for women who ignored ZANU(PF) scripts. International and local development organizations brought programmes and projects to women, even as their representatives sometimes expressed ambivalence about 'women' as a site of development focus. There have also been old gender practices, such as brideprice and men's once-exclusive rights to inheritance, intermingling with new venues in which average Zimbabweans shape their own rules, identities, behaviours, and destinies today.

In analysing Zimbabwe over the past nineteen years, I have found it useful to frame the many contractions and conflicting pressures exerted on 'women' (and other aspects of the country) in terms of overlapping discursive regimes of truth that specify what good Zimbabweans should be and do. I have named five regimes that have been in effect, in varying ways, at least since independence: a Marxist regime of promise, a liberal – pragmatist regime, an authoritarian regime of strength, an aid and development regime, and a gender 'tradition' regime. Each is organized around a different centre of force that has the capacity to declare true and false positions and to call considerable public attention to those declarations. Each regime can punish and reward people for behaviour that flaunts or reinforces regime-approved norms. Each also anoints true keepers of what it tries to promote as the authentic rules of Zimbabwean politics, economic, and society (Sylvester 1990; 1995a). Alongside the regimes, burrowing between the sanctions and inducements each has offered, are capillaries of power, where average people contest, shape, and accede to multiple messages about proper gender comportment (Sylvester 2000). That is, truth-saying power has produced its own sites and forms of resistance and compliance, and 'women' have been most often found in those capillary sites. This type of framework for the political economy of Zimbabwean relations is obviously beholden to the work of Michel Foucault (Rabinow 1984).

The chapter moves along overlapping regime tracks for 'women' in post-colonial Zimbabwe. It notices and puzzles over issues that have arisen around an identity that has historically been back-seated to 'men,' and has been earmarked by some post-colonial regimes for change and by others for stasis. The narrative specifically weaves through meanings of 'women' touted by the three regimes of truth that centre around varying parts of the ZANU(PF) government (liberal, Marxist, authoritarian), considers the ways 'women' are constituted by a regime of local cum international development, and stops periodically at sites of a gender regime of 'tradition' that permeates all the others. I draw examples of norms about 'women' from research I have conducted in Mashonaland factories, peasant and commercial fields, and reproduce literary words about 'women' in order to provide texture and context to the analysis.

The ensemble of regimes, and sites of 'women' acting within or outside their norms, results in a set of non-linear and plural narratives about 'women,' with no summing up point, no single identity marker crossing regimes or appearing in the self-identifying words of Zimbabwean 'women'. Multiple roads lead, in other words, towards and away from a variety of gender positions and understandings simultaneously. The point is to trace those positions and to notice that 'she' is a contested identity that moves in several directions at once through the moving picture that is Zimbabwe.

Contesting regimes pronounce on 'women'

> There should have been trumpets, truly there should have been. For was I – I Tambudzai, lately of the mission and before that the homestead – was I Tambudzai, so recently a peasant, was I not entering, as I had promised myself I would, a world where burdens lightened with every step, soon to disappear altogether? (Dangarembga 1988, 91)

Tambudzai, a character in Tsitsi Dangarembga's novel *Nervous Conditions* is narrating glee at learning of her acceptance into a private secondary school during the last years of Rhodesia. She expects the opportunity to carry with it great personal reward and few burdens. Many other 'women' may have had similar thoughts as Zimbabwe came into being. They may have said to themselves, 'once the armed struggle for independence ends, once a Zimbabwean government is in power and makes changes – leading the country to leap ahead of itself, to jump beyond the colonial and traditional past – women's burdens will lighten, there will be choices, the future will be one I can promise to myself and realize for myself' (for a sampling of views, see Zimbabwe Women's Bureau 1981; 1992). Such imaginative fictions about 'women,' and what could come their way, anticipated a turn into fact. In fact, what did come next was a pot-pourri of messages and policies – some expanding opportunities and some restricting them – about 'women' and their place, their true potential, and the traps that could hamstring a good 'woman' and bring her down in the new Zimbabwe.

Vacillating equivocations around 'women' in the new Zimbabwe have been traced, in part, to events of the armed struggle. Heike Schmidt (cited in Bhebe and Ranger 1996, 28), for one, has argued that the war for independence produced a variety of gender ambiguities that carried forward into the post-independence state and post-colonial era. It can be said that they incubated inside the cross-cutting nationalist agendas that dominated Zimbabwe's armed struggle (Sylvester 1990). What were those ambiguities?

It is clear that some 'women' fought in the war and thereby changed traditional notions about 'women' as reproducers, caretakers, cultivators, and mainstays of family when men were away in migrant labour. Other 'women' did not risk their lives for the war effort and yet gained from the outcome, because they were associated with powerful winning men. In rural areas, near the thick of the fighting, some lost everything and everyone. Others could go about their usual urban lives only minimally affected by the conflagration. Even 'women' who took an active part in the war effort had differing experiences. Some were press-ganged to fight. Some joined ZANLA or ZIPRA forces voluntarily and were later designated by the guerrilla forces as *chimbwidos* – girl leaders charged with overseeing and ensuring the material comfort and the safety of fighting comrades. They might be expected to 'go to the *poshito*' with one of them, which meant go off and have sex with a male comrade (Makande cited in Staunton 1990, 49); or they would manage the food preparation, supervise the fetching of wood, and carry weapons for the men. Most of this work accorded with usual expectations of what a woman was and what she properly should be doing for men (Kriger 1992).

In a situation where some gender expectations were transformed by the war and others were more or less unchanged, where some people fought and others did not, some supported the guerrillas and others did not, a clear picture of the post-colonial Zimbabwean 'woman' could not be outlined in and amongst the festivities of independence. More, despite loud trumpetings, the new government of Zimbabwe was not itself unified around 'a' vision of the future. Some members of what was an indigenized Rhodesian government inclined towards Robert Mugabe's Marxian – Maoist hopes for a socialist Zimbabwe, though time tells us that these were few and far between. Others had been trained abroad in neoclassical economics, biding their time until they could return to Zimbabwe to promote a liberal – nationalist course. Government officials could also be simple opportunists, who used government work to enhance family and personal fortunes.

We can look back and also see that the timing of Zimbabwe's birth put it in a squeeze with regard to 'women' and other policy areas. The year 1980 fell in the middle of the UN Decade for Women (1976–1985), the activities around which was broadcast the message that states must provide and safeguard rights and opportunities for women in employment, education, reproduction, health, and property realms. At the same time, the multilateral donor community, from which Zimbabwe hoped to garner some cash and credit, was entering its neoliberal phase. Northern states were in oil-related recession and the World Bank, their donor wing, was pulling back from McNamara's influential basic needs approach of the previous decade. Concerns for the fundamentals of daily life in developing societies were now left for alternative development NGOs to manage, while the big institutions turned to structural adjustment, an approach that would be criticized throughout the 1990s for its burdensome effects on 'women'.

Government resisted structural adjustment for a decade, and during that time did codify an Age of Majority (adulthood) Act that benefited women; it also rewrote the Industrial Relations Act so as to outlaw discrimination in pay and positions on the basis of sex. Equivocations, however, could be seen in the failure to add 'women' to the important category of 'landholders' in resettlement schemes. Messages in other areas, such as the direction the country's economy would go, were equally mixed. Carolyn Jenkins (1997) characterizes policies in the 1980s as including a little nationalization, a little land resettlement, careful safeguarding of existing economic interests, labour market interventions, increased spending on public services, the establishment of co-operatives, and changes to the legal status of women. As for broader society, it was tugged between old and new ways, with employers, for example, equivocating about new stipulations concerning maternity leave and child-feeding during work hours (Sylvester 2000). The 1990s brought more consumer goods and better transportation to average Zimbabweans, along with soaring inflation rates that near 65 per cent at the end of the millennium, unemployment that now stands at 50 per cent, one of the highest HIV-AIDS rates in the world, and extreme levels of corruption. It also brought forward the contestations and ambivalences that beset the country in the 1980s, because the regimes of truth around which Zimbabwean life was organized then persist in varying degrees of power now.

The short-lived Marxist promise

From the first day of Zimbabwean independence until the early 1990s, Robert Mugabe publicly held to the line that ZANU(PF) was a Marxist – Leninist party committed to leading the people to a scientific socialist future. The 'people' of most concern to this wing of the state, and its supporting social forces among some ex-combatants and leftists, were peasants and proletarians. The ZANU(PF) party-state did recognize that 'the People as a Nation cannot necessarily be homogeneous in respect of their cultural or racial backgrounds', but it added that 'this diversity should become more a source of our cultural wealth than a cause of divisive notions of groupist superiority philosophy' (ZANU(PF) 1980, 1309). ZANU(PF) never did flesh out the contents of its Marxist rhetoric and the ways it hoped to reconcile the People as a Nation with the class divisions in that nation, so that peasants and proletarians could ultimately triumph. Moreover, ongoing pressures from the multilateral donor community, urging the government to soften or give up on socialism as a vision, conjoined with international events to overtake local ambition in this area, especially once the Soviet bloc began to disassemble and the stature of Marxism to fall.

While the regime of Marxist promise existed, however, and it was effectively finished by 1989, 'women' were treated to two contradictory messages. First they were told that a socialist future would emerge through rural development and land redistribution, which suggested in class terms that cultivators (usually 'women') might gain considerable status as 'workers' in a peasant 'class'. Urban 'women' would also benefit from a greater acceptance of cities as places where both men and women should live and prosper, and where anti-discrimination laws would enable 'women' to join men in factory work and become 'proletarians'. 'Women' were encouraged by the Marxian stream of the state to form producer co-operatives and to work to make the future political economy of the country immanent in the present work of average people. That is, they were to become 'socialist man', by virtue of pooling resources and working in socialist-presaging relations of production that had often been cast around the figure of the male worker. Peasant, proletarian, and socialist 'women' would evacuate private spaces to join class identities associated with a life of production outside the home, which was the usual classical Marxist handling of the Woman Question.

Yet the regime of promise often undercut the producer message for women by also writing 'women', secondly, as the sole 'mothers' and 'family' people in the society. As late as 1990 the ZANU(PF) election manifesto, which still gestured to scientific socialism, maintained that women have the decisive role 'in maintaining the *family* as the basic social unit of our society' (ZANU(PF) 1990, 21, emphasis in original). 'Women' were promised a liberation associated with becoming honoured workers, but they were also officially sited in the household, a move that cut them off from the logic of the socialist promises. Such views also gave 'men' tacit permission to produce in places far from the household, thus reducing the likelihood that 'women' could step out of their homebody script and into a chain of work that could alter gender relations of production. The Marxist regime was soon eclipsed, but its renderings of 'women' as homebound creatures would reappear across other regimes of truth.

The effects of Marxist *promesses manquées* show up plainly in Zimbabwe's (barely) lingering co-operatives sector. In 1985, a government report found 470 all-women co-operatives scattered across the country (Chitsike 1985). Their ubiquity was high but their level of profitability was low. Poorly trained, poor to begin with, barely aware of what a co-operative did, of how one worked, 'women' had often been pressed by government or NGOs into forming these organizations of production in the early 1980s; and then they were left, by government at least, to make its dream come true by and for themselves. Vacillating, the government frequently shifted the oversight of co-operatives from department to department through the 1980s; and, in addition, it underfunded each new location for these enterprises relative to its other priorities (Sylvester 1991b). By the late 1980s, many rural and urban dwellers seemed to be in a co-operative, yet because few were making much money, 'co-operative' began to be seen as a designation for 'poor and demeaned women'. Novelist Chenjerai Hove captures this sense in his *Shebeen Tales: Messages from Harare* (Hove 1994, 31), when he says of some 'women' that 'when they saw they were getting old and no man ran after them, they formed a co-operative'.

When I met many co-operative 'women' in the late 1980s, for my research on women, production, and progress (Sylvester 2000), I learned that they had been trying to make a go of their enterprises on their own for years. They repeatedly asked me to find a donor for them, for they knew that Zimbabwe was crawling with NGOs. It would not be far-fetched to suggest that the co-operative sector limped on into the 1990s only because of the largesse of organizations such as the Zimbabwe Women's Bureau, the European Union, Silveira House, and international groups such as Partnership in Production, who did not always agree with the socialist message but did see the value in forming people into production groups. Nonetheless, a World Bank report (1992) charged that '[t]he actual contribution these public and private institutions have made to women's social and economic conditions is well below their potential'.

I read 'women's' interest in finding outside help and funding as a sign of their continuing interest in the co-operative way of working ('we get to think our own thoughts here,' I was told), sometimes an eagerness to be in production of some kind ('It's good to produce'), and also an indication that some among them were near to giving up. With a donor, 'we can do things by ourselves without doubting', said one 'woman'. That is, we can get on with our own agendas of production without wasting ourselves on limited enterprises. Without a donor – and 'donor' is not in the classical Marxist lexicon – many of the 'women' realized they were lacking the skills, money, and business experience to do more than make the effort, keep up the appearances, turn in a performance of 'co-operative'.

The enthusiasms around spaces where 'women' would do (great) things on their own, co-operatively, became one casualty of a Marxist dream that contested with interests of other sorts in the heads of, and in the policy realms managed by, Zimbabwean officials. By the late 1990s, fewer than half the co-operatives that Silveira House and the Zimbabwe Women's Bureau had sponsored in the 1980s were still in existence. Silveira House, a local Catholic charity, had shifted efforts from co-operative development to micro-enterprise development and micro-credit programmes (personal interview, December 1999). In the case of the Zimbabwe Women's Bureau, the shift was away from agendas dictated by the government, to 'development issues identified by the communities themselves', particularly, as suits their mission, those identified by local 'women' (Zimbabwe Women's Bureau 1998, 3).

Longer-lived liberal regime formulas

In 1988, a representative of an international donor organization in Zimbabwe told me that despite all the government talk about social-ism, ideology had not been an issue in the country because people had been pragmatic, positive, and mature. Signs of official pragmatism could be seen in the then constitution and in Zimbabwe's Westminster institutions, both of which came about when the war brought matters to a pragmatic end around a London negotiating table. At the end of that day, black Zimbabweans took charge of the government; they accorded protection for minority whites and granted liberal rights to all citizens. In the economy, a growth with equity theme reverberated through the decidedly inequitable economy Zimbabweans had inher-ited. From the mid-1980s, when the government published its *First Five-year National Development Plan, 1986–1990* (Government of Zimbabwe 1986a), to the introduction of a Structural Adjustment Programme in 1990, economic initiatives gave capital a leading, yet officially ambiguous, role in developing Zimbabwe. References to a future economy catering to peasants and proletarians abounded, for instance, while policies of state safeguarded large-scale farming by pro-hibiting the nationalization of private farms without compensation. The government also invited foreign capital to the country as long as it abided by a lengthy set of stipulations, including the entering of joint ventures with local concerns, use of local raw materials and processed inputs, and reliance on labour-intensive technology (Government of Zimbabwe 1982b, 1).

One other sign that a pragmatic to liberal regime co-existed with the Marxist regime of socialist promise was the ruling party's proclamation that 'women will enjoy equal rights with men in all spheres of political, economic, cultural, and family life' (ZANU[PF] 1980, 1310). With the Legal Age of Majority Act, 'women' could enter into contracts, including marriage, without seeking the permission of (or necessarily attracting the brideprice expected by) their lineages. The Matrimonial Causes Act of 1985 entitled 'women' to family property in cases of divorce. The Labour Relations Act of 1984 prohibited discrimination in wages, jobs, benefits, promotions, training, and retrenchment on the basis of sex. The laws made it clear that people called women could expect access to political, economic, and social arenas and thereby to resources. Wrote the poet Freedom T.V. Nyamubaya (1986, 22), 'She has the right/A right to say what she is/A right to say her dreams/She should not have to choose/The right that she is . . . '

Under the liberal – pragmatic regime, 'women's' success in throwing off old burdens and staking out new lives in Zimbabwe would depend on their knowledge of the political system, that is, on knowing how and where to direct political actions. This knowledge would be hard in coming, given that the new laws did not cut back on privileges for 'men' and did not protect 'women' if they sought to challenge the private sector or the class structure the pragmatic regime wanted to keep in balance. At rallies marking new national holidays, 'women' were told time and again by various government officials that they should co-operate with men, be patient, and take care of their families. In a sense they were told to use the liberal system judiciously or not at all. We might say that the pragmatism of the liberal regime equated 'women' with a set of interests directable towards the betterment of all Zimbabweans rather than towards the acquisition of resources that could enhance a group called women.

To illustrate ambiguities around the regime of pragmatism, consider the case of 'women factory workers' seeking to take a benefit that pragmatism had accorded them – one hour of child-feeding time per day with pay. Part of the Labour Relations Act stipulated that those with small children could take one hour of their workday – usually a half-hour in the morning and another half-hour in the afternoon – to breastfeed the infants. Employers could neither interfere with this practice nor reduce a 'woman's' wages if she took the benefit. Management and government, however, could put obstacles in the way by not providing child-minding facilities at work places. This was a particular problem in urban factories, which were usually located in industrial areas far removed from places of worker residence.

In a series of garment factories I visited in the late 1980s, 'women workers' grumbled to me about the hapless babyfeeding benefit and asked if I could help them raise the money for factory crèches. At the same time, they did more than complain. They also began to bring in their family sewing and to take one hour to work on these extracurricular garments – in full view of their supervisors (see Sylvester 1995b). When I asked them what they were doing, they would tell me they were 'sewing my husband's trousers', and that management would not do anything about this 'because we don't take our babyfeeding right'. Once I recognized the practice, I could see more and more incidences of it in Harare's clothing factories. It was a self-made benefit that apparently carried comparable worth, in the eyes of 'women', to the benefit they were not able to take. It was a substitute and more than that: even 'women' who did not have infants sewed their 'husband's trousers'.

With management tied into a Marxist-tinged Labour Relations Law, which made it impossible to fire workers without undertaking a long application process with the Ministry of Labour, these 'women' felt free to work out their designer benefit. They forged ahead until 1993, when codes of industrial conduct – another pragmatic tool – were introduced into factories. Negotiated by unions, management, and government personnel, the codes were meant to protect workers from arbitrary abuse or dismissal at a time when the structural adjustment programme was making it easier to retrench workers. The codes were also meant to give management the right to discipline or retrench workers who did not abide by the clearly written stipulations. One stipulation built into the clothing industry codes was that employees must restrict their work to materials provided by supervisors. This ended the 'women's' efforts to answer back to the empty babyfeeding benefit. Not having institutionalized their substitute benefit, it was easily swept away by the pragmatic regime that entered factory life in the 1990s. Pragmatism had bitten women on two sides.

The omnivorous regime of strength

One could argue, borrowing the ideas of James Scott (1990, 18), that Marxism and liberal pragmatism were the two public transcripts in the 1980s – and liberal – pragmatism into the mid-1990s – that presented 'the *self*-portrait of dominant elites as they would have themselves seen'. The regime of strength, by contrast, gathered force first in colonial practices *vis-à-vis* blacks, then as a guerrilla war-fighting strategy for independence, and then around the backrooms of Zimbabwe's official politics. It became very evident during the military campaign (the Gukurahundi) ZANU(PF) waged against its rival party, PF-ZAPU, in Matabeleland. Since that time, the regime of strength *aficionados* had used money and influence to help politicians and friends get rich, stay in power, and impose their will on the people. It is a regime based on a logic of insider indispensability – the inside being ZANU(PF), and especially the Mugabe wing within it. That regime has raised its head throughout the post-colonial period in Zimbabwe, waxing and waning as the fortunes of ZANU(PF) seem to waver.

Jenkins (1997, 578) argues that various styles of authoritarianism tend to unfold where there are ethnic divisions, weak political institutions, a shallow sense of nationhood, limited technical and administrative capacity, unfulfilled popular aspirations, and a certain economic dependence on other nations. In Zimbabwe, all these conditions prevailed at independence and have persisted intermittently through the 1990s. During the 1980s there were highly publicized incidents of insider privilege and patronage, such as the Willowgate scandal. Reports Nyamubaya (1986, 44) through her X-ray mouth, 'He shuts himself up in his own room/Obsessed with his itching thoughts of wealth/He alone has worked for!/ A few extra dollars from the masses contract . . .'

There were also rough, intermittent government crack-downs on organized labour and against rival parties. In 1997 it was said that ZANU(PF) thugs tried to do in the general-secretary of the Zimbabwe Congress of Trade Unions (ZCTU), Morgan Tsvangirai, for leading a coalition of forces opposed to ZANU(PF) tactics and rule. ZANU(PF)'s campaign in the 2000 elections also featured considerable (and well-documented) violence against the Movement for Democratic Change, leading several donor countries finally to pull the plug on aid to Zimbabwe. The Netherlands cited chronic violations of human rights in Zimbabwe, economic mismanagement, and the government's ill-considered 11 000 troop involvement in the Congo civil war. Italy cancelled a US$22 million electrification project, claiming that it could not operate in the climate of rampant corruption. Even before the latest omnivorous acts of authoritarianism, Nyamubaya (1986, 58) wrote pre-sciently, and sadly, about being 'born in a country/once called Rhodesia by the Rhodesians/now it's called Zimbabwe by Zimbabweans . . . What's the difference, anyway?'

Of course there have been beneficiaries of ZANU(PF)'s authoritarian power. Among them have been wives, female relatives, and political servants of regime insiders, such as members of the ZANU(PF) Women's League. 'These women' have enjoyed the spill-over status, resources, and life-styles that accompany friendship with Zimbabwe's latest indispensables. Indeed, one of the biggest beneficiaries of strength has been Mugabe's young second wife, Grace, whose shopping trips to South Africa can be reason enough for the first family to commandeer commercial flights. It is more difficult to ascertain the exact ways that others have materially benefited from their support for the ruling insiders. It is evident, however, that rewards of some sort pertain when women turn out to praise-sing Mugabe when he returns from overseas visits, many wearing garments imprinted with his face. In a country where husbands can try to prevent rural women from attending training meetings in the cities (Sylvester 2000), it is suddenly OK for rural women to attend ZANU(PF) rallies in Harare, Masvingo, or Bulawayo. Some Mugabe supporters have even cast him as a person of such weight that they pay him tribute by carrying pots of water on their heads *while walking on their knees* towards the ZANU(PF) dias.

More commonly, authoritarianism has downsides for 'women', and these have been most evident whenever the exercise of 'women's rights' has threatened to disorder the rules of insider/outsider place. 'Women' seen alone in the city streets at night have been picked up for prostitution, even when they have been simply working late in their offices. Those who have sought to exercise their voting rights on behalf of candidates from parties other than ZANU(PF) have been harassed by members of the ZANU(PF) Women's League, known to go door-to-door in some high-density areas such as Chitungwiza asking 'women' who they intend to support (Sylvester 2000). And although the Agricultural Finance Corporation (AFC) claimed in the late 1980s to be very willing to give loans to 'women farmers', even when they were not the official heads of most communal area and resettlement households, the gemstone monies often went to white clients. An official of that lending body unself-consciously informed me in 1990 that 'if it's a particularly good client, we even have money for school fees. This is usually the case for commercial farmer [men] . . . We don't do this for everyone.' The others, presumably, would disrupt the rules of insider trust, so why bring them in? The same AFC official, not recognizing his double entrendre, said, 'we don't want to burden people with too much credit'. Co-operatives were also made to conform to rigid, outer-directed rules before they could register with the government. The rules emphasized hierarchy within communalism (often including a gender hierarchy) and conformity to a set of general principles. Perhaps because these rules did not encourage a messier but potentially more equitable form of decision politics, Francis Chinemana (1987, 15) could find that 'males' representation [on co-operative committees] is approximately 20 per cent higher than their representation within total membership numbers' in 1987.

A particularly interesting case of the regime of strength surrounds rural farming groups that operate under the auspices of the Ministry of Agriculture's Group Development Area Schemes. The groups comprise mostly 'women', owing to the lingering colonial tradition of contracting 'men's' labour out of rural areas for work in the cities. Thoroughly regimented by the extension service, several communal area villages form committees and send representatives to an umbrella committee for the area, the ward, and to a district agricultural committee. Michael Drinkwater (1991, 236) tells us that '[i]n the way Agritex operates, "proven agricultural practices" are passed down the organization's hierarchy from subject-matter specialists (SMS) to agricultural extension officers (AEOS) to extension workers (EWS) to members of farmer groups, sometimes through farmer training leaders (FTLS)'. Not surprisingly, one official described local farm groups in Mashonaland in tones that praised similar discipline: 'Six to eight people live near each other and help each other plow, harvest, etc. They plan an itinerary to do one person's plowing on Monday, another person's on Tuesday and so on. They are also expected to organize their own transport and fertilizers and work together. The successful ones wear uniforms, organize singing choirs, compose their own songs with messages to promote, and sometimes compete.'

I talked to 'women' in three farming groups in Mashonaland East Province and heard them describe their projects as miniature regimes of strength. Well in line with the Ministry's approved chain of command, each group produced a chair, a vice-chair, treasurer, vice-treasurer, and a secretary. They worked diligently together too, in much the way the agricultural official described. Yet rather than feeling burdened by imposed rules, most of the 'women' I spoke to radiated a palpable energy. They worked enthusiastically and embraced discipline, saying, in the words of one, 'we can now help ourselves by rotating work and doing things collectively'. Moreover, they were creative in their adaptations of the rules of group leadership, with one group rotating posts by gender. Their responses to my questions suggested that if they had more power in national politics, far from setting aside the rigid and uncreative models that engulfed them, they would, in fact, replicate the regime of strength's rule-setting tendencies; but in that case, they would change the agenda and '*make* men go for family planning', '*make* men who impregnate girls marry those girls', 'reduce school fees', and 'lower prices of everything'. In effect, they would command the rules of strength and wield them to bring justice to 'women' and, through them, to the countryside. One cannot say that such 'women' were victims of the regime of strength, for that is not the way they saw themselves. They were, however, hemmed in, depended on external experts for advice, and often thought the few local men about were indispensable to the leadership of their groups.

The regime of eligibility for development

After independence, and the lifting of UN sanctions against the country, donors and NGOs landed in mass to provide resources for income-generating projects, co-operatives, basic needs programmes, training, and so forth; indeed, Chinemana (1987) found that approximately 125 sources of funds existed for co-operatives alone by the mid-1980s. Their resources underwrote rural and urban development projects that shaped peasants and city-folk into eligibility for modernity and trained them for economic viability in a development process that was not often of their own making (Verhagen 1987). Local regimes of truth, grounded in and around the state and its arms, often vied with NGOs for the power to pronounce the authentic path to development. The picture of who was doing what for whom and where quickly cluttered, as trade unions, workers committees, government consultants, and even factory managers became potential agents of aid and 'women's' development.

Each organization comprising the regime of eligibility has taken positions that can mirror one or more of the local regime truths about 'women'. Through interviews with 50 aid agencies in Zimbabwe, I learned, for instance, that many organizations were focusing at least some of their attention in the late 1980s and early 1990s on 'women'. These usually came at their missions from a women in development (WID) or women and development (WAD) angle; the first pragmatically seeks to integrate women into development activities ongoing in the country, and the second, again pragmatically, seeks to empower women by encouraging them to organize production around their daily tasks. Organizations that then projected these liberal modes of thinking included the Zimbabwe Women's Bureau and the Swedish aid agency, Swedish International Development Authority (SIDA). Other organizations did not set their sights on 'women', because they saw 'women' as already equal to men. An official from Christian Care said, 'we have community programmes and the majority of people we work with are women'.

There have been Marxists about too, in the Zimbabwe Project and the Organization of Collective Co-operatives of Zimbabwe (OCCZIM). Their activities have focused on workers in a way that precludes particular attention to 'women'. Said a representative from OCCZIM, 'it's not good for women to form their own co-operatives because that's feminism and it causes divisiveness'. Some organizations have not given 'women' much thought at all in project design for reasons, perhaps, of unstated adherence to the regime of gender, which marks out some bodies as more important than others. Said the representative from CUSO, the Canadian University Students Overseas in 1988, 'when I think of co-operatives, I think of men'. The regime of eligibility could be powerful in the late 1980s and early 1990s, but it was also hit-or-miss in its movements around 'women'. My recent interviews with a few members of the local NGO community suggest that this distribution of perspectives has not changed much.

The case of a weaving co-operative in Harare illustrates the cluttered and ambiguous picture of eligibility, even though it has a reasonably happy ending. In the early 1970s, a group of women wanted to learn marketable skills and decided to form a club to think about their options. Later, an advisor from the then Rhodesian City Council, which was located across the street from where the 'women' were meeting, contacted the group and began to teach the members weaving. It was the time when Rhodesia was worried about the armed struggle and tried, most belatedly, to compensate for years of neglect through various Community Development Programmes. The Council suggested the 'women' form a bona fide producer co-operative rather than remain bound to a formless weaving club. In 1976 the group did so, but by then there were 100 'women' involved and nowhere near the number of buyers to sustain their efforts. Between 1979 and 1983, the co-operative's energy fell as it lost most members. Finally it ceased functioning altogether, except for four members who checked in periodically on the two looms the City Council had purchased for them. These members were on the verge of selling the looms when a story about their plight appeared in the newspaper and attracted the attention of the new Ministry of Youth, Sport, and Culture. Ministry officials assisted the remaining four weavers to craft a grant proposal for a SIDA programme. The application was successful, and in 1983 the weavers received Z$14 000 as well as a Swedish woman trainer, who was with them until 1986. Through this assistance, the weavers were able to purchase two more looms at a cost of Z$600 each, which boosted their productivity. At the time I first encountered the Harare Weaving Co-operative, in 1988, there were 22 members working 8 looms to make rugs and household cloths for tourists. The chairwoman of the co-operative said the enterprise brought in Z$25 000 for 1987, which was distributed to the weavers according to the number of pieces each produced.

In this case, a local government agency formed the 'women' into a weaving co-operative, but did not offer the follow-through necessary to get the co-operative producing effectively; these were the last days of Rhodesia, after all, and the government was preoccupied with security issues. Another set of helpers in the post-independence period was better positioned to assist the 'women', and the climate was such that there was international money chasing relatively few formed projects. Donors literally plucked the group of weaving 'women' out of obscurity and then out of bankruptcy, turning them into a post-colonial urban *cause célébre*. Still, the individual weavers I interviewed expressed a degree of ambivalence about the otherwise solvent co-operative. One told me that the members had never been taught how to repair the looms and that spare parts, such as metal handles, were difficult to get. Another said that in 1985 the chairperson of the co-operative did not come to work regularly but continued to get paid anyway by the Swedish advisor; finally the members expelled the recalcitrant member. Also, after years of assistance, one member told me that 'not many of us can read and write, although most go to school at night, with books paid for by a co-operative education fund'. I asked several members whether the 'women' there wanted power. I was told that 'women want employment, not political power', and also that 'women are women – they don't want power'. Overall, the vacillations of the early days of this co-operative only partially dissolved into the normal disputes and equivocations of daily work. In this success story of the late 1980s, some 'women' felt empowered by the external help and some simply laboured away at the looms, indifferent to the development fuss that had contributed to their opportunity, indifferent to matters of gender, ambivalent about what 'women' could accomplish.

As the Soviet bloc fell apart in the early 1990s, one often heard Zimbabweans say that all the donors had run off to East Europe. Money for co-operatives did fall off, but it was also the case that low returns on investments in most co-operatives, coupled with the government's introduction of a structural adjustment programme, and its increasingly suspicious posture towards international NGOs, swept some international development projects aside. But not entirely. Hove wrote (1994, 115) that '[d]onor agencies and governments feature daily on television and in the newspapers, pouring their begged-for money into our national coffers. Thus we become a nation of beggars whose hands are fully stretched to receive every cent from the wealthy nations of the North. No word about our national identities, our aspirations and perceptions, nothing.' Says Nayamubaya more poetically in her 'Western Expatriate in Africa' (1986, 56):

> Away from narrow roads and crowded housing,
> Away from rain and snow in winter,
> With millions of unemployed at home
> Good at foreign, poor at home affairs,
> How determined is your determination?
> Your good heart needs repairing:
> Africa, a dumping ground of the dollar debris . . .

And the 'women' who received both the dollars and the debris? For some of them it has been a big shrug or a matter of slow and tortuous progress (Sylvester 1999).

A ubiquitous gender regime too

A multifaceted gender regime permeates and interpenetrates the others. It combines aspects of pre-colonial 'tradition,' such as the brideprice practice, with the modern sexual division of labour introduced by colonial rule; and it shows up the lingering colonial tendency for 'men' of different classes (African 'men' and white colonial 'men' too) to form a tacit alliance around the shared interest in controlling 'women' (Schmidt 1992; Barnes 1992; Jeater, 1993; Gaidzanwa 1993). This regime has predefined, in the sense of providing a tradition for, many of the gender issues encrusted in Zimbabwe's diverse politics of truth today.

Viewed benignly, the gender regime 'merely' enforces a commonplace designation for two types of bodies: there are women and there are men and each has his or her job. The results of such designations, though, are rarely benign. 'Women' commercial farm workers, for instance, complained to me in 1989 that they were not taken on as 'permanent workers'. Only the men, they told me, can be in that category. The 'women' were made to be 'casuals', 'seasonals', and 'contract workers', lesser designations all. 'Women' who declare themselves lesbians have been subject throughout the 1990s to government denunciations (some of them backed by rallies attended by Women's League members). And then there are some women who defend 'traditional' gender distinctions, seeing 'women's' true places as in their husband's household or under his control.

One way of looking at the gender regime is in terms of a patriarchal content. Jeanne Henne (1988, 36) has written about a long-standing patriarchal mode of production in Africa that undercuts the idea that 'traditional' African production was communal, with 'no basis for denying any family member free access to the means of production; thus . . . no material basis for intrahousehold exploitation and no basis for class'. Her research has located persistent inequalities in labour time and consumption among different household members, a finding that leads her to argue that in the patriarchal mode of production, effective possession of the means of household-based production is monopolized by a class of patriarchs who are socially recognized as heads of household and/or extended family production units. The dependent class – wives, unmarried daughters, sons, and junior siblings of the patriarchal class – is denied free access to the means of production on the basis of ideological and political criteria which allow the patriarch class to set the terms on which women and dependent males gain access to the means of production (Henne 1988, 37, 38).

The gender regime follows from a patriarchal mode of production. It links control over material conditions of household participation and production with the political and ideological truths that produce and maintain dominant – subordinate relations of gender. Yvonne Vera (1994, 75) captures it in her short story, 'An Unyielding Circle': 'Knees! Knees! A woman must bend on her knees to give food to a man. What kind of woman is this? The woman, not wanting to argue with the drunken men, does as she is told, and the group breaks into applause.'

Surely it is the gender regime that is responsible for one of the latest set-backs for 'women' in Zimbabwe. In an April 1999 High Court decision, 'African women' were made subject to customary or traditional law in the area of inheritance, reduced in status to junior men. The 5–0 decision against a 'woman' complainant, who had sued her half-brother for ownership of her deceased father's land, flew in the face of Zimbabwe's constitutional stipulations and liberal pledges of 'women's' equality with men. It also violated several international human rights treaties Zimbabwe had signed, not the least being the Convention on the Elimination of All Forms of Discrimination against Women. Arguing that 'women' leave their families after marriage, and therefore cannot use inheritance to better the lives of natal relatives, the court let stand what it called an 'African' or 'Shona' tradition that gives inheritance precedence to men. Local and international groups spoke out about the decision and wrote to the High Court in protest, only to find that the justices termed their concerns 'contemptuous' (Nizkor 1999).

Galvanized by the court decision, and against the backdrop of activities to draft a new constitution in 1999, a variety of groups (including the Women's Action Group, Zimbabwe Women's Resource Centre and Network, The Musasa Project, The Zimbabwe Women and the Law Association, Zimbabwe Women's Bureau, and others) formed a women's coalition to push for a better deal for 'women' in a new legal framework. One concern has been to ensure that 'women' have the right to hold land in their names, something that has not been the usual case in the resettlement areas. The coalition has also been bold in calling for the end of violence against women in households and for debates on tradition in pre-colonial society. They argue in both cases that male adjudicators interpret gender traditions in ways that are erroneous, favourable to 'men,' and endangering of 'women's' rights and safety.

Gender considerations have interacted across all the regimes in Zimbabwe. They have not subordinated all Zimbabwean people called women to the same degree: 'childless white women', for example, have been long accustomed to privileges of inheritance and age of majority *vis-à-vis* African counterparts. The gender regime has been strong enough, however, to ensure that it is still widely accepted that people called men are kings of castles and kraals. More than the other regimes, this one has tended to cross race, class, region, ethnicity, religion and regime, albeit not in a uniform way.

Sense-making 'women'

That there are many positions surrounding 'women' in Zimbabwe can be interpreted either as a positive factor of governance or a sign of chaos; and sometimes a bit of both, depending on the speed with which the messages change. Loosely based on several postmodernist arguments, one could say that equivocations about gender identity and behaviour are better than strict and rigid rules of position. Vacillations, equivocations, and ambiguities can lead to more democratic openness and tolerance for alterity. 'Women', once shackled to onerous duties and constrained parameters of identity, can work the contradictions to move around, rearrange their locations and their work, challenge the expectations of others and survive (Brown 1991). Indeed, the opportunities presented by meandering regimes of truth have carried some Zimbabweans to altered positions within households and society at large. In other cases, ambiguous 'womanhood' has caught people in travails of mobility that intensify the effort of getting by on a daily basis, supporting a child, improving skills, or persuading one's supervisor to make her a permanent rather than a temporary piecework employee; indeed, how can a 'woman worker' become 'permanent' when the messages about her place in society are kept in motion, in impermanence? Some 'women' therefore refuse the equivocations and take a stand within a regime, for or against 'women'.

Do 'women' need to be seen as universal subjects of a range of human rights or specified capabilities before they can have the freedom necessary to carve out their choices of identities, mobilities, and resource options (Nussbaum and Glover eds. 1995)? This is the debate, both inside Zimbabwe and internationally, and there is much equivocation about it. Of course everyday 'women's' stories, and the debates and the ambivalences spun off them, are far from exhausted – although many 'women' may be everlastingly tired of struggles about 'simple' issues of gender. Vera (1994, 75–78) continues her tale in a way that brings our narratives to a culminating point of everyday tension:

Under the market shed, close to where the men are sitting, someone turns on a battery radio and soft lilting music fills the cold afternoon air. As she moves away [from the men who told her to kneel] the woman beats her arms angrily about her, sending the dust off her skirts . . . 'I can handle any woman, any woman,' a man says, waving his arms drunkenly about, as though some woman has already challenged him . . . She wove a silence that protected and consoled her, postponing the moment when she would have to endure her anguish . . . 'Maize! Maize! Maize!' The men's voices intruded on their silence.

But 'she' and her friends are telling the story, no? 'She' is there, weaving the silence of the other market 'women' in and among words. She is taking up space, working the coals that grill the maize, raking them to separate out the ashes, building the fire anew. She is complying with expectations and contesting them, equivocating and vacillating about what she should be and do next. Although surrounding regimes configure her ('can handle any woman'), in fact 'who knows how many secrets one will uncover, after a lot of raking in forbidden spaces?' (Vera 1994, 77).

9

Foreign and Security Policy of Zimbabwe: From Independence to the DRC

Donald P. Chimanikire

Introduction

To write about factors determining the foreign policies of African states is not easy. It is a task beset by a number of problems. One is the newness of most of them as sovereign independent states. It has not been possible for them to build up any tradition, or any firmly established pattern of interests behind their foreign policies (Aluko 1977, 1). Unlike their counterparts in Europe and in the United States, the governing elites, and indeed in many cases the presidents alone, in Africa have extensive control over the foreign relations of their countries. The reasons for this are not hard to see. Being new in the international system many African states still have to carve out for themselves established interests in the international arena. Consequently, there is nothing like a traditional pattern of external behaviour. Furthermore, there are no serious domestic institutional restraints on the behaviour of the African governing elites.

The African presidents or heads of state are extremely powerful. Indeed, governments in Africa, even where the military is not in power, are highly personalized. The field of foreign affairs is often regarded as the special preserve of the president. In some cases, the President acts as his own foreign minister, and where a separate office has been established for foreign affairs, the minister may remain his courier rather than an important figure in the formulation of foreign policy (Aluko 1977, 10).

Foreign policy in Zimbabwe, too, 'is set at the highest level by the President and articulated either by him or by the Minister of Foreign Affairs' (Government of Zimbabwe 1999c). Even though increasingly often 'a number of ministries and bodies are involved' (Government of Zimbabwe 1999c), what might be called 'deliberate' foreign policy is formulated by the President alone or in cabinet or in consultation with the Minister of Foreign Affairs. At his pleasure, the President might involve in a minor way other cabinet members. The Parliament of Zimbabwe and organs of the ruling Zimbabwe African National Union – Patriotic Front (ZANU(PF)) – have a minor role in formulating the broader and general outlines of foreign policy (Kitikiti 1993, 2).

At the time of independence, the Ministry of Foreign Affairs had a very limited operational base. It served only the narrow interests of a minority pursued by the past Rhodesian regimes. The operational base narrowed even more in 1965 when Ian Smith declared Unilateral Declaration of Independence (UDI), a move that was inevitably followed by the isolation of the Rhodesian government on the part of the international community. As a result, Rhodesia's foreign relations were mainly aimed at maintaining links with the apartheid regime of South Africa and a few other reactionary governments.

Since 1980, Zimbabwe has expanded the range and scope of its diplomatic representation abroad. These missions are located in the industrialized countries, in Africa and the rest of the developing world. Zimbabwe has witnessed the steady increase of its foreign missions, which total over 70 (*Zimbabwe News*, April 1989, 37). However, due to the budget deficit, President Mugabe has recently directed that all its missions should justify their existence on economic grounds.

Principles of Zimbabwe's foreign policy

The attainment of independence in 1980 brought about numerous changes to Zimbabwe. These not only involved the restructuring of Zimbabwe's society, but also entailed the transformation of a government structure that had served the interests of a minority into one that represented the interest of the majority.

In order to understand the principles of Zimbabwe's foreign policy today, one needs to take into account the 'revolutionary origins' (Government of Zimbabwe 1999c) of the armed liberation struggle of the Patriotic Front led by Robert Mugabe and Joshua Nkomo. These principles can be loosely stated as follows:

- sanctity of the right to life and self-determination and defence of national sovereignty;
- equity in the distribution of national wealth;

- anti-imperialism;
- equality of sovereign states and non-interference in the internal affairs of other states;
- justice in the international division of labour as well as in the distribution of gains from international trade;
- peaceful resolution of internal and international conflicts; and
- elimination of poverty, underdevelopment and obstacles to self-sustaining development (Kitikiti 1993, 2).

In the list, the principles of self-determination and sovereignty can hardly be overemphasized. In 1999 the Minister of Foreign Affairs noted, 'We support very strongly the principles of the right to self-determination of peoples and of non-interference in the internal affairs of other states, particularly where such interference is not for self-evident humanitarian or other moral imperatives but the convenience or self-interest of a bigger power or any other state' (Government of Zimbabwe 1999c).

Zimbabwe, a beneficiary of the determination of the Organization of African Unity (OAU) that all of Africa had to be free if the independence of any African country was to have meaning, could not stand on the sidelines as the great battle between the forces of freedom and independence and those of racism and colonialism raged in the sub-continent. Zimbabwe subscribed financially to the OAU Liberation Committee. One of the very first foreign policy decisions of independent Zimbabwe was to recognize the Saharawa Liberation front as the legitimate government of the Saharan People's Republic (Nkiwane 1999, 204).

Support for liberation in Africa

It is a truism that where a country is situated has implications for its external behaviour. As Solomon Nkiwane has pointed out, the geographical location of Zimbabwe in Southern Africa is a crucial factor in Zimbabwe's foreign relations. Zimbabwe is a land-locked country, surrounded by four immediate neighbours. These are Botswana in the southwest, South Africa in the south, Mozambique in the east and Zambia in the north. In addition, to these neighbouring countries must be included Namibia which, through its Caprivi Strip, at Zimbabwe's extreme western point, needs to have its point of convergence with Zambia, Botswana and Zimbabwe clarified. (Nkiwane 1997, 8.) Since the bulk of Zimbabwe's trade is with extra-African countries, an easy and reliable access to the coast is of paramount importance. Consequent upon this, Zimbabwe has tried to maintain cordial relationships with countries through whose territories its exports and imports must pass. For example, Zimbabwe has to maintain friendly relationships with South Africa to survive, and this will remain so irrespective of the ideological orientation of the leaders in power in Zimbabwe (see Aluko 1977, 12).

During the twenty years of Zimbabwe's independence, the Southern African sub-regional environment has largely been characterized by conflict. In the 1980s there was the conflict inherent in Africa's unfinished quest for independence, evident in the continuing struggles of independence and self-determination by the peoples of Namibia and South Africa. There were the conflicts occasioned by the desire of the apartheid state to create chaos in the territories of its neighbours to the north in order to buy time for apartheid. These included Mozambique Resistance Movement (RENAMO) banditry in Mozambique, support for Union for the Total Independence of Angola (UNITA), raids into Botswana, Zambia, Lesotho, Mozambique and Swaziland, and sponsorship of banditry by super-Zapu and other elements and the beaming of hostile propaganda against Zimbabwe through 'Radio Truth'.

The existence of a hostile neighbour required that Zimbabwe had to join other members of the international community in deploring the apartheid system and demanding its destruction. Zimbabwe in this regard took a frontline position in calling for the isolation of the Pretoria regime through the imposition of comprehensive mandatory sanctions by the international community (*Zimbabwe News*, April 1989). It believed strongly that it was its duty to support unreservedly the liberation struggle which was being waged by the ANC and Pan African Congress (PAC) in South Africa, and South West Africa Peoples' Organization (SWAPO) in Namibia. There was the moral duty to the Namibian and South African people, who expected solidarity and support from their more fortunate cousins to the north. And, ultimately, there was supreme national interest on the part of Zimbabwe, which being situated in the volatile region itself could not expect normal intercourse with all its neighbours, economic development, and economic and social well-being of its people as long as the violence and its cause were not removed.

Zimbabwe's approach to the regional environment was therefore based on principles. These principles emanated not only from the national ethos of Zimbabwe, but also from the Charters of the United Nations and the OAU. OAU required all African countries to do everything in their power to rid the continent of colonialism. Zimbabwe did everything consistent with its means to bring independence and majority rule to Namibia and South Africa. During Zimbabwe's terms in the Security Council, first in 1983–1984 and in then 1991–1992, Zimbabwe championed the cause of removing threats to peace in Southern Africa. As chairman of the Non-Aligned Movement (NAM), Zimbabwe helped launch the Africa Fund whose main aim was to assist not only the liberation movements in Namibia and South Africa, but also the Southern African states threatened by Pretoria's policy of destabilization.

As part of the non-aligned group at the United Nations, Zimbabwe pushed hard for a United Nations Transition Group (UNTAG) team that could ensure free and fair elections in Namibia in March 1990, and for the Harare Declaration on Southern Africa, adopted by the OAU *ad hoc* Committee on Southern Africa. The latter was eventually adopted by the UN General Assembly as the definitive blueprint of a negotiated solution to the South African question. The document set out how an ideas climate conducive to negotiations could be created in apartheid South Africa, achieving democratic transformation and readmitting South Africa into the international community. Apartheid was correctly labelled the root cause of the conflict in Southern Africa. Thus the cornerstone of fighting for peace and security in Southern Africa was to fight apartheid (Jokonya 1992, 3, 4; see also Patel 1987).

Botswana, Zambia, Tanzania and Zimbabwe agreed to support Mozambique, which faced RENAMO destabilization. But only Zimbabwe and Tanzania were able to send troops there. Botswana provided logistical support. From 1982 Zimbabwean soldiers protected Zimbabwe's outlet to the sea, the Mutare–Beira oil pipeline, which was undoubtedly the lifeline of its economy (*Zimbabwe News*, April 1989, 38). Zimbabwe's close relationship with Mozambique was reflected in a defence agreement and a one-time flourishing semi-official Zimbabwe–Mozambique Friendship Association. The 1981 joint declaration of the Zimbabwe–Mozambique Friendship Association regarded an attack against Mozambique as an attack against Zimbabwe. On this basis a Special Task Force was deployed to guard the Beira corridor but its role soon increased. Zimbabwean troops protected the Nyamapanda route, which was essential to the economy of Malawi. In August 1985, Mugabe gave an open-ended commitment to the survival of Mozambique by stating that Zimbabwe would deploy up to 30 000 troops if necessary. In the same month ZNA launched an airborne assault on the Goronga base at Casa Banana and in November 1985 Zimbabweans overran RENAMO's territorial base at Pungwe and Nyarunyaru. Zimbabwean military involvement in Mozambique increased by 7000–10 000 troops in 1988. President Samora Machel's death in an air crash in October

1986 only stiffened Mugabe's resolve to stand by the Frelimo government (Stoneman and Cliffe 1989, 187, 188). It was only in the course of
the peace process in Mozambique that Zimbabwe withdrew its troops
from there in 1993.

One should realize that despite Zimbabwe's hardline position against
apartheid, its policy towards South Africa walked a narrow tightrope,
constrained by fear of the consequences of provoking open hostility
and economic or military reprisals. Besides, a large part of the
Zimbabwean white community had close relations with the whites in
South Africa (Nkiwane 1999, 209). Zimbabwe denied the ANC permission to establish bases on its territory, merely allowing offices in Harare.
The ANC headquarters thus remained in Lusaka. In the light of subsequent South African commandos' bloody raids on Botswana, Lesotho
and Mozambique aimed at the ANC but killing nationals as well, this
seemed to be justified. The murder of ANC representative Joe Gqabi and
attacks on ANC offices in Harare were warnings of how much worse
things could be (Stoneman and Cliffe 1989, 183).

Zimbabwe was a founder member of SADCC in 1980. This was an
organization whose primary objective was by peaceful means to reduce
Southern African countries' dependence on apartheid South Africa, as
well as to consolidate and strengthen economic ties among independent nations in the region. Zimbabwe has played an important role in
SADCC/SADC, providing its first two executive secretaries, and fulfilling
its responsibility for the regional food security portfolio.

The prominent role that Zimbabwe assumed in the fight against
apartheid was noticed all over the world (Nkiwane 1999, 210).
Paradoxically the tragic existence of a hostile neighbour was precisely
the factor that gave enormous prestige to Zimbabwe in international
forums. As stated by the Minister of Foreign Affairs in 1999, 'we made
it embarrassing to have relations with South Africa for Third World
countries within the OAU and NAM. Within the UN we were able to
have the Security Council impose various sanctions and other measures
against the country. . . . That in this period Zimbabwe became the
Chairman of the NAM (1986–1989) and of the Commonwealth (1991)
is indicative of the effectiveness of our campaign and recognition by
other countries of the centrality of our country in the resolution of the
conflict in Southern Africa. Having the chairman in Southern Africa
also in itself brought the world spotlight on the region' (Government of
Zimbabwe 1999c).

In 1997 Zimbabwe chaired the OAU. Zimbabwe has also been active
in the Group of 77 (G77) and the Group of 15 (G15.) In 1995, President

Mugabe was nominated to chair the World Solar Commission to oversee and guide the World Solar Summit Process.

Active non-alignment and the changing global context

The conflict in Southern Africa also involved the superpower dimension. This was most striking in the case of Angola where, having determined that the Luanda government was supported by Moscow, the United States government went to great lengths to support the UNITA banditry. It was also generally reflected in the Western support for conservative governments in the region, including the racist white regime, on the grounds that the forces of liberation were sympathetic to Moscow or, at the very least, that Moscow was sympathetic to the forces of liberation. Outside Southern Africa, Zimbabwe tried to pursue a policy of non-alignment, which resulted in opposition to the USSR and US policies (Stoneman and Cliffe 1989, 190). Zimbabwe refused to appear a 'client state' of any other power.

Guided by this policy, in 1983 Zimbabwe took the decision to abstain in the UN Security vote following the shooting down of South Korean Airline KAL 007 by the Soviet Union. This decision was taken, neither because Zimbabwe believed that the Soviets were right in their actions, nor because Zimbabwe believed that it had been sent on a spying mission. The decision to abstain was taken, because the event had taken on an East–West outlook. However, Zimbabwe opposed the Soviet Union's involvement in Afghanistan and Vietnam's in Cambodia. When the US invaded Grenada in 1983, Zimbabwe condemned the move as a violation of basic international law and principles. Just as Zimbabwe opposed apartheid, so it condemned Zionism in the Middle-East (*Zimbabwe News*, April 1989, 38). Nicaragua and Cuba can be mentioned among countries that were supported by Zimbabwe, because they 'faced interference in their internal affairs by the big Powers in the context of the Cold War' (Government of Zimbabwe 1999c). In 1990, Zimbabwe condemned the Iraq invasion in Kuwait (Nkiwane 1999, 205).

Since the end of the Cold War and apartheid, the challenges of Zimbabwe's foreign policy have changed dramatically. Although traditional policy issues such as anti-imperialism and self-determination continue to be relevant, the tone and idioms used to articulate those foreign policy interests have been affected by the global geo-political restructuring and the attainment of majority rule in South Africa. The emergence of a unipolar world dominated economically by the US and US-controlled international organizations has tilted the focus of economic policy to the multilateral spheres. The Uruguay Round of Trade

Negotiations has created new obligations, which challenge national sovereignty in such sensitive policy areas as relations with multi-national enterprises. Zimbabwe's future development options are likely to be constrained by international obligations, which the country has to accept in order to preserve the global environment.

Under the leadership of President Mugabe, Zimbabwe has attempted to safeguard its interests in such areas as peace and international trade through regional arrangements. For example, Zimbabwe's goal to achieve full employment and economic development has been linked to the country's diplomatic capacity to achieve the objectives set forth by the Southern African Trade Community, the Common Market for Eastern and Southern Africa (COMESA), the Preferential Trade Agreement (PTA) and Abuja Treaty on the African Economic Community (AEC). Zimbabwe has also taken an active part in negotiations on the World Trade Organization (WTO) and the future of the EU–ACP co-operation

The most striking example of Zimbabwe's foreign policy assuming a regional outlook in the post-apartheid and post-Cold War world is the country's interest in regional security, including its involvement in the DRC. Simultaneously there have been tremendous pressures on the President to redirect the substance of Zimbabwe's policy from foreign to domestic problems.

Zimbabwe's involvement in the war and President Mugabe's way of handling the domestic political and economic problems, which culminated in the election year 2000, have worsened Zimbabwe's international reputation. It needs to be noted that Zimbabwe's relations with most members of the Commonwealth have been excellent and until recently this was also the case with the industrialized countries, including the Nordic countries, Britain, Germany, Italy and the Netherlands, which are among the major trading partners of Zimbabwe.

For example, in March 2000 the British High Commission in Harare clashed with Zimbabwe Customs Authorities, which decided to verify the contents of the British diplomatic consignment. The incident was widely reported in the international media and led to the brief recall of the British High Commissioner to London. According to the Zimbabwean Minister of Foreign Affairs, such a decision was in line with 'an unprecedented anti-Zimbabwe crusade' of the British 'Junior Minister' at the Foreign Office. This crusade was said to include discouraging foreign investments in Zimbabwe and trying to influence the IMF, African Development Bank as well as the donor community generally not to disburse funds to Zimbabwe (Government of Zimbabwe

2000b). The language used by the Zimbabwean government was exceptionally harsh, manifesting the Zimbabwean leadership's anger towards
the British position.

In June 2000 the US Senate introduced a Bill entitled 'Zimbabwe
Democracy Act 2000'. The Bill proposed to prohibit assistance or debt
relief from being extended to Zimbabwe by the US government. It also
opposed any assistance to Zimbabwe by international financial institutions in which the US is a member. Zimbabwe decided to actively lobby
other SADC states about the harmful implications of such a Bill to the
whole Southern African region.

Britain and the United States are among the leading countries of the
Western donor community, which provides a bulk of development aid
to Zimbabwe and even more importantly has enormous influence in
the international financial institutions. In an attempt to check and con-
strain the powers of President Mugabe, the Western policy of political
and economic conditionality has effectively instrumentalized
Zimbabwe's serious economic problems. So far the net result of conditionality, however, has been rather counterproductive. If not for other
reasons, this is so, because it grossly contradicts one of the guiding
principles of President Mugabe's foreign policy thinking: that of self-
determination.

Zimbabwe's involvement in the DRC conflict

Immediately after assuming power in the Democratic Republic of Congo,
President Laurent Kabila joined SADC in order to integrate his country's
development and enormous resources with those of Southern African
states. By the same token, Kabila wanted to become less dependent on
DRC's neighbours in Eastern Africa: Rwanda and Uganda. At the beginning of August 1998, this newest member of SADC was invaded by
Rwanda and Uganda in collaboration with local rebels. The major motive
behind the invasion was to install a government subservient to the
Rwandese and Ugandan governments. From their point of view, Kabila
had proved to be 'uncontrollable' and had to be removed at all costs.

This was tantamount to the violation of sovereignty and territorial
integrity of the DRC. The invasion negated and violated principles of
international law: the right of nations to self-determination, the right to
self-preservation and the right to determine one's fate without coercion.
The DRC therefore invited SADC to assist in fighting the aggression.
Already in 1995 the Inter-State Defence and Security Committee
(ISDSC), an institution of the SADC organ on Politics, Defence and

Security, had adopted a resolution to take collective action in case of attempts to remove governments of the member states by military means.[1]

On 18 August 1998, the ISDSC (that is defence ministers) after a thorough analysis of the situation in the DRC resolved to deploy troops in support of the legitimate government. The Committee unanimously agreed that those who were ready had its blessing to intervene. The meeting, however, was not participated in by South Africa, which had earlier emphasized the importance of a negotiated solution to the Congo crisis. According to some observers, Zimbabwe's eagerness to decide about the issue in South Africa's absence reflected Zimbabwe's aspirations to get control over SADC military operations and to balance South Africa's regional hegemony. There were many who thought that Mugabe was trying to make his little Zimbabwe again a 'big brother' in Southern Africa, or a small 'King maker' – against protestations of Mandela in bigger South Africa. President Mandela, however, did not question the legitimacy of the ISDSC decision. Already in September, Mandela said that SADC unanimously supported Zimbabwe's, Namibia's and Angola's military intervention in the DRC (see Kennes, Laakso and Schraeder 2000).

According to the government of Zimbabwe, this was a matter of principle involving Zimbabwe's own national interest: 'Today it may be the DRC that is aggressed and tomorrow it could be Zambia. If we do not resist the aggressor in the DRC who will help Zimbabwe when the monster threatens it?' (Government of Zimbabwe 1999c). However, it needs to be noted that the Zimbabwean army had provided material help to Kabila's AFDL forces already during the 1996–1997 war in Congo/Zaire.

Inside Zimbabwe, the decision to send troops to the DRC raised criticism. Among the critics was the National Convention for Change (NCC), a coalition of Zimbabwean opposition parties. It threatened to take the government to court in order to challenge the legal basis of the decision-making procedure regarding intervention. The NCC's argument was that the decision to be involved in the DRC was made unilaterally by President Mugabe without any consultation in Parliament as required by law.

Probably the leaders of Zimbabwe, Angola and Namibia wanted to deploy troops quickly, because any delay could have led to the fall of Kinshasa. Later, Chad under a bilateral agreement with the DRC government deployed in the north. The military effort was directed towards opening and securing the DRC's lifeline, its only route to the sea and to repulse the rebel advance to Kinshasa. Zimbabwe and Namibia directed operations from Kinshasa and Angola from the coast, ultimately trapping the rebels in between and delivering a devastating blow, crushing the Kinshasa invasion decisively. The SADC Allied Forces established a task force headquarters in Kinshasa. The Allied Forces brought normalcy to Kinshasa and resumption of road, railway, waterway transportation, fuel and electricity supply. The rebels took advantage of the lull after their defeat in the western front, prompted by the desire of the Alliance to seek a peaceful resolution to the conflict, and made territorial gains in the eastern DRC. The SADC Allied Forces were eventually deployed in the eastern DRC to thwart any further enemy territorial gains.

The SADC intervention in the DRC is consistent with Article 51 of the UN Charter regarding collective security by member countries in the event of external aggression. The UN Security Council on 12 April 1999 adopted resolution 1234 (1999) expressing its commitment to preserve the national sovereignty, territorial integrity and political independence of the DRC (for the full text of the UN Security Council resolution 1234 see *DRC War Bulletin* No. 2, 1999).

The intervention was also consistent with the OAU Harare Declaration of 1997 regarding the removal of the government by force of arms. Precedents of intervention on behalf of victims in Africa are abundant, including the above-mentioned SADC support for Mozambique, which received worldwide acclaim. The Economic Community of West African States (ECOWAS) intervened to restore the elected government of Sierra Leone and also in the Liberation crisis. Those who argue as to why only three SADC countries intervened in the DRC should know that out of 16 countries in ECOWAS only 5 sent troops. SADC has intervened twice in Lesotho, first in 1996 by pursuing a diplomatic solution. In 1998 the SADC endorsed military intervention by South Africa and Botswana to restore law and order.

SADC intervention in the DRC therefore upholds the principles of international law relating to aggression and the UN Charter, OAU and SADC resolutions. According to the Zimbabwean government, the intervention serves as a deterrent to would-be aggressors and creates an enabling environment for self-determination and self-preservation (*DRC War Bulletin* No. 1, 1999). This maiden attempt to provide a purely African solution to an African problem must perforce succeed, as the consequences of failure are too ghastly to imagine: some adventurous states could henceforth violate OAU and SADC protocols with impunity (*Zimbabwe Mirror*, 25 June–1 July 1999).

However, given this legal background of Zimbabwe's intervention and its ideological justification, economic motivation behind the interest of the Zimbabwean government to aid the DRC should not be excluded. As a matter of fact, the Zimbabwean business fraternity were the first to send a morale-booster to the soldiers in the DRC, while a number of civil society groups have made critical note of the business interests dragging Zimbabwe into that war (*Daily News*, 29 July 1999).

It is interesting to note that Zimbabwe's import of electricity from the Inga Dam on the mighty Congo River notwithstanding, until recently there has been very little economic co-operation between Zimbabwe and Congo/Zaire. Now the examples are plenty. When added to the fact that a large part of the previously state-owned enterprises in Zimbabwe are controlled by high-ranking politicians and army officers, it might well be that the long-term commercial interests of Zimbabweans in the DRC form an important impetus behind its involvement in the war.

Already before the war, the Zimbabwean government company 'Zimbabwe Defense Industries' was sending supplies to the DRC army through 'Zvinavashe Transport' of general Zvinavashe. Zimbabwe's Agricultural and Rural Development Authority has been awarded huge areas of farming land in the DRC. In July 2000, at the time when Zimbabweans were eagerly waiting for the deputy appointments for the new government, President Mugabe himself headed a commercial delegation to Lumumbashi. An agreement between the Zimbabwe Electricity Supply Authority's and Snel of the DRC was claimed to result in savings of up to Z\$38 million (US\$1 million) for Zimbabwe on electricity imports each month. During the same visit the national airlines of both countries agreed to start joint ventures not only between the two countries, but also with regard to connections to South Africa and Europe. Further co-operation concerned the maintenance of the Congolese airports. A Zimbabwean bank had also opened a branch in the DRC in order to finance trade between the two countries (*The Herald*, 14 July 2000; BBC, 25 July 2000; see also Kennes, Laakso and Schraeder 2000).

The most important business co-operation, however, is probably taking place in the mining sector. The examples of the Zimbabwean businessman Billy Rautenbach's scandalous involvement in the Gecamines, a big mining company in Katanga, and the failed attempt of Oryx Diamonds to get listed on the London stock exchange, are examples that have got a lot of publicity. Oryx was connected with Zimbabwean army officers and accused of selling 'conflict diamonds' by the British government (BBC, 12 June 2000).

More recently, the Zimbabwean and DRC governments have announced joint business ventures in diamond and gold mining through companies that will be run by military officers. Defence Minister Moven Mahachi is quoted as having said, 'instead of our army in the DRC burdening the treasury for more resources, which are not available, it embarks on viable projects for the sake of generating the necessary revenue' (BBC, 25 July 2000). In the long term, perhaps fighting on Kabila's side is Zimbabwe's and SADC's way of keeping multinationals away from African resources so that Africans can use them without Western meddling. This might have succeeded. Yet, these resources cannot be mobilized for African development without peace. Besides, whatever business opportunities there are in the DRC for the Zimbabwean government and ordinary businessmen and women, it is unlikely that they will generate profits without investments, time and adequate experience in the maddeningly difficult business environment of the DRC.

Cost of the war

In August 1998, Zimbabwe deployed 3000 soldiers in the DRC but the figure has since risen to 11 000. Some Zimbabweans, including parliamentarians, are opposed to the whole deployment just when Zimbabwe is going through its worst crisis in two decades. The reasons for these sentiments centre on the losses that Zimbabwe has been bearing, and the fact that Zimbabwe has no good reason to be in the DRC anyway. Many are concerned about the economic costs of the war. (*Zimbabwe Mirror*, 25 June – 1 July 1999). The IMF, which has been withholding balance of payments support for Zimbabwe, has asked the government to explain the funding of the DRC military incursion. Thus it is not surprising that the government has been reluctant to release details of the cost of the DRC war to the taxpayers. Defence Minister Moven Mahachi is even on record as saying the war was being financed by the DRC itself.

However, the budget overview for the 1997/98 financial year prepared by Minister of Finance Herbert Murerwa for the Parliamentary Budget Committee in June 1999 indicated that the expenditure on Zimbabwe's commitment in the DRC had increased from Z\$35 million a month in 1998 to above Z\$70 million a month in 1999.

In October, the British *Financial Times* claimed that Zimbabwe had misled the IMF over the costs of the war in order to be able to obtain a loan from the IMF. Zimbabwe had told the IMF it spent US\$3 million a month, but the paper quoted a government document indicating that more than US\$25 million was spent a month. *The Financial Gazette* revealed that Zimbabwe had lost \$200 million worth of military equipment in the war (BBC, 25 July 2000). In September 2000, the Minister of Finance Simba Makoni told Parliament that Zimbabwe had spent about

Z$10 billion (US$263 million) on the war. According to him this was unsustainable. Later in the year, there were reports on worrying delays on the payments of subsistence allowances to the troops in the DRC (*Zimbabwe Standard Online*, 5 November 2000).

Irrespective of the exact sums, there is no doubt that the financial resources being channelled to the DRC intervention have created budgetary constraint for essential public services, which have been severely strapped because of a cash shortage. As an example, the Health and Child Welfare Ministry was allocated a paltry Z$3.53 billion in the 1999 budget, against a bid for Z$5.6 billion. The health sector is also cash strapped: the Minister Timothy Stamps asked for a supplementary allocation but he was given only Z$200 million, which his ministry had already exhausted. A sum of Z$70 million a month (Murerwa's figures from June 1999) would have rescued the Ministry of Health and Child Welfare for the rest of the year. Based on the same figures, one can note that the cost of keeping Zimbabwe's troops in the DRC for three months in 1999 was slightly more than what the Treasury allocated the Parirenyatwa Group of Hospitals for the whole year. The hospital asked for Z$585 million but was given only Z$200 million. A single month's spending on the soldiers in the DRC is almost double what was allocated to United Bulawayo Hospitals in the financial year of 1999.

Ceasefire agreement

The failure to score a quick military victory, which was apparently expected both by the rebel side and the SADC Allied Forces on Kabila's side, is becoming a factor contributing towards a negotiated solution. The rebel movement itself has since split between those led by Wamba dia Wamba, and keen to find a national solution, and those backed by Rwanda. Uganda, which now backs Wamba dia Wamba's group, appears more ready for negotiations than Rwanda, which for serious internal problems cannot afford such a commodity unless compelled to by those who have so far aided her warring mission.

The SADC allied forces cannot fight on indefinitely and, for Zimbabwe in particular, the DRC issue has become inextricably bound up with serious political and economic considerations at home. Kabila has been saved and, with every month since August 1998, the DRC state appears less and less fragile. However, Kabila cannot indefinitely bask in the sunshine of the military support of his allies.

It is against this background that the peace process can gather momentum (*The Financial Gazette*, 15 July 1999). For all the militant rhetoric and war victories by the opposing sides, it must have become clear to Kabila, as it has been to everyone else, that his political survival could only be guaranteed by the Congolese themselves and not by Angolans, Namibians or Zimbabweans.

The eagerly awaited peace accord was signed in Lusaka on 10 July 1999 and guns were expected to have fallen silent. Leaders of Southern African Development Community allied countries – Angola, the DRC, Namibia and Zimbabwe – signed the peace pact on the one hand, while leaders of the invading countries – Rwanda and Uganda – signed on the other. Sharp personal clashes within the rebel camp, which almost threatened to scuttle the peace efforts, forced the mediator, Zambian President Frederick Chiluba, to defer the rebel signing ceremony to a later date (*Zimbabwe Mirror*, 25 June–1 July 1999).[2] However, one year after the signing of the document there is still no effective cease-fire.

Assuming that a cease-fire will be reached, real work must begin to ensure that guns fall silent throughout the vast Central African nation and that the country is given an opportunity to find permanent solutions to its recurrent instability. It is only through genuine and palatable democracy that the former Zaire, looted and plunged into three decades of anarchy by Mobutu Sese Seko and his followers, will emerge from its seemingly endless bloodletting into durable peace and stability. There is no magic solution to Congo's deep-seated woes other than allowing the popular will of the people to define the course of its history. Military interventions, however well planned and executed, will never guarantee permanent peace.

The Southern African region has learnt some lessons from the developments in the bloody war in the DRC. The war has also succeeded in revealing the existence of differences and camps within the region. Zimbabwe is now wiser after involving itself in a conflict that it could have avoided. It seems that the best option would have been to get the UN involved (*The Herald*, 28 June 1999).

Conclusions

During its independence, Zimbabwe has adopted an active role in international politics. It continues to promote its security and economic interests via regional arrangements. In this respect, Zimbabwe's foreign and security policy has not changed significantly. One major explanation for this is that the leadership has remained the same over the twenty years of independence. No other political party has ever ruled Zimbabwe apart from the ZANU(PF). Most of that time opposition parties in Zimbabwe have been very weak and deeply divided. Civic groups have not been eager to be active in the field of the official foreign policy of Zimbabwe. Foreign and security policy formulation has been the preserve of the President.

The international environment of Zimbabwe's foreign policy, however, has changed. Therefore, Zimbabwe's position in it has also changed. After the end of apartheid, the Southern African region is no more in the focus of international politics. By the same token, however, the economic potential of the region is keenly monitored. It is the 'enabling environment' for business (in the vocabulary of the World Bank) that matters when Zimbabwe embarks on its third decade as an independent state. And indeed, the government of Zimbabwe is recognizing that new issues are broadening the frontiers of its diplomacy. The diplomatic environment itself has become extremely complex (Kitikiti 1993, 10). As noted by the Minister of Foreign Affairs, although Zimbabwean foreign policy is still led by the President 'even private citizens affect and influence foreign policy . . . What our academics may say, for instance, in the various seminars they attend at home and abroad each year can lend credence or remove the same from the pronouncements of the official purveyors of foreign policy' (Government of Zimbabwe 1999c).

In the future, a particular challenge to the Zimbabwean foreign policy is to respond to the rather tarnished image of the country in the Western media. The Minister continued 'How we are perceived by the world is affected, in part, by the very organization of our society, by legislation intended purely for domestic ends e.g. the Land Acquisition Act which in our case is deliberately and mischievously misrepresented by certain sectors of the world media' (Government of Zimbabwe 1999c). This task might not be an easy one. Yet, as this chapter shows, Zimbabwe has capacity and experiences on which to build a foreign policy tradition that is able to respond to the changing international and domestic circumstances.

Notes

1. In principle the organ has a mandate to function independently of other SADC structures. President Mugabe is its first chairman. The broad objectives of the organ are to further regional co-operation in conflict prevention, management and resolutions; peacemaking, peacekeeping and peace enforcement; defence and security co-operation; and political/diplomatic co-operation at the regional and international levels. At least to a certain extent the question is about a military alliance.

2. The six-point plan, which was a culmination of six weeks of negotiations, called the warring parties to observe a troop standstill on all fronts, remaining in the positions that they occupy at the moment when this agreement comes into force. It also provides for the deployment of UN and OAU who would be given a mandate to disarm renegade forces. These include the Lord's Resistance Army, which carries out guerrilla attacks in Uganda, and Interahamwe Hutu militiamen and former Rwandan government soldiers who orchestrated the slaughter of an estimated 800 000 people in Rwanda's 1994 genocide. The documents also calls for the deployment of UN and OAU peacekeeping monitors and observers, the exchange of prisoners of war, the formation of a Congolese National Army incorporating the two main rebel groups, and the announcement of a timetable for the pullout of all foreign forces (*The Herald*, 12 July 1999).

10
The Media in Zimbabwe: The Struggle between State and Civil Society

Helge Rønning

Introduction

On 6 October 2000, after police on the instructions of the Minister of Information had raided the first private radio station in Zimbabwe, the independent newspaper *The Daily News* opened its editorial of the day with the following words: 'THERE always seems to be an element of panic and hysteria in the government's reaction to new developments on the media front, whether it is in broadcasting or newspapers.' In an exemplary manner the media policies and media situation in Zimbabwe reveal the contradictions between the authoritarian and democratic impulses in the political development of the country. It is symptomatic of a conflict between the state and civil society.

Zimbabwe Mass Media Trust enters the media scene

The history of the Zimbabwe Mass Media Trust (ZMMT) may serve as an entry point into an analysis of the contradictory relationship between the government and the press (Saunders 1991). The Zimbabwe Mass Media Trust was created by the new independent Zimbabwean government in January 1981 as an articulation of its media policy. The background was a dissatisfaction with the situation in the national press. The two daily newspapers in the country, *The Rhodesian Herald* in Salisbury and *The Bulawayo Chronicle* in Bulawayo, were at independence owned by the South African Argus company's chain of newspapers.[1] It was obvious to everyone that this was an arrangement that had to change. A major South African media chain which at the same time controlled the major English language newspaper in the apartheid state, even if these papers voiced a cautious form of critique of apartheid, could not continue to control the print media in a country that saw itself as being in the forefront of the struggle against apartheid. And while the two papers under the Smith regime quite often were censored, and attempted to uphold principles of editorial independence, they were nevertheless seen as part of the Rhodesian establishment. In January 1981 the 43.2 per cent of the stock in the newspaper company held by South African investors was bought at a cost of Z$2.7 million (US$5 million) and placed by the government under the control of a new entity called the Zimbabwe Mass Media Trust. The old Argus company was also renamed Zimbabwe Newspapers Ltd (Zimpapers) and it owned the two dailies in Harare and Bulawayo, Sunday papers in the same cities, and a weekly paper in Mutare. The money to buy the shares was put up by the Nigerian government; it is, however, unclear whether all the money was ever transferred to Zimbabwe.

The creation of the ZMMT solved an initial policy dilemma for the ZANU(PF) government when it came to acquiring the Argus shares and finding a new structure to replace the previous ownership model. The dilemma was how to decolonize the foreign-owned media while maintaining some national stake in them without the direct intervention of the state. If the media were 'indigenized' the question remained as to which local interests should be allowed to control them? On the one hand, it was not in line with ZANU(PF) policies to privatize the press, and there were powerful sectors of the party that wished to nationalize the press. On the other hand, the government was reluctant to face charges of exerting undue influence over the media, particularly as ZANU(PF) had criticized the Argus press for being in the service of the UDI regime. If the Ministry of Information were to have a controlling influence in the management of the restructured Zimpapers, this could have cast doubt on ZANU(PF)'s commitment to traditional democratic freedoms, to which they had promised to adhere during the Lancaster House negotiations with Britain.

The Trust was intended to serve as a vehicle not just for changing the staff and editorial policy of the papers, but also to oversee the transition in the management and operation of the public print media from white minority control to serving the interests of the broad section of Zimbabwean society. It was emphasized by the government that the press should be a free press responsible to the national interest and should in principle be mass-oriented, nationally accessible and non-partisan in content.

The ZMMT was supposed to serve two interests at the same time, to manage a press which was formally tied to the development aspirations of the government. But also committed to the independence of the press. The trust was thus constituted as a non-governmental, non-party, non-profit making Trust, with a constitutionally prescribed non-partisan Board of Trustees. It was to have administrative and financial autonomy and the government would not interfere in the running and management of its affairs. Subsequently, the trust entered into a business relationship with other Zimbabwean private investors, who to a large degree consisted of factions of domestic white capital that had figured as the commercial stalwarts of white Rhodesia. This was the situation until 1986 when the Trust obtained 51 per cent of the shares in the company. In addition the Trust was given control of the new national news agency ZIANA, the new school of journalism (later transferred to Harare Polytechnic as a department), and later it acquired the national book-selling chain Kingston's. In the early 1990s, it set up a chain of local newspapers the Community Newspaper Group that partly were taken over from previously private (white) owners, and partly were newly started with funding from among others UNESCO, later to fold.

Initially, the trustees (a maximum of seven and a minimum of three) were appointed by the government. Thereafter, the board was designed to be self-perpetuating, naming on its own any new members to replace former members who ceased because of resignation, death or other reasons to sit on the board. Regulations prohibited the inclusion of members of parliament, the uniformed services or the public service on the board. An administrative secretariat headed by an executive secretary vested with responsibility for running the day-to-day affairs of the Trust was set up. From the very beginning, the structure of ZMMT had inherent contradictions in relation to the Trust's autonomy as the Deed of Donation was made by the government and was subject to amendment by the government. As long as the government retained that monopoly to amend the deed, there was very little that could be done by other actors to secure the independence of the Trust. It appears to be legally free, but it is in practice bound to the government, and its legal autonomy could be changed at any time whenever it is unfavourable to the government. The requirement that the Trust had to furnish the government with reports of its annual accounts and other further information details of its operations, etc. also potentially compromised its autonomy.

At its inception, ZMMT may be interpreted as being, together with the restructuring of the Zimbabwe Broadcasting Corporation (ZBC), the most important practical expression of ZANU(PF)'s line of decolonizing, nationalizing and democratizing the media. However, as the party's project of acquiring total hegemonic control of both the political sphere, the state and civil society with the explicit aim of introducing the one-party state unfolded in the 1980s, the ZMMT and its component media became increasingly submerged in political struggles for leadership in state and civil society. The Trust's appearance as a neutral buffer between the state and the ruling party on the one hand, and an independent public press and civil society on the other became more and more hollow. There were a number of factors at play here, but among them were ZMMT's growing structural dependence on the state for financial planning, economic and political support. The most important factor in the relegation of the Trust to a secondary function in the running of the public press was its financial insecurity which at times bordered on severe crises.

Very early in its existence, the Trust was to encounter problems on a number of fronts because of its internal financial and political weaknesses, which was linked to the growing presence of the Ministry of Information in the direct supervision of the public media and the Trust itself. Correspondingly, the ZMMT was increasingly distanced from real control of the media placed under its authority. This may be illustrated by the relationship between the Trust and Zimpapers. After the creation of the Trust, a tripartite decision-making structure emerged at Zimpapers consisting of the Trust, the Ministry and the new black senior management at Zimpapers, who there is no doubt was closely allied to the ZANU(PF) leadership, and to a large degree acted to secure the interests of the ruling party in controlling the national press (Rusike 1990, Saunders 1991).

The conflict between the principle of editorial and journalistic independence on the one hand, and the urge to put the press under state and party control on the other, had come to the forefront already in the 1980s in a number of cases which led to the dismissals and removals of editors and journalists in Zimpapers. In addition, there is the clear partisan coverage that Zimpapers, to a lesser or greater degree, gave (and gives) of political events in Zimbabwe, including blatantly skewed, or scant and nonexisting reporting of opposition to, grievances with, and demonstrations and strikes against the government and the ruling party, as well as uncritical praise of the party and its leadership. The effective subjection of the ZMMT to the state and ruling party must be seen as maybe the most important casualty of the ruling party's invasion of nominally autonomous public institutions.

In December 2000, it was decided to dissolve the ZMMT. This had been on the books for some time, partly because the companies controlled by the Trust were in economic difficulties. This was the case for Zimpapers, which had lost circulation and advertising in 1999 and 2000, and for ZIANA which for all practical purposes had been bankrupt for some time, as well as for the Community Newspaper Group which, together with other businesses in the country, suffered under the difficult economic conditions in the country. But more important was that the Ministry of Information was abolished in September, and the functions that related to ZMMT had been transferred to the Information and Publicity Department in the President's Office headed by the Minister of State for Information and Publicity Professor Jonathan Moyo. The liquidation of the Trust was implemented at a meeting of the trustees as the legal circumstances around it made it impossible for the Minister to disband it himself. But there is every indication that it was done because it was felt that the institution no longer served any purpose as a vehicle for giving the government control of the official media a veneer of respectability. The control is now direct from the President's Office through the handpicked boards of the different entities that fell under the former trust. It has been indicated that a new structure would be set up to combine ZIANA, the Zimbabwe Information Services and the Community Newspaper Group, effectively making them into even more of a government mouthpiece.

Willowgate – Zimpapers' first attempt at investigative journalism

The history of the ZMMT is closely linked to the most important media enterprise that was under its domain – Zimpapers. It is in relation to the national press that the problems of the Trust and its lack of real independence are most clearly illustrated. This relationship consists of a row of conflicts over editorial independence leading to the sacking of editors, and of government interference in the daily running of the papers. The first clear incident in this saga took place in 1983 when the legendary Zimbabwean journalist, the late Willie Musarurwa, was sacked as editor of *The Sunday Mail* for giving prominent coverage to what was called the opposition, that is ZAPU. In 1987, Henry Muradzikwa, then editor of *The Sunday Mail*, later editor-in-chief of the national news agency ZIANA, published an article that was critical of the treatment of

Zimbabwean students in Cuba at a time when the then Cuban foreign minister was visiting Zimbabwe. He was punished by being 'promoted' to group projects manager at head office.

The most important case and what served as a major contribution to the opening up of the Zimbabwean media after Independence, however, was the so-called 'Willowgate' scandal which broke in *The Chronicle* in Bulawayo in 1988. This exposure of corruption may serve as an exemplary tale of how professional journalism may contribute both to the democratic process and to an increased awareness of professional standards among journalists. First, it is a case of how one courageous editor Geoffrey Nyarota, and his colleagues, partly through having good contacts with, and legitimacy within, a number of circles with access to information on corrupt practices, managed through professional journalistic work to expose serious corruption high up in government. Second, it is an indication of how dissatisfaction with such practices created an alliance between the press, honest civil servants and the public, which may be seen as an example of how this in itself may serve as a safeguard against governmental malpractice.

There are several reasons why it was *The Chronicle* that exposed how ministers and other high officials abused their right to buy cars from the assembly plant at Willowgate in the industrial areas of Harare, and in a situation of strict regulations on the sale of cars, resold them at a high profit. One reason is that *The Chronicle* is published in Bulawayo where dissatisfaction with the ZANU(PF) government had been strong through the 1980s. This was linked to a number of factors of which two interrelated aspects were of particular importance. In the elections of 1980 and 1985, Matabeleland had voted heavily for PF-ZAPU which became the opposition party. Partly because of that, but also because of as yet not properly clarified reasons, Matabeleland in the early 1980s was subjected to gross repression and as many as 20 000 people were killed in massacres carried out by the notorious 5th Brigade in cleansing operations against so-called dissidents, who were thought to be old members of the ZAPU army (ZIPRA). Well-known ZAPU politicians had also been jailed under the emergency laws. Secondly, at the time there was a hesitant atmosphere in the Zimbabwean political sphere in general because of the unity accord signed between ZANU(PF) and PF-ZAPU in December 1987. This had led to a certain opening of the debate particularly around the issue of the one-party state. Thirdly, the general disillusionment with the politics of the government was growing in wide circles. Thus the Willowgate case may be interpreted as how a broader political situation led to the testing of the limits of government control within the official press.

The public outcry and the pressure by independently minded politicians within the ruling party and from wide circles in Zimbabwean civil society led to President Mugabe setting up a commission of inquiry under the leadership of Justice Sandura in January 1989. The commission's findings resulted in the resignation of five ministers and civil servants, and Nyarota and his journalists were praised for their investigation. This is an example of the importance of an independent judiciary for the democratic process. However, Geoffrey Nyarota had at the time already been relieved of his editorship and moved to an administrative position at the headquarters of Zimpapers in Harare. He had tested the limits of the official press, and overstepped them.

The ZANU(PF) government and editorial independence at Zimpapers

Geoffrey Nyarota was, however, not to be the last editor in Zimpapers to be removed from his position because he exercised editorial independence. In early 1998, the editor of *The Herald* Tommy Sithole was removed from his post and 'promoted' to director of business projects and public relations at the Zimpapers head office. This case was remarkable for many reasons not least because Sithole for many years had been known as a loyal party supporter with close ties to the President. He had through his 15 years at the helm of the paper defended and promoted government policies.

The events that brought about his fall were the protests and strikes in 1997 and 1998, which also resulted in some cautiously independent reports in *The Herald* on issues such as police brutality in quelling demonstrations, government's mismanagement of the economy, as well as the wastage of public funds. This development of editorial attitudes at *The Herald* finally led to sharp editorial comments in January 1998 following the violent food price riots. The background to the editorials was partly that Mugabe and government ministers had accused the labour movement and the whites of fomenting the unrest. The editorials stated among other things that to accuse ZCTU or 'ethnic groupings' was a form of delusion. Scapegoating was not the solution to the problem, and the government should face the existing crisis in the country head-on.

After Sithole's demise, the editor of *The Sunday Mail* Charles Chikerema was made editor. He, however, died after a short period and was replaced by the Director of Information Bornwell Chakaodza in May 1998, and he served as the editor till after the elections in June

2000. Then he was sacked in August/September in a major shake-up at Zimpapers due both to economic and political circumstances. The circulation and advertising revenue of *The Herald* and the other Zimpapers dropped in the period leading up to the elections, and there were also misgivings among the staff, reported in the independent press, about the blatantly partisan reporting in the papers during the election and referendum campaigns. After the elections, Chakaodza tried to introduce a less partisan attitude in the papers, and he even wrote an article welcoming the presence of MDC members in the Parliament. The conclusions in the analysis of the reporting in the Zimbabwean media of the election campaign by the Media Monitoring Project[2] clearly indicated that Zimpapers were severely biased in their reporting of the election campaign and the election itself.

The change in attitude must be understood on the basis of several developments in the Zimbabwean press environment. One is the rise of a much stronger independent press, particularly a competing daily *The Daily News*, which in 2000 outsold *The Herald* drastically. Another is that Zimpapers was losing money and encountered serious economic problems, which were a result of both the competition on the newspaper market, and of the general economic crisis in the country. Chakaodza and those who agreed with him hoped to change the situation by moving Zimpapers away from the government line. This resulted in the firing of everyone in top positions on the Harare papers – Chakaodza and his deputy editor Thomas Bvuma, the editor of the *Sunday Mail* Pascal Mukondiwa, the chairman of the board Nelson Samkange, who was replaced by Tommy Sithole – a retired newspaper administrator, whose experience went back to the pre-independence Argus days, replaced the chief executive.

There are lessons to be learned from this long story of conflicts between government and editors, who in many cases started out as being loyal supporters of the party and the government, then discovered that a newspaper's legitimacy is not based on being a mouthpiece for a government but rather on being an observer and reporter of events in society, where a variety of viewpoints and perspectives are being expressed, and that responsible journalism has to be independent and critical.

The independent press in Zimbabwe

On Christmas Day 1994, the last issue of Zimbabwe's first independent daily – *The Daily Gazette* – appeared. The saga of the paper is of great significance for the understanding of the relationship between state-controlled newspapers and the private press, and the role of the market in relation to the press in Southern Africa. When it folded, *The Daily Gazette* had existed for a little over two years. The first issue appeared Monday, 5 October 1992. In his publisher's statement, Elias Rusike declared that the new newspaper was dedicated to national unity, a mixed economy and democratic rights. But more than anything else there was an emphasis on the independence of the paper, and on its right in the interest of the nation to criticize the government, individual ministers, political parties, business interests and private individuals. The newspaper did not see itself as an oppositional paper, but as an alternative to what was called the government-controlled press. The paper would concentrate on issues, not people, and pursue an objective, balanced and fair form of journalism, in the interest of bringing the truth to the public.

The Daily Gazette aimed at becoming a modern hard-hitting popular newspaper mixing political news and comments with typical tabloid material in the form of sensationalism and particularly crime-stories. While *The Herald* in its staidness and avoidance of popular and critical journalism may be seen as a poor copy of British or rather South African quality newspapers, *The Daily Gazette* might be likened to a British tabloid in the *Daily Mirror* tradition. In its first week of existence, the paper carried a number of stories revealing abuse of power and corruption in public institutions. Many Zimbabweans interpreted this as a sign of the appearance of a more open society, and that it would be possible to gain more insight into the goings-on behind the closed doors of power. On the other hand, it became clear very early on that the paper lacked sufficient resources to undertake the kind of investigative journalism that it had set out to do. Much of the material in the paper consisted of stories from news agencies, and poorly researched reports, of an often sensationalist kind, and also a form of snooping journalism which showed little respect for the privacy of individuals, based on very weak sources.

From the very beginning, *The Daily Gazette* had severe logistical problems such as a lack of telephone lines and equipment, not enough vehicles, and so on. It also had problems with distribution, acquiring enough advertising, in short with establishing a sufficiently strong basis for the continuation of the paper. It also became clear after the paper had folded, that the financial basis for the launching was weak. The proprietors probably did not have enough capital to sustain the paper for more than a year. The experiment with *The Daily Gazette* thus tapped the publishing company – Modus – for most of its resources and left it to all intents and purposes more or less bankrupt when the paper ceased publication. At its launch the print run was 40 000, it peaked at 55 000, and was at the time of its folding probably around 20 000. Contributing to the fall of the paper were high interest rates, soaring production costs and restricted consumer demand that led to shrinking margins. Furthermore, there is no doubt that *The Daily Gazette* in trying to break Zimpapers' monopoly was confronted by a government jealous of its privileged access to the national press, and that this also had as a consequence that it was met with attempts to make its existence as difficult as possible. This probably took the form of trying to influence potential advertisers not to advertise in the paper. Although evidence is scant, there exist indications that both parastatal and private businesses were wary of placing ads in *The Gazette* for fear of antagonising the government. It should be borne in mind that the liberalization of the Zimbabwean economy had not developed as far then as it had towards the end of the 1990s.

The chequered history of *The Daily Gazette* is in many ways central to the history of an independent press in Zimbabwe. The paper grew out of Modus publications, whose history goes back to 1959. Its main publication before the start of the daily was the weekly *The Financial Gazette* whose roots go back to 1956. During UDI it was called *The Rhodesian Financial Gazette* and it was in many ways a mouthpiece for the Rhodesian Front. In 1979, it was bought by a group of liberal white investors – Clive Murphy, and Nigel and Rhett Butler. In 1982, they hired a very capable and liberal-conservative journalist Clive Wilson as editor, and he started upgrading the paper with new staff and equipment. In the course of a few years the paper became not only the most important voice of the mainly white business community, but also came to be regarded as the paper for alternative opinion in the country in general, in spite of the fact that it never pursued a popular form of journalism. It increased its circulation in the course of five years from around 4000 to 20 000, and it was an economic goldmine that attracted a lot of advertising.

In 1989, Modus publications and *The Financial Gazette* were bought by a group of three black investors under the leadership of Elias Rusike, who until then had been group managing director of Zimpapers. They hired Geoffrey Nyarota as editor of *The Financial Gazette*, and he began changing the paper's profile to be more involved in political news reporting, starting a special supplement *The Weekend Gazette* which later became a separate publication and formed the basis for *The Daily Gazette*.

In 1991, Nyarota was fired as editor – it has never been established for what reasons – but he later won compensation in a court case for being unfairly dismissed. At about the same time, Modus bought a new printing press, and the preparations for starting the daily had begun. The publication of *The Financial Gazette*, however, continued all the time, its editorial independence gradually coming under pressure from the owners of Modus, who were under pressure from their creditors at the government-controlled Zimbank. Staff and infrastructure were pared back sharply, in a desperate attempt to cut costs and stay afloat. In the wake of this, and the management's increasing admonition to ease up on criticism of the government and ruling party, the editor Trevor Ncube and several other senior editorial staff left the paper in 1996. However, *The Financial Gazette* continues to be an important voice of especially the black business community and it maintains its independent editorial line under the very able editorial leadership of Francis Madongwa, and his deputy editor Basildon Peta. Particularly in the run up to the referendum and the elections in 2000, the paper did a formidable job of political reporting.

What then did *The Daily Gazette* achieve during its short life? Probably the most important result was that the paper proved that it was possible to challenge the monopoly of Zimpapers, and that it was feasible to create alternative, more open forms of journalism. Thus the paper, together with other alternative media, developed a form of critical journalism which at its best definitely has contributed to the opening up of Zimbabwean society.

In May 1996, a new weekly newspaper hit the streets in Harare. It was called *The Zimbabwe Independent* and it came in the wake of the crisis in the independent press after the collapse of *The Daily Gazette* and *The Sunday Gazette*. The paper was an attempt to revive the private sector press that had been severely eroded, and to widen the scope and national reach of published opinion. The editorial line of *The Independent* has from the very beginning included support for meaningful 'black empowerment' measures, for economic reform programme, and consistent criticism and exposure of government mismanagement, corruption and abuse of power. The newspaper proved to be a success: it reached a circulation of 25 000 after a little more than a year. The publishers bought a second-hand press, and also started a Sunday paper *The Sunday Standard* in April 1997. Under the editorship of Mark Chavunduka, the paper adopted a style that may be characterized as a form of up-market populist entertainment journalism. The market for both the 'Independent' papers is the professional urban sector, but its impact is doubtlessly larger than its circulation indicates.

The Independent was set up with the backing of solid capital, management and editorial resources (including a translocated senior editorial team from Modus, headed by former *Financial Gazette* editor Trevor Ncube). The leading investors were Clive Murphy and Clive Wilson. Since they sold their controlling interest in Modus, they consolidated a new publishing company and developed a national distribution agency that was used to support *The Independent*. Clive Murphy withdrew from the company early in 1999, and in August 2000 Trevor Ncube took over Wilson's shares.

In addition to the *Financial Gazette* and the two 'Independent' papers, the weekly independent Zimbabwean press also consists of *The Zimbabwe Mirror* that started publication in December 1997. It had its background in an intellectual and academic Trust built up around the monthly magazine *Southern African Political and Economic Monthly (SAPEM)*. In the beginning it bore the marks of its background in intellectual circles and lacked a journalistic style, but it has developed and may now be characterized as an informed, analytical paper with sharp articles. Its editorial line, under the leadership of the politically influential and flamboyant intellectual Ibbo Mandaza, may be characterized as a form of radical nationalism and quite different from the business-based attitude of its competitors. Its political message which may be characterized as critical of, but with an affinity to ZANU(PF), also gives it access to information about what goes on inside the party in a way that none of its competitors can. It supported the government over the referendum, and also reported the election from a position of government support, but also from a critical distance. The paper's greatest challenge and problems probably lie in an insufficiently developed infrastructure and distribution network. A readership survey in 2000 estimated its readership to be around 87 000 per week. In November the same year, reports were published that *The Mirror* planned to become a daily.

The tendencies to open up and diversify the Zimbabwean press were reinforced in July 1998 when plans for establishing both a new daily newspaper and a chain of local newspapers in Zimbabwe were announced. The company behind the initiative, Associated Newspapers of Zimbabwe (ANZ [PVT] Ltd), intended to spend 65 million Zimbabwean dollars on launching a new national daily newspaper – *The Daily News* – to be printed simultaneously in Harare and Bulawayo and 5 local weeklies in urban centres around the country employing about 100 journalists in addition to technical and advertising personnel. Behind these ambitious plans were local journalists and editors such as Geoffrey Nyarota and Wilf Mbanga, who for many years ran the

Community Newspaper Group. By 30 March 1999, all the papers had been launched.

One of the most interesting aspects of the project was its economic background. Behind it was a consortium of Zimbabwean institutional, corporate and private investors, backed by companies and individuals with publishing interests in the United Kingdom, New Zealand and South Africa. Among the foreign investors were: the Bank of Scotland; Tindle Newspapers, one of Britain largest publishers of local and regional papers; Cross Graphics, a British supplier of printing and associated equipment; Allied Press, New Zealand's largest private media group; Commonwealth Publishing Ltd, which publishes a range of publications in several Commonwealth nations. Originally, the South African newspaper group Independent Newspapers, controlled by the Irish magnate Tony O'Reilly, was supposed to be among the investors, but early in 1999 it was announced that the group had withdrawn from the project.

The ANZ papers ran into economic difficulties early in their existence. The problems were in part due to the general difficult economic situation in Zimbabwe. To invest in media in a situation of economic decline is extremely difficult, as the media industry in general, and press in particular, is very susceptible to changes in the overall economy, and there exists a conventional wisdom that a retracting market is one in which the market media will suffer very soon. In addition, it turns out that the growth and development of the independent media in the Southern African region has been frustrated over the years by many obstacles which include overregulation by government and limited access to finances, and hyper-inflation in many of the region's economies, including Zimbabwe in recent years.

Nevertheless, there is no doubt that the problems to a large degree had their roots in over-optimistic plans and projections for economic viability, particularly of the local papers. Partly they stemmed from an organizational process and practice that was not geared to the complexities of running a major newspaper house. The press the group had acquired arrived too late and had serious problems in its initial production phase. The distribution system was not up to standard. And there are also reasons to believe that the company was undercapitalized for the size of the operation. Early in its existence, ANZ went through very difficult changes and crises. The group had to close most of its local papers, all of which were launched before *The Daily News*, and drop their Saturday and Sunday editions. They had to fire many of their journalists, and others left. And the management was restructured.

The crisis was particularly grave in September 1999, when the group was rescued by Southern Africa Media Development Fund (SAMDEF) through a soft loan of US$300 000. SAMDEF was set up as an outgrowth of MISA (Media Institute of Southern Africa) to strengthen, through financial, technical and training support, the capacity of the SADC region's independent media to become self-sustaining professional, and economically viable, media operations. The support is to be geared to emergent independent media enterprises in the sub-region that are not in a position to raise commercial loans or raise sufficient collateral to run their enterprises in a professional and business-like manner and service or ultimately repay its loan or other obligations to SAMDEF. ANZ was the first major project in southern Africa to qualify for this sort of assistance after an extensive investigation into the possible sustainability of the company had been conducted.

This was due to the fact that already at the time of the SAMDEF rescue operation *The Daily News* steadily increased its circulation and under the referendum campaign it grew tremendously, at the same time as the circulation of *The Herald* dropped. This was a tendency that continued during the election campaign. In June, just before the election, *The Daily News* reached a circulation of 129 500 copies, while *The Herald* was down to 87 647. Since mid-1999, the paper has also attracted significant advertising. This tendency has continued after the elections. The paper is being published every day, and also has an Internet edition, and has established itself as Zimbabwe's most important newspaper. It played a very significant role as a counterweight to *The Herald's* blatantly partisan election reporting, by adopting a professional journalistic attitude and particularly highlighting incidences of violence and the abuse of power. The editor's office was also the object of an attempted bombing in April 2000. Its reporting led ZANU(PF) supporters and officials to accuse it of being an opposition paper, but the monitoring reports of the election coverage do not establish this to any great degree.

With the success of the paper in the Zimbabwean public sphere, and its economic recovery, it then came as a great surprise to the Zimbabwean media scene when in November 2000 the paper was threatened economically by none other than SAMDEF. The reason for this action was very complex. But it no doubt involved much politicking and a form of consorted action by SAMDEF leadership and forces within Zimbabwe with connections to ZANU(PF) who controlled minor shareholding posts in ANZ. At the same time as this action against the paper was instigated, there were other actors who wanted to get into the company. Chief among these was a consortium of indigenous investors led by Strive Masiyiwa, who had built a successful cellular company, Econet, after winning a long legal wrangle with the government. He moved to Johannesburg in 2000 after stating that he feared the political climate in Zimbabwe. His company runs telecommunications operations in, among others, Malta, Botswana, Lesotho and Tunisia. The group around Masiyiwa saw the newspaper as a good investment opportunity. This would also reduce the level of foreign shareholding in ANZ to 30 per cent.

The history of ANZ has many interesting aspects: among others it may be seen as an example of how the market can further media diversity. Particularly interesting is the fact that it is foreign media capital that provided the impetus for greater media pluralism in Zimbabwe. This aspect, however, also provoked the most worrying response from the government: both the Minister of Information Chen Chimutengwende and the Minister of Industry and Commerce Nathan Shamuayirira criticized the project for being foreign-dominated and for having the potential of destabilizing the political order and of furthering oppositional political agendas. In early 1999, Chimutengwende also stated that he was considering introducing rules against foreign investments in Zimbabwean media and restrictions on the right of international donors to support media in the country. The ANZ initiative suggests that in the interest of media pluralism it is necessary to adopt a pragmatic position to what often may be seen as fundamental doctrines in relation to restrictions on foreign ownership and media concentration.

Such principles must be applied in relation to historical circumstances and contexts, and it is to a large degree true that in Africa it is the market media that are independent. It is characteristic of the relationship between the government and the press in monolithic systems that representatives of the rulers tend to attack the independent press regularly on the basis of two sorts of arguments: either that they represent a divisional threat to national unity and cohesion, or that they purvey slander and lies. An example of the first attitude is to be found in regular attacks on the independent press in Zimbabwe from both the ZANU(PF) press and ministers.

The private press, national security issues and foreign interventions

In January 1999, a very serious attack on the independent press occurred, the implications of which are much more far-reaching than being only a conflict between the press and the government. It started when *The Standard* on 10 January claimed that there had been an attempted military coup in the army and that 23 officers had been arrested. The newspaper reported that the plans for the coup had their background in widespread dissatisfaction in the army and in Zimbabwean society with the country's involvement in the civil war in the Democratic Republic of Congo. Some days after the publication of the story, military police stormed the offices of the paper, and subsequently arrested the editor – Mark Chavunduka – and the reporter Raymond Choto who had written the story. They were severely tortured during the nine days they were in military detention. During the torture and interrogation, the military police wanted to know who the military sources were and especially the alleged link with South African military intelligence. The police, furthermore, wanted to know the funding of the two independent papers and the military police and air-force sources used. The two journalists were transferred to the civil police and formally charged only after a judge had ruled that their arrest was unconstitutional and that they should be released forthwith. That did not take place till some days later, and after the Minister of Defence Moven Mahachi had been threatened with being taken to court for contempt because he had stated that his ministry did not take orders from courts. When they appeared in court the journalists were charged under the Law and Order (Maintenance) Act, a law introduced by the Smith regime and aimed at suppressing African nationalism before independence. Its terms cover the publication of 'false news' and 'spreading alarm and despondency'. The state alleged that the story was not verified and was meant to tarnish the image of the Zimbabwe Defence Forces and cause public disorder. However, Chavunduka and Choto in their statements to the police denied that their story was bound to cause 'alarm, despondency and public disorder' since the alleged coup was quelled. They also said they took reasonable steps to verify the story with the Defence Ministry without success. Two days later, the publisher of the group, Clive Wilson, was also arrested, only to be released after a weekend in custody without being charged. When the case finally came to court, the journalists were acquitted.

Whatever the true version of the coup story, the events are an example of the ongoing conflict between the Zimbabwean government and the independent media. The struggle between the government and independent press in Zimbabwe over how to interpret the crisis-ridden situation in the country particularly in relation to the country's heavy engagement in the civil war in the Congo did not end with this. Three weeks later the editor and three journalists from *The Zimbabwe Mirror* were also arrested for having written about the dissatisfaction within the army with the military engagement in the Congo.

In relation to the coverage of the war in the Congo, the Ministry of Information is considering introducing the censorship of stories dealing with military matters; ironically, that was the reason behind the introduction of censorship in Ian Smith's Rhodesia. Furthermore, the setting up of an official press council and licensing arrangements for the press have also been hinted at. And real and possible donor support for independent Zimbabwean media has been attacked vehemently as foreign interference in internal political affairs. This happened when Sweden gave support for the starting up of the monthly magazine *Horizon* in 1991. The SIDA grant of Z$450 000 attracted the ire of the party and the government, questions were asked in Parliament, the Swedish ambassador was called to explain the matter to the then Minister of Foreign Affairs Nathan Shamuyarira, and the issue may have cost Sweden a place on the Security Council because it lost the support of Zimbabwe in its campaign. SIDA justified the grant by maintaining that it saw a pluralistic media system as a prerequisite for democratic development, and that this was consistent with Swedish development co-operation policies.

There have been several cases of arrests of journalists over the years, and they all point to the fact that it is characteristic of the relationship between the government and the press in monolithic systems that representatives of the rulers tend to attack the independent press regularly on the basis of two sorts of arguments: either that they represent a divisional threat to national unity and cohesion, or that they purvey slander and lies. An example of the first attitude is to be found in regular attacks on the independent press in Zimbabwe from both the ZANU(PF) press and ministers. They include accusations that the independent media had a well-calculated programme to destroy the country and the ZANU(PF) government, and statements to the effect that even if the government fully recognizes the freedom of the press as enshrined in the constitution of Zimbabwe, it also has the responsibility to protect the nation from malicious misinformation deliberately intended to create instability by some newspapers because of financial greed, and that the independent press has a hidden agenda.

Developments like these confirm what the independent media and human rights organizations have alleged since the early 1990s, namely that the government treats all non-official media as an opposition party, and as enemies of the state. It is a conflict that illustrates how a power-conscious and increasingly corrupt authoritarian government feels threatened by open media. But this again then also makes it difficult for the media to ally themselves with possible outside donors, as it may imply an increased potential for conflict between the government and the international community, as well as confirming government suspicion of the propaganda of the independent media as being a tool of foreign and anti-government interests. The Zimbabwean government and the Zimbabwean media have over the years been in constant conflict over how to regulate and influence media policies, as regards the economic and political situation as well as ethics. There have been attempts to set up both statutory and voluntary media councils. The latest attempt is a media advisory panel that was appointed by the government in December 2000, which was met by suspicion in the independent press over whether it would serve only to legitimize the government hegemony over the national media, the most important and strictly governmental of which is the Zimbabwe Broadcasting Corporation (ZBC), whose history and organizational structure have their roots in the colonial era.

There still is a colonial legacy to ZBC. The legal basis of the corporation was until October 2000, when the President signed a new temporary law, the Rhodesian Broadcasting Act of 1957 as amended in 1974. The law gave ZBC a monopoly to broadcast in the country and placed authority over broadcasting firmly in the hands of the political authorities. Under the Act, ZBC is assigned a monopoly status and accountability to the Minister of Information, Posts and Telecommunications (MOI). This minister is also responsible for advising the President on whom to appoint to the Board of Governors. The Board of Governors, in turn, is responsible for mapping broad policy decisions. ZBC is financed through a combination of licence fees, advertisements and government grants. This Act restructured the broadcasting arrangement that was in existence during the so-called Central African Federation. A British royal commission recommended a new broadcasting authority along BBC lines with explicit autonomy. But the Act placed the final authority, politically and financially, in the hands of the government, and leaving the autonomy – so to speak – to the goodwill of practical policies, or to political culture. Consequently, during the Rhodesian Front (RF) and UDI years the Rhodesia Broadcasting Corporation (RBC) developed into an institution very much like the South African Broadcasting Corporation under apartheid, and during the liberation war it became an outright racist propaganda machine for the Ian Smith regime (Zaffiro 1984, 75).

The electronic media

At independence in 1980, a BBC task force was commissioned to examine the existing television and radio services and assess the likely future requirements of broadcasting in an independent Zimbabwe. Particular reference was made to the feasibility of expanding the broadcasting services to reach the whole population and all parts of the country. The report indicated that one of the main problems was that the RBC had institutionalized a form of control which was outdated and insensitive to the interests of the majority of Zimbabweans.

Organizationally a new centralized board of management was recommended, and finally that the corporation needed restructuring and expensive capital and technical expansion. The government accepted most of the recommendations and the result was that the ZBC became financially and politically dependent upon the government. Shortly after independence most of the white staff left the ZBC and new people loyal to the new government were appointed. Many of them had their background in the radio stations operated by the liberation movements in Zambia and Mozambique. The content of the broadcasting changed. But the fundamental style of the institution was more or less the same, and has remained so ever since. As under UDI, broadcast policy plays a central role in the management of political change and legitimization efforts. Professional and political attitudes and loyalties at the ZBC appear inseparable. Politicians approach the corporation with their own interests in mind and the ZBC must respond to official interests, even at the price of being reduced at times to a sycophant of the regime (Zaffiro 1984, 217). Thus there exists a basic continuity between broadcasting before independence and after.

The report argued that the programming of the ZBC should be strengthened in such a way that it would fully reflect the interests and cultural diversity of the totality of the people of Zimbabwe and serve the nation as a unifying force. Following these general principles the BBC task force made the following basic recommendations, for the use and development of radio: that the then existing radio services be renamed, reorganized and re-launched as three national networks transmitting from Harare; that one of these should be an around-the-clock FM station called Radio 3, broadcasting primarily music but also news and topical affairs of special interest to the young; that one FM channel be used to provide a new national educational service – Radio 4; one channel should broadcast in African languages and have a programme that partly catered for a developmental agenda, and one, Radio 1, should broadcast in English. Once developments of greater priority had been achieved, the ZBC and the government might wish to consider the possibility of establishing local, or community, radio stations in certain centres of the country. (This is a suggestion that was never realized.)

In the first decade after independence, radio broadcasting in Zimbabwe followed a recipe of a mixture of news and information programmes that during elections were highly government-oriented, but otherwise had a certain developmental journalistic angle to them, particularly on Radio 4, the educational radio channel, and Radio 2, the African language channel. Entertainmentwise, the programming on radio consisted of a mixture of music, radio drama, and ring-in programmes. More or less the whole country is being covered by radio signals. In the border areas with South Africa a significant part of the population tune into South African stations. In the 1990s, it became steadily clearer that particularly news reporting on ZBC radio was biased, and the influence of developments within the press played an important role here. And in order to get information about developments in Zimbabwe many people listened to the BBC's African service.

TV is both a commercial and a strictly government-controlled medium (Andersen 1997, Manhando 1997). It is thus subjected to both the controls of the market and the state. A consequence of this is that news and current affairs reporting is characterized by an absence of controversial and investigative journalism. After independence in 1980, plans were envisaged for a two-channel system, where TV1 was supposed to be the vibrant entertainment channel for the whole country, while TV2, which was set up in 1986, was to be developed into a serious educational and informative channel, with no commercial breaks. However, this policy did not work well, and TV2 became a 'repeater' channel, repeating programmes aired on TV1. The weakest point was that TV2 was only accessible to a small urban population in Harare and the surrounding areas. TV2 became an absorber of scarce financial resources.

Only around 25 per cent of Zimbabwean households have their own television set, and, as one would expect, high education and income groups own a high percentage of the total number of sets. Between 60 and 70 per cent of the population in the big cities watch television more than five days a week. A common way of watching is with neighbours and friends. A set is shared by many people in private homes or at beer-halls, bars, and so on. The core viewer, however, lives in a big city, is relatively young, well-educated and has a good income, and thus may be characterized as 'middle class'. What is here referred to as the 'middle class', is – or has the potential of being – the central political agent in the process of development or change in Zimbabwe. It is from this 'class' that the 'political class' of the ruling party is recruited, and it is through groups within the same 'class' that the present formalities of a multi-party system in theory, but not in practice, may be changed and attain real democratic political substance. It is from this social grouping that initiatives that may constitute a challenge to the hegemonic position of the ruling party will come, and in this possible struggle the prime medium of the 'middle class' – television – is of some importance. And consequently, the government is wary of relinquishing control over it. Increasingly, however, people turn to cable and satellite television in order to gain access to a wider choice of programmes, and companies such as the South African Multi-choice, which among others carries M-net, are gaining ground all the time.

Through the 1990s, the ZBC experienced a number of crises of a managerial, organizational and economic kind involving the misappropriation of funds, bad management, and corrupt practices. In addition, particularly TV lost audiences to satellite broadcasting. In 1997, a British consultant – Peter Ibbotson – was asked to assess the situation of broadcasting in Zimbabwe, and also to look into the commercial viability of the ZBC. In the report it was stated that for all practical purposes the corporation was bankrupt. There was an accumulated backlog of Z$100 million, which the corporation said was due from the government, and it was needed to save the ZBC in spite of its monopoly (Ibbotson 1996; *Africa Film & TV News Flash*, 30 May 1997). The government seemed, however, very reluctant to pay. It was, furthermore, pointed out that the ZBC seemed to be an inefficient and costly organization to run, for example debt servicing and administrative overheads absorbed 63 per cent of the corporation's earned income. A conclusion which may be drawn from the report was that the state was no longer willing, or able, to put its financial muscle behind the ZBC. As a consequence, the institution was (and still is) left in a financial squeeze, which can only be solved through more commercials. But commercials presuppose listeners and viewers, and therefore the ZBC has to put up a schedule that can function as a nice environment for adverts. In the long term, this market logic will affect the programming of the corporation. In general terms, this is the condition of most public service broadcasters all over the world after the breakdown of the broadcasting monopoly. The ZBC is in a difficult position, not between dependence on the state and the political establishment and freedom, but between degrees and various types of dependence and direct government interference, something that was particularly noticeable during the campaign around the referendum and the 2000 election campaign, when the ZBC served as a propaganda apparatus for the government.

The 'Ibbotson report' recommended that the airwaves should be opened to competition, that private broadcasting should be introduced, and that a separate Regulatory Authority should be set up which should have the task of drawing up, advertising and allocating detailed licences to broadcasting. By 1999, however, the recommendations had not yet been implemented. It is indicative of the role of the ZBC, and particularly its contradictory positions as regards commercialism and state control, that the only recommendation from the report that was implemented was that ZTV2 was made available to three private broadcasters, two of which folded after a short time, and important interests in the remaining channel seem to have close links with the ruling party. The government did not want to open up for independent radio.

Since mid-January 1999 the Zimbabwean print and broadcast media have been monitored under a project, Media Monitoring Project Zimbabwe, supported and set up by Article XIX, Media Institute of Southern Africa (MISA), and the Catholic Commission for Justice and Peace in Zimbabwe (CCJPC). Its weekly reports conclude that on average only 6 per cent of the stories in ZBC TV newscasts can be said to be fair and balanced; between 68 and 80 per cent of the stories are based on only one source, and roughly half the stories are characterized as 'the voice of ZANU(PF)'. The struggle over the control of the total programming of the ZBC is continuous. In a court ruling early in 1999, it was decided that ZBC TV was obliged to air adverts for alternative political forces. The court ruled that the sole public TV channel has no right to dictate content or ban views that differ from the government's.

On 22 September 2000, there was another ruling by the Supreme Court that completely changed the legal situation of Zimbabwean broadcasting. The court ruled that it was unconstitutional for the government to uphold its broadcasting monopoly, and that the company that had brought the case against the government, Capitol Radio, could operate and provide a broadcasting service within the country. Which the radio company subsequently did, and started transmitting. The government answered on 4 October by passing a Presidential Powers (Temporary Measures) Broadcasting Regulations 2000, and consequently banned Capitol Radio for, among other reasons, compromising national security. The same day, police raided the station and the homes of the broadcasters and dismantled and impounded their equipment. The court battle over the issues continues. But the new law shows clear signs that the government was not prepared to give up its control over broadcasting until after the presidential elections in 2002. The new law provides for a Broadcasting Authority of Zimbabwe to be set up. The Minister of State for Information and Publicity in the President's Office appoints members of the authority that will recommend whether licences are issued or refused before the Minister makes the final decision whether to issue licences to any person wishing to provide a broadcasting service. The provisions are very restrictive and it was characterized as 'a miracle for any application to be approved unless the applicant has "friends in high places", or is prepared to forget the fairness and balance that is the cornerstone of all journalism and the dissemination of information in a democracy' (*The Daily News*, 6 October 2000). In addition, the law also includes requirements that are clearly anti-democratic, such as that one hour is to be devoted to governmental information on stations that obtain a licence.

New restrictive laws further curtail the media

The run-up to the 2002 elections was not only characterized by political arguments and rhetoric hurled by politicians at each other and the electorate. Also, the media was in the firing line from political parties and their associates. However, even if representatives of the opposition and the regime both used strong words and harsh techniques when attacking their media critics, two significant differences exist. First, the extent of the opposition's criticism was significantly more limited compared to the government's. This was primarily due to the opposition's very limited means of communication and resources. Second, the regime's attack of the media was much more encompassing and vicious. In their arsenal could be found introduction of Draconian media laws, destruction of properties and harassment of journalists. Several of these actions could be regarded as standard operation procedures of the ZANU(PF) regime when election is around the corner. However, the intensity and dedication to this destructive mission displayed by the Minister of Information Jonathan Moyo and his colleagues during the various stages of the 2002 election were significant. This behaviour effectively prevented the media from fulfilling its important democratic role of scrutinizing and reporting on politicians and their policies. This time around, the wrath of the Mugabe regime also became very tangible for the international media, in particular the BBC.

New draconian media law: the Access to Information and Protection of Privacy Act

The government tried to introduce several new pieces of legislation prior to the 2002 elections, which would dramatically curtail the flow of information. The more significant ones were the Access to Information and Protection of Privacy Act and the Public Order and Security Act.

The Public Order and Security Act gives wide-ranging discretion to the police. Among other things, the police are given the powers to arrest people who are not carrying identity cards at public meetings. Senior police offers also have the powers to disperse public meetings whenever they deem it legitimate. Of more concern to media practitioners is the fact that filing reports that could undermine the authority of the President, or making abusive or false statements against the President could render a heavy fine and/or a long prison sentence. The Public Order and Security Act is there not only to protect the good name of the President. Also, to utter words, display writing or perform an act that could be regarded as obscene, threatening or insulting or intended to provoke a breach of peace, could be enough for the police to act.

One of the more controversial media laws was introduced to the Zimbabwean Parliament in December 2001. The Access to Information and Protection of Privacy Bill was intended to curb not only the activities of Zimbabwean journalists but also of foreign news media trying to report on events inside Zimbabwe. When representatives of both national and international media organizations learned about the actual content of the Bill, they condemned it in harshest possible terms. More surprisingly, senior members of the ruling party also criticized segments of the Bill. It's a matter of fact that the Parliamentary Legal Committee declared parts of the law as unconstitutional. The Chairman of the Committee Dr Eddson Zvobgo said, among other things, that the law gave too much power to the Minister of Information. Judicial and investigative powers, which should remain with the police force and the courts, were especially mentioned.

Members of the independent and international media organizations stressed other areas of grave concern to them. It was suggested that national journalists had to be accredited by a government-appointed commission, the Media Commission. These licences need to be renewed on an annual basis and could be revoked at any time by the Media Commission. Reasons to revoke a journalist's licence could be that s/he is deemed to spread rumours or falsehoods. Furthermore, should the

Media Commission decide that a published article is based on cabinet deliberations, or information that could harm the law enforcement process or be a threat to national security, the journalist would lose her or his licence. To make sure that journalists don't gain access to such information, the Bill also barred public institutions from releasing information relating to intergovernmental relations and activities.

Journalists were not only running the risk of losing their right to work, but also severe financial penalties could be meted out by the authorities (Z$100 000). In addition, a journalist could also face a two-year prison sentence should s/he be convicted of violating this new media law.

Because of the severe internal and external criticism, the Bill had to be amended before it was passed by the Parliament on 31 January 2002. In spite of the reconciliation between members of the Parliamentary Legal Committee and the ZANU(PF), President Mugabe didn't sign the law before the elections. It was only after he had been re-elected in March 2002 that he finally signed the document and made it a legally binding act.

However, in spite of this delay, the Zimbabwean police had *de facto* already begun implementing the law before Mugabe signed the Bill on 15 March 2002. Still, a surge in legal actions taken against both local and international journalists followed the enactment of the Access to Information and Protection of Privacy Act, which indicates that the Mugabe regime has no intention of easing its pressure on critical media practitioners.

Conclusions

The struggle at the beginning of the twenty-first century over broadcasting illustrates yet again the conflict between ZANU(PF)'s and Mugabe's authoritarian tendencies, and the democratic legacy of the struggle against the Rhodesian regime has always been a factor in Zimbabwean political life. The democratic impulse in Zimbabwean society has been expressed mainly by the numerous civic organizations in the country, a vocal, intellectual community, churches and human rights organizations, and a small, but vocal, independent press. In addition the judiciary has been independent and principled in its defence of the constitution. This has, in spite of everything, kept Zimbabwean society relatively open. And it is the struggle over maintaining this open room and extending it which is currently behind, and has always been a factor in, the conflict between President Mugabe and the ZANU(PF) leadership on the one hand and the independent press on the other: an authoritarian state ideology poised against the democratic agenda of a multifaceted civil society.

Notes

1. At independence the two papers changed their names to respectively *The Herald* and *The Chronicle*.
2. The Media Monitoring Project (MMPZ) is a joint initiative of three organizations: the Zimbabwe chapter of the Media Institute of Southern Africa (MISA), the Catholic Commission for Justice and Peace in Zimbabwe (CCJPZ) and ARTICLE 19, the International Centre Against Censorship, which is based in Johannesburg and London. The project has a particular interest in those sections of the media that are financed out of public funds, since these have an obligation to serve the needs of the entire community. However, the privately owned media are also subject to scrutiny. The MMPZ began operations in January 1999, monitoring all news and current affairs coverage in the publicly owned media – the Zimbabwe Broadcasting Corporation and Zimbabwe Newspapers (1980) Ltd. From June 1999 it extended full monitoring to the private media. From the beginning of January 2000 until after the referendum the MMPZ's work focused almost exclusively on coverage of the constitutional debate and referendum. The project had a similar focus on the 2000 parliamentary election (see http://www.icon.co.zw/mmpz).

Bibliography

Adams, M., E. Cassidy, J. Cusworth, M. Lowcock and F. Tempest (1996) *Report of ODA Land Appraisal Mission to Zimbabwe, 23 September – 4 October 1996'*, Harare: Overseas Development Agency.

African Development Fund (1986) *Appraisal Report for the Mid-Zambezi Valley Rural Development Project*, African Development Fund, Agricultural and Rural Development Department.

Alexander, Jocelyn (1996) 'Things Fall Apart, The Centre Can Hold: Processes of Post-war Political Change in Zimbabwe's Rural Areas', in Bhebe and Ranger (eds).

Alexander, Jocelyn and JoAnn McGregor (1999) 'Representing Violence in Matabeleland, Zimbabwe: Press and Internet Debates', in Tim Allen and Jean Seaton (eds) *The Media of Conflict*, London: Zed.

Alexander, Jocelyn, JoAnn McGregor and Terence Ranger (2000) *Violence & Memory: One Hundred Years in the 'Dark Forests' of Matabeleland*, Portsmouth, NH: Heinemann and London: James Currey.

Aluko, Olajide (1977) 'The Determinants of the Foreign Policies of African States', in Olajide Aluko (ed.) *The Foreign Policies of African States*, London: Hodder and Stoughton.

Amin, Nick (1992) 'State and Peasantry in Zimbabwe since Independence', *European Journal of Development Research*, 4(1): 112–162.

Amsden, Alice (1993) *Asia's Next Giant: South Korea and Late Industrialisation*, New York: Oxford University Press.

Andersen, Michael Bruun (1997) 'The Janus Face of Television in Small Countries: The Case of Zimbabwe', *Critical Arts* 2: 28–45.

Astrow, Andre (1983) *Zimbabwe: A Revolution That Lost Its Way?*, London: Zed.

Banana, Canaan S. (ed.) (1989) *Turmoil and Tenacity: Zimbabwe 1890–1990*, Harare: The College Press.

Barnes, Teresa (1992) 'The Fight for Control of African Women's Mobility in Colonial Zimbabwe, 1900–1939', *Signs: Journal of Women in Culture and Society* 17(3): 586–608.

Berridge Anthony (1993) *ESAP & Education for the Poor*, Silveira House Social Series No. 5, Gweru: Mambo Press.

Bhalla, Ajit, Rob Davies, Margaret Chitiga-Mabugu, Ramos Mabugu and Jacob Kaliyati (1999) *Zimbabwe: Globalization, Liberalization and Sustainable Human Development*, UNDP/UNCTAD Country Assessment Report (First Draft).

Bhebe, Ngwabi and Terence Ranger (1996) 'Volume Introduction: Society in Zimbabwe's Liberation War', in Bhebe and Ranger (eds).

Bhebe, Ngwabi and Terence Ranger (eds) (1996) *Society in Zimbabwe's Liberation War*, London: James Currey, Portsmouth, NH: Heinemann and Harare: University of Zimbabwe Publications.

Bijlmakers, Leon A., Mary T. Bassett and David M. Sanders (1998) *Socioeconomic Stress, Health and Child Nutritional Status in Zimbabwe at a Time of Economic Structural Adjustment: A Three-year Longitudinal Study*, Research Report No. 105, Uppsala: Nordic Africa Institute.

Bijlmakers, Leon A., Mary T. Bassett and David M. Sanders (1996) *Health and Structural Adjustment in Rural and Urban Settings in Zimbabwe*, Research Report No. 101, Uppsala: Nordic Africa Institute.

von Blanckenburg, Peter (1994) *Large Commercial Farmers and Land Reform in Africa: The Case of Zimbabwe*, Aldershot: Avebury.

Bloch, Eric (1994) 'Indigenisation – Is It Failing?' *The Financial Gazette*, 15 September.

Bond, Patrick (1998) *Uneven Zimbabwe: A Study of Finance, Development and Underdevelopment*, Trenton, NJ, and Asmara: Africa World Press.

Bourdillon, Michael (1991[1976]) *The Shona Peoples: An Ethnography of the Contemporary Shona, with Special Reference to Their Religion*, revised edition, Harare: Mambo Press.

Bourdillon, M.F.C. (1987a) *The Shona Peoples. An Ethnography of the Contemporary Shona, with Special Reference to their Religion*, revised edition, Gweru: Mambo Press.

Bourdillon, M.F.C. (1979) 'Religion and Authority in a Korekore Community', *Africa* 49: 172–181.

Bratton, Michael (1986) 'Farmer Organizations and Food Production in Zimbabwe', *World Development* 14(3): 367–384.

Bratton, Michael and Nicolas van de Walle (1997) *Democratic Experiments in Africa: Regime Transitions in Comparative Perspective*, Cambridge: Cambridge University Press.

Brown, Wendy (1991) 'Feminist Hesitations, Postmodern Exposures', *Differences: A Journal of Feminist Cultural Studies* 3(1): 63–84.

Burgess, Stephen F. (1997) *Smallholders and Political Voice in Zimbabwe*, Lanham, MD: University Press of America.

Burton, John W. (1986) 'The Means to Agreement: Power or Values', in Diane B. Bendahmane and John W. McDonald Jr. (eds) *Perspectives on Negotiation: Four Case Studies and Interpretations*, Washington, DC: Foreign Service Institute, US Department of State.

CCJP/LRF (1997) *Breaking the Silence, Building True Peace: A Report on the Disturbances in Matabeleland and the Midlands 1980 to 1988*, Harare: CCJP and LRF.

Central Statistical Office (1998) *Poverty Assessment Study*, Harare: CSO.

Chan, Stephen with the assistance of Chanda L.J. Chingambo (1992) 'Democracy in Southern Africa: The 1990 Elections in Zimbabwe and 1991 Elections in Zambia', *The Round Table* 322: 183–201.

Cheater, A.P. (1990) 'The Ideology of "Communal" Land Tenure in Zimbabwe: Mythogenesis Enacted?', *Africa* 60: 188–207.

Chinemana, Francis (1987) *Women and the Co-operative Movement in Zimbabwe*, Report for the Ministry of Co-operative Development, Harare: Government Printer.

Chipika, Stephen (1990) 'Agricultural Technology in Zimbabwe: The Smallholder's Choice', *Appropriate Technology* 17(1): 22–25.

Chisvo M. and L. Munro (1994) *A Review of Social Dimensions of Adjustment in Zimbabwe, 1990–94*, Harare: UNICEF.

Chitsike, L.T.A. (1985) *A Report on the Review, Study and Effective Coordination of Co-operatives*, Harare: Government Printers.

Chivore, B. (1990) *Teacher Education in Post-independent Zimbabwe*, Harare: ZIMFEP.

Chung, Fay and Emmanuel Ngara (1985) *Socialism, Education and Development – A Challenge to Zimbabwe*, Harare: Zimbabwe Publishing House.

Cliffe, Lionel (1991) 'Were They Pushed or Did They Jump? Zimbabwe and the World Bank', *Southern Africa Report*, March.

Colclough, Christopher and Keith Lewin (1993) *Educating all the Children: Strategies for Primary Schooling in the South*, Oxford: Clarendon Paperbacks.

Collier P. (1995) 'Resource Allocation and Credibility', part of *Interim Report of the AERC study on Regional Trade and Trade Liberalization in Sub-Saharan Africa*.

Compagnon, Daniel (1999) 'Discours et pratiques de "l'indigenisation" de l'économie: une comparaison Zimbabwe – Malaisie', *Revue Internationale de Politique Comparée*, 6(3): 751–776.

Cowen, Michael and Liisa Laakso (2002) 'Elections and Election Studies in Africa', in Michael Cowen and Liisa Laakso (eds) *Multi-party Elections in Africa*, Oxford: James Currey and New York: Palgrave.

CZI (1990) *Export Incentives and Institutional Support for Industry*, Harare: Zimbabwe Banking Corporation.

Dambo Research Unit, Loughborough University, UK (1987) 'Utilisation of Dambos in Rural Development: A Discussion Paper', unpublished report, University of Zimbabwe.

Dangarembga, Tsitsi (1988) *Nervous Conditions*, London: The Women's Press.

Darnolf, Staffan (1997) *Democratic Electioneering in Southern Africa: The Contrasting Cases of Botswana and Zimbabwe*, Göteborg: Göteborg University Press.

Dashwood, Hevina (1996) 'The Relevance of Class to the Evolution of Zimbabwe's Development Strategy, 1980–1991', *Journal of Southern African Studies* 22(1): 27–48.

Davidow, Jeffrey (1984) *A Peace in Southern Africa: The Lancaster House Conference on Rhodesia, 1979*, Boulder: Westview.

Davies Rob and Sanders David (1988) 'Adjustment Policies and the Welfare of Children: Zimbabwe, 1980–1985', in Giovanni A. Cornia, Richard Jolly and Frances Stewart (eds) *Adjustment with a Human Face: Protecting the Vulnerable and Promoting Growth*, Vol. 2, New York: UNICEF and Oxford: Oxford University Press.

Derman, W. (1995) *Changing Land-use in the Eastern Zambezi Valley: Socio-economic Considerations*, report submitted to World Wide Fund for Nature – Zimbabwe and the University of Zimbabwe Centre for Applied Social Sciences.

Derman, W. (1993) 'Recreating Common Property Management: Government Projects and Land Use Policy in the Mid-Zambezi Valley, Zimbabwe', unpublished paper, Harare: Centre for Applied Social Sciences.

Derman, W. and J. Murombedzi (1994) 'Democracy, Development, and Human Rights in Zimbabwe, A Contradictory Terrain', *African Rural and Urban Studies* 1: 119–43.

Diamond, Larry, Juan J. Linz and Seymour Martin Lipset (eds) (1988) *Democracy in Developing Countries, Vol. 2: Africa*, Boulder: Lynne Rienner.

Dorsey, Betty Jo (1989) 'Educational Development and Reform in Zimbabwe', *Comparative Education Review* 33(1): 40–58.

Drinkwater, Michael (1991) *The State and Agrarian Change in Zimbabwe's Communal Areas*, London: Macmillan and New York: St Martin's.

Evans, Michael (1992) 'Making an African Army: The Case of Zimbabwe', in Norman Etherington (ed.) *Peace, Politics and Violence in the New South Africa*, New York: Hans Zell.

Evans, Michael (1988) 'Gukurahundi: The Development of the Zimbabwe Defence Forces, 1980–1987', *Strategic Review for Southern Africa* 10(1): 1–37.

Fauré, Yves A. and Jean-François Médard (1995) 'L'Etat-business et les politiciens entrepreneurs, néo-patrimonialisme et 'big men': économie et politique', in Stephen Ellis and Yves A. Fauré (eds) *Entreprises et entrepreneurs africains*, Paris: Karthala-Orstom.

Foster, Philip (1965) 'The Vocational School Fallacy in Development Planning', in Arnold Anderson and Mary Jean Bowman (eds) *Education and Economic Development*, Chicago: Aldine.

Gaidzanwa, Rudo (1999) *Voting with Their Feet: Migrant Zimbabwean Nurses and Doctors in the Era of Structural Adjustment*, Research Report No. 111, Uppsala: Nordic Africa Institute.

Gaidzanwa, Rudo (1993) 'Citizenship, Nationality, Gender and Class in Southern Africa', *Alternatives: Journal of Humane Governance and Social Transformation* 18(1): 39–60.

Garbett, K. (1977) 'Disparate Regional Cults and a Unitary Field in Zimbabwe', in R. Werbner (ed.) *Regional Cults*, London: Academic Press.

Garbett, K. (1969) 'Spirit Mediums as Mediators in Valley Korekore Society', in J. Beattie and J. Middleton (eds) *Spirit Mediumship and Society in Africa*, London: Routledge & Kegan Paul.

Garbett, K. (1966) 'The Rhodesian Chief's Dilemma: Government Officer or Tribal Leader', *Race* 8: 307–426.

Gibbon, Peter (1995) 'Introduction: Structural Adjustment and the Working Poor in Zimbabwe', in Gibbon (ed.).

Gibbon, Peter (ed.) (1995) *Structural Adjustment and the Working Poor in Zimbabwe*, Uppsala: Nordic Africa Institute.

Godana, T. and Ben Hlatswayo (1997) 'Privatisation and Commercialisation of Public Enterprises', a study commissioned by the ZCTU and FES, January 1997, Harare.

Government of Zimbabwe (2000a) 'Land Issue in Zimbabwe', http://www.gta.gov.zw/Land%20Issues/LAND.htm.

Government of Zimbabwe (2000b), 'Minister of Foreign Affairs Honourable I.S.G. Mudenge on Zimbabwe – UK Relations', 15 March, http://www.gta.gov.zw/foreign%20affairs/Zim_UKrelations.htm.

Government of Zimbabwe (1999a) *Discussion Paper on the Vision of Local Government in Zimbabwe*, draft, January, Ministry of Local Government and National Housing.

Government of Zimbabwe (1999b) *Rural District Councils Capacity Building Programme, Fourth Six Monthly Programme Review Report* 1st January to 30th September 1999, draft, November, Ministry of Local Government and National Housing.

Government of Zimbabwe (1999c) 'Minister of Foreign Affairs on Zimbabwe's Foreign Policy', Harare, 20 January.

Government of Zimbabwe (1998a) *The Report of the Commission of Inquiry into the Administration of the War Victims Compensation Act*, Harare: Government Printer.

Government of Zimbabwe (1998b) *Zimbabwe Programme for Economic and Social Transformation (ZIMPREST)*, Harare: Government Printer.

Government of Zimbabwe (1994a) *Census 1992 – Zimbabwe National Report*, Harare: Central Statistical Office.

Government of Zimbabwe (1994b) *Commission of Inquiry into Appropriate Agricultural Tenure Systems, under the Chairmanship of Professor Mandivamba Rukuni, Volume One: Main Report*, Harare: Government Printer.

Government of Zimbabwe (1992) *War Veterans Act*, Harare: Government Printer.

Government of Zimbabwe (1991) *Framework for Economic Reform, 1991–95*, Harare: Government Printer.

Government of Zimbabwe (1990a) *Economic Policy Statement: Macro-economic Adjustment and Trade Liberalisation Including the Budget Statement*, Harare: Government Printer.

Government of Zimbabwe (1990b) *Annual Report of the Secretary for Primary and Secondary Education, 1988*, Harare.

Government of Zimbabwe (1989) *Report of the Commission of Inquiry into the Establishment of a Second University Campus*, Harare: Government Printer.

Government of Zimbabwe (1987) *Education Act 1979*, Harare: Government Printer.

Government of Zimbabwe (1986a) *First Five-year National Development Plan, 1986–1990*, Harare: Government Printer.

Government of Zimbabwe (1986b) *Socio-economic Review of Zimbabwe 1980–1985*, Harare: Ministry of Finance, Economic Planning and Development.

Government of Zimbabwe (1985) *Government of Zimbabwe's Five Years of Achievement: A Proud Record of Public Service 1980–85*, Harare: Government Printer.

Government of Zimbabwe (1983) *National Manpower Survey, Vol. 1, 1981*, Harare: Ministry of Manpower Planning and Development.

Government of Zimbabwe (1982a) *Transitional National Development Plan, 1982/83–1984/85*, Vol. 1, Harare: Government Printer.

Government of Zimbabwe (1982b) *Foreign Investment: Policy, Guidelines and Procedures*, Harare: Government Printer.

Government of Zimbabwe (1982c) *Report of the Commission of Inquiry into the Agricultural Industry*, chaired by Gordon Chavanduka, Harare.

Government of Zimbabwe (1981) *Growth With Equity: An Economic Policy Statement*, Ministry of Finance, Economic Planning and Development, Government Printer.

Government of Zimbabwe (1980) *War Victims Compensation Act*, No. 22, Harare: Government Printer.

Graham-Brown, Sarah (1991) *Education in the Developing World: Conflict and Crisis*, London: Longman.

Green, Reginald H. and Xavier Kadhani (1986) 'Zimbabwe: Transition to Economic Crisis, 1981–1983: Retrospect and Prospect', *World Development* 14(8).

Gunning Jan W. and Clever Mumbengegwi (eds) (1995) *The Manufacturing Sector in Zimbabwe: Industrial Change Under Structural Adjustment*, University of Zimbabwe and University of Amsterdam.

Gustafsson, Ingemar (1987). *Schools and the Transformation of Work: A Comparative Study of four Productive Work Programmes in Southern Africa*, University of Stockholm Institute of International Education.

Gustafsson, Ingemar (1985) *Zimbabwe Foundation for Education with Production, ZIMFEP: A Follow-up Study*, SIDA Education Division Documents No. 29, Stockholm: SIDA.

Gwinyayi, Albert Dzinesa (2000) 'A Comparative Study of the British Empire Service League, Rhodesia (B.E.S.L.) and the Zimbabwe National Liberation War Veterans Association (Z.N.L.W.V.A.) 1989–1999', BA Honours history thesis, University of Zimbabwe.

Hadenius, Axel (1993) *Democracy and Development*, Cambridge: Cambridge University Press.

Hammar, Amanda (1998) 'Speaking with Space: Displacements and Claims in the Politics of Land in Zimbabwe', paper presented at CODESRIA General Assembly, Dakar, 14–18 December.

Hanlon, Joseph (1988) 'Destabilisation and the Battle to Reduce Dependence', in Stoneman (1988c).

Hatchard, John (1993) *Individual Freedoms & State Security in the African Context: The Case of Zimbabwe*, Harare: Baobab Books.

Hawkins, Anthony M. (1995) 'Lessons of Adjustment from Zimbabwe', in Kapoor (1995b).

Henne, Jeanne (1988) 'The Material Basis of Sexism: A Mode of Production Analysis', in Sharon Stichter and Jane Parpart (eds) *Patriarchy and Class: African Women in the Home and the Workforce*, Boulder: Westview.

Herbst, Jeffrey (1992) 'The Dilemmas of Land Policy in Zimbabwe', in Simon Baynham (ed.) *Zimbabwe in Transition*, Stockholm: Almqvist & Wiksell International.

Herbst, Jeffrey (1990) *State Politics in Zimbabwe*, Berkeley and Los Angeles: University of California Press; Harare: University of Zimbabwe Publications.

Holtzclaw, Heather (2000) 'Place, Race, and Politics: Understanding Zimbabwe's Land Invasions', paper presented at the African Studies Association Annual Meeting, Nashville, TN, November.

Horton S., R. Kanbur and D. Mazumdar (1991) 'Labour Markets in an Era of Adjustment: An Overview', World Bank PRE Working Paper Series, WPS 694.

Hove, Chenjerai (1994) *Shebeen Tales: Messages from Harare*, Harare: Baobab Books.

Hyden, Göran (1983) *No Shortcuts to Progress: African Development Management in Perspective*, London: Heinemann.

Ibbotson, Peter (1996), 'Report delivered in Oxford 18 December 1996', unpublished consultancy report for ZBC, Harare.

IBDC (1993) 'Background Paper', unpublished mimeo, Harare, December.

ILO (1993) *Structural Change and Adjustment in Zimbabwe*, Geneva: ILO.

IMF (1993) *World Economic Outlook*, Washington, DC: IMF.

Jeater, Diana (1993) *Marriage, Perversion, and Power: The Construction of Moral Discourse in Southern Rhodesia, 1894–1930*, Oxford: Oxford University Press.

Jenkins, Carolyn (1997) 'The Politics of Economic Policy-making in Zimbabwe', *Journal of Modern African Studies* 35(4): 575–602.

Johnson, David (1990) 'The Politics of Literacy and Schooling in Zimbabwe', *Review of African Political Economy* 48: 99–107.

Jokonya, Tichaona (1992) 'Zimbabwe's Foreign Policy and Its Thrust on Peace and Security in Southern Africa', unpublished report of proceedings of the seminar on peace and security in the Southern African Region, Institute of Development Studies, University of Zimbabwe, 11–13 March.

Kadhani, Xavier and Reginald H. Green (1985) 'Parameters as Warnings and Guide-posts: The Case of Zimbabwe', *Journal of Development Planning* 15.

Kaplinsky, Raphael and Anne Posthuma (1993) 'Organisational Change in Zimbabwean Manufacturing', mimeo.

Kapoor, Kapil (1995a) 'Overview of the Seminar', in Kapoor (1995b).

Kapoor, Kapil (ed.) (1995b) *Africa's Experience with Structural Adjustment: Proceedings of the Harare Seminar, May 23–24, 1994*, World Bank Discussion Papers 288, Washington, DC: World Bank.

Kennes, Erik, Liisa Laakso and Peter Schraeder (2000) 'Congo Crisis: Background and International Dimension', unpublished manuscript.

Kitikiti, Nicholas (1993) 'Ministry of Foreign Affairs Current Training Programme', unpublished paper presented at the Zimbabwe Institute of International Affairs inaugural seminar, Kadoma Ranch Motel, 26–28 May.

Kriger, Norma (forthcoming) *Guerrilla Voices: Power and Privilege in Zimbabwe*, Cambridge: Cambridge University Press.

Kriger, Norma (2000a) 'War Victims Compensation: Collusion Between Zimbabwean Ex-combatants and Government', *Journal of African Conflict and Development* 1: 35–45.

Kriger, Norma (2000b) 'Transitional Justice as Socioeconomic Rights', *Peace Review* 12(1): 59–65.

Kriger, Norma (1992) *Zimbabwe's Guerrilla War: Peasant Voices*, Cambridge: Cambridge University Press.

Laakso, Liisa (2002) 'When Elections are Just a Formality: Rural – Urban Dynamics in the Dominant-party System of Zimbabwe', in Michael Cowen and Liisa Laakso (eds) *Multi-party Elections in Africa*, Oxford: James Currey and New York: Palgrave.

Laakso, Liisa (1999) *Voting Without Choosing: State Making and Elections in Zimbabwe*, Acta Politica 11, University of Helsinki Department of Political Science.

Lall, Sanjaya (1990) *Building Industrial Competitiveness in Developing Countries*, Paris: Development Centre of the Organisation for Economic Co-operation and Development.

Lan, David (1985) *Guns & Rain: Guerrillas and Spirit Mediums in Zimbabwe*, Harare: Zimbabwe Publishing House.

Lehman, H.P. (1990) 'The Politics of Adjustment in Kenya and Zimbabwe: The State as Intermediary', *Studies in Comparative International Development* 25(3).

Lemon, Anthony (1988) 'The Zimbabwe General Election of 1985', *Journal of Commonwealth & Comparative Politics*, 26(1): 3–21.

Libby, Ronald (1987) *The Politics of Economic Power in Southern Africa*, Princeton: Princeton University Press.

Lind, Agneta (1995) *Desk Study of the Education Sector in Zimbabwe*, Sida Education Division Documents No. 66, Stockholm: SIDA.

Lindauer, David L., Oey A. Meesook and Parita Suebsaeng (1988) 'Government Wage Policy in Africa: Some Findings and Policy Issues', *World Bank Research Observer* 3(1).

Lynam, T.J.P., J. Chitsike, M. Howard, P. Hodza, M.A. Khumalo and W. Standa Gunda (1996) 'Assessing the Contributions of Renewable Resources to the Livelihoods of Communal Area Households in the Zambezi Valley of Zimbabwe', paper presented at the Pan-African Symposium on Sustainable Use of Natural Resources and Community Participation, Harare, 24–27 June.

McGregor, JoAnn (1995) 'Introduction', *Environment and History* 1: 253–56.

Mackenzie, Clayton (1988) 'Zimbabwe Educational Miracle and the Problems It Has Created', *International Review of Education* 34(3): 337–353.

MacKinlay, John (1990) 'The Commonwealth Monitoring Force in Zimbabwe/Rhodesia, 1979–1980', in Thomas G. Weiss (ed.) *Humanitarian Emergencies and Military Help in Africa*, London: Macmillan.

Makumbe, John (1999) *Development and Democracy in Zimbabwe: Constraints of Decentralisation*, Harare: Southern Africa Printing & Publishing House.

Makumbe, John (1991a) 'The 1990 Zimbabwe Elections: Implications for Democracy', in Mandaza and Sachikonye (1991).

Makumbe, John (1991b) 'Zimbabwe Elections 1990: An Overview', *University of Zimbabwe Department of Political and Administrative Studies Election Studies Project Occasional Paper Series* 1(3).

Makumbe, John and Daniel Compagnon (2000) *Behind the Smokescreen: The Politics of Zimbabwe's 1995 General Elections*, Harare: University of Zimbabwe Publications.

Mamdani, Mahmood (1996) *Citizen and Subject: Contemporary Africa and the Legacy of Late Colonialism*, London: James Currey.

Mandaza, Ibbo (1986a) 'The State and Politics in the Post-white Settler Colonial Situation', in Mandaza (1986b).

Mandaza, Ibbo (ed.) (1986b) *Zimbabwe: The Political Economy of Transition 1980–1986*, London and Dakar: CODESRIA.

Mandaza, Ibbo and Lloyd M. Sachikonye (eds.) (1991) *The One-party State and Democracy*, Harare: SAPES Books.

Manhando, Susan (1997) *Broadcasting in a Deregulated Southern Africa: Zimbabwe's Efforts to Engage with Technological Change in Electronic Media*, University of Oslo, Department of Media and Communication.

Maposa, Isaac (1995) *Land Reform in Zimbabwe*, Harare: Catholic Commission for Justice and Peace.

Mararike, Claude G. (1999) *Survival Strategies in Rural Zimbabwe: The Role of Assets, Indigenous Knowledge and Organisations*, Harare: Mond Books.

Masters, William A. (1994) *Government and Agriculture in Zimbabwe*, New York: Praeger.

Mhone G. (1999) 'Towards A National Employment Policy For Zimbabwe: A Proposed Policy Framework', discussion paper prepared for ILO/SAMAT, September.

Mhone G.C.Z. (1993) *The Impact of Structural Adjustment on the Urban Informal Sector in Zimbabwe*, Geneva : ILO.

Mitchell, Diana (1997) 'Gongos on the March in Zimbabwe', *Frontiers of Freedom* 11: 4–5.

Mkandawire, Thandika (1985) '"Home Grown" Austerity Measures: The Case of Zimbabwe', *Africa Development*, 10(1/2).

Mlambo, A.S. (1997) *The Economic Structural Adjustment Programme: The Case of Zimbabwe, 1990–1995*, Harare: University of Zimbabwe Publications.

Moore, David (1992) 'The Ideological Formation of the Zimbabwean Ruling Class', *Journal of Southern African Studies* 17(3).

Morande, Felipe and Klaus Schmidt-Hebbel (1994) 'Zimbabwe: Fiscal Disequilibria and Low Growth' in William Easterly, Carlos Alfredo Rodriguez and Klaus Schmidt-Hebbel (eds) *Public Sector Deficits and Macroeconomic Performance*, New York: Oxford University Press, published for the World Bank.

Morande, Felipe and Klaus Schmidt-Hebbel (1991) 'Macroeconomics of Public Sector Deficits: The Case of Zimbabwe', World Bank Policy, Research, and External Affairs working papers, WPS 688.

Moyo, Jonathan (1992) *Voting for Democracy: A Study of Electoral Politics in Zimbabwe*, Harare: University of Zimbabwe Publications.

Moyo, Sam (2000) *Land Reform under Structural Adjustment in Zimbabwe: Land Use Change in Mashonaland Provinces*, Uppsala: Nordic Africa Institute.

Moyo, Sam (1995) *The Land Question in Zimbabwe*, Harare: SAPES Books.

Moyo S (1986) 'The Land Question', in Mandaza (ed.) (1986b).

Moyo, Sam, John Makumbe and Brian Raftopoulos (2000) *NGOs, the State & Politics in Zimbabwe*, Harare: SAPES Books.

Moyo, Sam, Peter Robinson, Yemi Katerere, Stuart Stevenson and Davison Gumbo (1991) *Zimbabwe's Environmental Dilemma: Balancing Resource Inequities*, Harare: ZERO.

Mudzi, Tracey (1998) 'Education in Zimbabwe: A Situational Analysis', Report for DFIDCA.

Mugabe, Robert G. (1989) 'The Unity Accord: Its Promise for the Future', in Banana (1989).

Munro, William A. (1998) *The Moral Economy of the State: Conservation, Community Development, and State Making in Zimbabwe*, Athens, OH: Ohio University Press.

Mupedziswa, Rodrick and Perpetua Gumbo (1998) *Structural Adjustment and Women Informal Sector Traders in Harare, Zimbabwe*, Uppsala: Nordic Africa Institute Research Report No. 106.

Murombedzi, J.C. (1992) *Decentralization or Recentralization? Implementing CAMP-FIRE in the Omay Communal Lands of the Nyaminyami District*, Harare: University of Zimbabwe Centre for Applied Social Sciences.

Murombedzi, J. (1991) 'Wetlands Conservation under Common Property Management Regimes in Zimbabwe', Harare: University of Zimbabwe Centre for Applied Social Sciences, NRM Occasional Papers.

Murombedzi, J. (1990) *The Need for Appropriate Local Level Common Property Resource Management Institutions in Communal Tenure Regimes*, Harare: University of Zimbabwe Centre for Applied Social Sciences.

Musemwa, Muchaparara (1995) 'The Ambiguities of Democracy: The Demobilisation of the Zimbabwean Ex-combatants and the Ordeal of Rehabilitation, 1980–1993', in Cillers, Jakkie (ed.) *Dismissed: Demobilisation and Reintegration of Former Combatants in Africa*, South Africa: Institute for Defence Policy.

Muzulu J. (1993) 'Exchange Rate Depreciation and Structural Adjustment: The Case of the Manufacturing Sector in Zimbabwe, 1980–91', unpublished PhD thesis, University of Sussex.

Närman, Anders (1991) *Education, Training and Agricultural Development in Zimbabwe*, Paris: UNESCO.

Ncube, Welshman (1991) 'Constitutionalism, Democracy and Political Practice in Zimbabwe', in Mandaza and Sachikonye (1991).

Ncube, Welshman (1989) 'The Post-unity Period: Developments, Benefits and Problems', in Banana (1989).

Ndlela, Dan B. (1984) 'Sectoral Analysis of Zimbabwe Economic Development with Implications for Foreign Trade and Foreign Exchange', *Zimbabwe Journal of Economics* 1(1).

Nherera, Charles (1998) 'Post-independence Reform Policies and Vocationalization of Secondary-school Education in Zimbabwe', in Lene Buchert (ed.) *Education Reform in the South in the 1990s*, Paris: UNESCO.

Nizkor International Human Rights Team (1999) 'Letter from the Supreme Court of Zimbabwe in Response to Several Women's Human Rights Organizations', May 26, HURINet – The Human Rights Information Network.

Nkiwane, Solomon M. (1999) 'Zimbabwe's Foreign Policy', in Stephen Wright (ed.) *African Foreign Policies*, Boulder: Westview.

Nkiwane, Solomon M. (1997) 'Background to Zimbabwe's Foreign Relations', in Solomon Nkiwane (ed.) *Zimbabwe's International Borders: A Study in National and Regional Development in Southern Africa*, Harare: University of Zimbabwe Publications.

Nordlund, Per (1996) *Organising the Political Agora: Domination and Democratisation in Zambia and Zimbabwe*, Uppsala: Uppsala University Press.

Nussbaum, Martha and Jonathan Glover (eds) (1995) *Women, Culture and Development: A Study of Human Capabilities*, Oxford: Clarendon Press.

Nyamubaya, Freedom T.V. (1986) *On the Road Again*, Harare: Zimbabwe Publishing House.

Nyawata Obert I. (1988) 'Macroeconomic Management, Adjustment and Stabilisation', in Stoneman (1988c).

Nzuwah, Mariyawanda (1980) 'Conflict Resolution in Zimbabwe: Superpower Determinants to the Peace Settlement', *Journal of Southern African Affairs* 4(4): 389–400.

Ødegaard, Anne (1998) *Brukerfinansiering og Skoledelkelse: En Studie av Brukerfinansierings Mulige Effekt på Skoledeltakelsen for Barn fra Lavintektshushold i Zimbabwe*, Hovedoppgave i Samfunnsgeografi, University of Oslo.

Pakkiri, Logan (1989) 'Education Policies and Economic Development in Zimbabwe', *Zimbabwe Journal of Educational Research* 1(3): 280–303.

Palmer, R.H. (1990) 'Land Reform in Zimbabwe, 1980–1990', *African Affairs* 89: 163–181.

Patel, Hasu H. (1987) 'South Africa's Destabilisation Policy', *The Round Table* 303: 302–310.

Psacharopoulos, George and William Loxley (1985) *Diversified Secondary Education and Development: Evidence from Colombia and Tanzania*, Baltimore: Johns Hopkins University Press.

Psacharopoulos, George and Maureen Woodhall (1985) *Education for Development: An Analysis of Investment Choice*, Washington, DC: Oxford University Press.

Rabinow, Paul (ed.) (1984) *The Foucault Reader*, New York: Penguin Books.

Raftopoulos, Brian (2000) 'Problematising Nationalism in Zimbabwe', *Zambezia* 26(2): 115–134.

Raftopoulos, Brian (1999) 'The State, Politics and the Indigenisation Process in Zimbabwe: Class Formation Behind Closed Doors, 1990–1996', unpublished seminar paper, Harare: University of Zimbabwe Institute of Development Studies.

Raftopoulos, Brian (1996), 'Fighting for Control: The Indigenization Debate in Zimbabwe', *Southern Africa Report* 11(4): 3–7.

Raftopoulos, Brian (1992) 'Beyond the House of Hunger: Democratic Struggles in Zimbabwe', *Review of African Political Economy* 54: 59–74.

Raikes, Philip (1988) *Modernising Hunger*, London: Catholic Institute for International Relations.

Ranger, Terence (1993a) 'The Communal Areas of Zimbabwe', in T.J. Basset and D.E. Crummey (eds) *Land in African Agrarian Systems*, Madison: University of Wisconsin Press.

Ranger, Terence (1993b) 'The Invention of Tradition Revisited', in Terence Ranger and Olufemi Vaughan (eds) *Legitimacy and the State in Twentieth-century Africa, Essays in honour of A.H.M. Kirk-Greene*, London: Macmillan.

Ranger, Terence (1989) 'Missionaries, Migrants and the Manyika: The Invention of Ethnicity in Zimbabwe', in Leroy Vail (ed.) *The Creation of Tribalism in Southern Africa*, London: James Currey.

Ranger, Terence (1985a) *Peasant Consciousness and Guerrilla War in Zimbabwe: A Comparative Study*, London: James Currey, and Harare: Zimbabwe Publishing House.

Ranger, Terence (1985b) *The Invention of Tribalism in Zimbabwe*, Gweru: Mambo Press.

Ranger, Terence O. (1982) 'Survival, Revival and Disaster: Shona Traditional Elites under Colonialism', paper presented to the Round Table on Elites and Colonisation, Paris.

Rattsø, Jørn and Ragnar Torvik (1998), 'Zimbabwean Trade Liberalisation: Ex Post Evaluation', *Cambridge Journal of Economics* 22: 325–346.

Rensburg, Patrick van (1974) *Report from Swaneng Hill: Education and Employment in an African Country*, Uppsala: Dag Hammarskjöld Foundation.

Rice, Susan Elizabeth (1990) 'Commonwealth Initiative in Zimbabwe, 1979–80: Implication for International Peacekeeping', unpublished PhD in Philosophy, Oxford University.

Riddell Commission (1981) *Commission of Inquiry into Incomes, Prices and Conditions of Service*, Harare.

Riddell R.C. (1979) 'Alternative Development Strategies for Zimbabwe', *Zimbabwe Journal of Economics* 1(3).

Robertson, John (1992) 'The Economy: A Sectoral Overview', in Simon Baynham (ed.) *Zimbabwe in Transition*, Stockholm: Almqvist & Wicksell International.

Roe, Emmory (1992) 'Report on the Amalgamation of District Councils and Rural Councils', Harare: University of Zimbabwe, Centre for Applied Social Sciences, CASS Occasional Paper Series – NRM.

Rotberg, Robert (2000) 'Africa's Mess, Mugabe's Mayhem', *Foreign Affairs* 79(5): 47–61.

Rothchild, Donald (1999) 'Ethnic Insecurity, Peace Agreement, and State Building', in Richard Joseph (ed.) *State, Conflict and Democracy in Africa*, Boulder: Lynne Rienner.

Rukobo, Andries Matenda (1991) 'Misplaced Emphasis in the Democracy Debate', in Mandaza and Sachikonye (1991).

Rusike, E.T.M. (1990) *The Politics of the Mass Media: A Personal Experience*, Harare: Roblaw.

Sachikonye, Lloyd (1999) *Restructuring or De-industrialization? Zimbabwe's Textile and Metals Industries*, Uppsala: Nordic Africa Institute Research Report No. 110.

Sachikonye, Lloyd M. (1990) 'Industrial Relations Crisis: An Anatomy of Recent Strikes in Zimbabwe', *Southern Africa Political and Economic Monthly*, September.

Sandbrook, Richard (1985) *The Politics of Africa's Economic Stagnation*, Cambridge: Cambridge University Press.

Saunders, Richard Gerard (1991) 'Information in the Interregnum: The Press, State and Civil Society in Struggles for Hegemony, Zimbabwe 1980–1990', PhD thesis, Carleton University.

Schatzberg, Michael (ed.) (1984) *The Political Economy of Zimbabwe*, New York: Praeger.

Schmidt, Elizabeth (1992) *Peasants, Traders, and Wives: Shona Women in the History of Zimbabwe, 1870–1939*, London: James Currey.

Scoones, I. and B. Cousins (1991) *Contested Terrains: The Struggle For Control over Dambo Resources in Zimbabwe*, London: Drylands Programme, IIED.

Scott, James (1990) *Domination and the Arts of Resistance: Hidden Transcripts*, New Haven: Yale University Press.

Searle, Peter (1999) *The Riddle of Malaysian Capitalism: Rent-seekers or Real Capitalists?* Honolulu: University of Hawaii Press.

Seegers, Annette (1986) 'Revolutionary Armies of Africa: Mozambique and Zimbabwe', in Simon Baynham (ed.) *Military Power: Politics in Black Africa*, London: Croom Helm.

Shadur, Mark A. (1994) *Labour Relations in a Developing Country: A Case Study on Zimbabwe*, Aldershot: Avebury.

Shaw, Timothy M. (1989) 'Corporatism in Zimbabwe: Revolution Restrained', in Julius Nyang'oro and T. Shaw (eds.) *Corporatism in Africa: Comparative Analysis and Practice*, Boulder: Westview.

Shaw, William H. (1986) 'Towards the One-party State in Zimbabwe: A Study in African Political Thought', *Journal of Modern African Studies* 4(3): 373–394.

Sibanda, Arnold (1988) 'The Political Situation', in Stoneman (1988c).

Singer Hans (1992) *Research of the World Employment Programme: Future Priorities and Selective Assessment*, Geneva: International Labour Organisation.

Sithole, Masipula (1988) 'Zimbabwe: In Search of a Stable Democracy', in Diamond, Linz and Lipset (1988).

Sithole, Masipula (1986) 'The General Elections 1979–1985', in Mandaza (1986b).

Skålnes, Tor (1995) *The Politics of Economic Reform in Zimbabwe, Continuity and Change in Development*, London: Macmillan.

Soames, Rt. Hon. Lord (1980) 'From Rhodesia to Zimbabwe', *International Affairs*, 56(3): 405–419.

Spierenburg, Marja (2000) 'Social Commentaries and the Influence of Adherents: The Role of the *Mhondoro* Cult in the Struggle over Land in Dande (Northern Zimbabwe)', in R. Van Dijk., R. Reis and M. Spierenburg (eds) *The Quest for Fruition through Ngoma, Political Aspects of Healing in Southern Africa*, London: James Currey; Athens, OH: Ohio University Press.

Spierenburg, Marja (1995) 'The Role of the Mhondoro Cult in the Struggle for Control over Land in Dande (Northern Zimbabwe): Social Commentaries and the Influence of Adherents', Harare: University of Zimbabwe Centre for Applied Social Sciences, NRM Occasional Papers Series.

Staunton, Irene (ed.) (1990) *Mothers of the Revolution*, Harare: Baobab Books.

Stedman, Stephen John (1991) *Peacemaking in Civil War: International Mediation in Zimbabwe, 1974–1980*, Boulder: Lynne Rienner.

Stoneman, Colin (1993) 'The World Bank: Some Lessons for South Africa', *Review of African Political Economy* 58: 87–98.

Stoneman, Colin (1989) 'The World Bank and IMF in Zimbabwe', in Bonnie K. Campbell and J. Loxley (eds) *Structural Adjustment in Africa*, Macmillan.

Stoneman, Colin (1988a) 'A Zimbabwean Model?' in Stoneman (1988c).

Stoneman Colin (1988b) 'The Economy: Recognising the Reality', in Stoneman (1988c).

Stoneman, Colin (ed.) (1988c) *Zimbabwe's Prospects: Issues of Race, Class, State and Capital in Southern Africa*, London: Macmillan.

Stoneman, Colin and Lionel Cliffe (1989) *Zimbabwe: Politics, Economics and Society*, London and New York: Pinter.

Strachan, Brigid (1993) *The Impact of Regressive Action Employment Policy on Redressing Racial and Gender Imbalances in the Labour Market in Zimbabwe*, Harare: University of Zimbabwe Centre for Applied Social Sciences.

Sylvester, Christine (2000) *Producing Women and Progress in Zimbabwe: Narratives of Identity and Work from the 1980s*, Portsmouth, NH: Heinemann.

Sylvester, Christine (1999) '"Progress" in Zimbabwe: Is "It" A "Woman?"' *International Feminist Journal of Politics*, 1(1): 89–118.

Sylvester, Christine (1995a) '"Women" in Rural Producer Groups and the Diverse Politics of Truth in Zimbabwe,' in Marianne Marchand and Jane Parpart (eds) *Feminism/Postmodernism/Development*, London: Routledge.

Sylvester, Christine (1995b) 'African and Western Feminisms: World-traveling the Tendencies and Possibilities', *Signs: Journal of Women in Culture and Society* 20(4): 941–969.

Sylvester, Christine (1991a) *Zimbabwe: The Terrain of Contradictory Development*, Boulder: Westview; London: Dartmouth.

Sylvester, Christine (1991b) '"Urban Women's Cooperatives," "Progress," and "African Feminism" in Zimbabwe', *Differences: A Journal of Feminist Cultural Studies* 3(1): 39–62.

Sylvester, Christine (1990) 'Simultaneous Revolutions: The Zimbabwean Case', *Journal of Southern African Studies* 16(3): 452–475.

Sylvester, Christine (1986) 'Zimbabwe's 1985 Elections: A Search For National Mythology', *Journal of Modern African Studies* 24(2): 229–255.

Tamarkin, M. (1990) *The Making of Zimbabwe: Decolonization in Regional and International Politics*, London: Frank Cass.

Tandon, Yash (1984) 'The Post-colonial State', *Social Change and Development* 8.

Taylor, Scott D. (1999) 'Race, Class, and Neopatrimonialism in Zimbabwe', in Richard Joseph (ed.) *State, Conflict, and Democracy in Africa*, Boulder: Lynne Rienner.

Tengende, Norbert (1994) 'Workers, Students and the Struggles for Democracy: State – Civil Society Relations in Zimbabwe', unpublished PhD dissertation, Roskilde University, International Development Studies.

Thomas, Stephen J. (1992) *The Legacy of Dualism and Decision-making: The Prospects for Local Institutional Development in CAMPFIRE*, Harare: Centre for Applied Social Sciences and the Branch of Terrestrial Ecology, Department of National Parks and Wildlife.

Thompson, Carol (1984) 'Zimbabwe in Southern Africa: From Dependent Development to Dominance or Cooperation?' in Schatzberg (1984).

Toye, John (1996) *Structural Adjustment and Employment Policy: Issues and Experiences*, Geneva: ILO.

UNDP (1996) *Human Development Report*, New York and Oxford: Oxford University Press.

UNDP (1990) *Human Development Report*, New York and Oxford: Oxford University Press.

UNIDO (1986) *The Manufacturing Sector in Zimbabwe*, Vienna: UNIDO.

Vanhanen, Tatu (1990) *The Process of Democratization: A Comparative Study of 147 States, 1980–88*, New York: Taylor & Francis.

Vera, Yvonne (1994) *Why Don't You Carve Other Animals*, Harare: Baobab Books.

Verhagen, K. (1987) *Self-help Promotion: A Challenge to the NGO Community*, Amsterdam: Cebemo.

de Waal, Victor (1990) *The Politics of Reconciliation: Zimbabwe's First Decade*, Cape Town: David Philip

Weiner, D., S. Moyo, B. Munslow and P. O'Keefe (1991) 'Land Use and Agricultural Productivity in Zimbabwe', in N.D. Mutizwa-Mangiza and A.H.J. Helmsing (eds) *Rural Development and Planning in Zimbabwe*, Aldershot: Avebury.

Weitzer, Ronald (1990) *Transforming Settler States: Communal Conflict and Internal Security in Northern Ireland and Zimbabwe*, Berkeley: University of California Press.

Werbner, Richard (1991) *Tears of the Dead: The Social Biography of an African Family*, Edinburgh: Edinburgh University Press.

Wetherell, Iden (1994) 'Fatal Flaws in Indigenisation', *The Financial Gazette*, 15 September.

Wetherell, Iden (1993) 'ZANU(PF)'s Zidco a Model for Thebe', *Weekly Mail*, 30 July.

Wild, Volker (1997) *Profit Not for Profit's Sake: History and Business Culture of African Entrepreneurs in Zimbabwe*, Harare: Baobab Books.

World Bank (1997) *Country Assistance Strategy for Zimbabwe*, Southern Africa Department, Africa Region.

World Bank (1996) 'Poverty in Zimbabwe: Current Knowledge and Issues for the Future', mimeo.

World Bank (1995) 'Performance Audit Report: Zimbabwe Structural Adjustment Program', World Bank Operations Evaluation Department, June.

World Bank (1993a) *Demobilization and Reintegration of Military Personnel in Africa: The Evidence from Seven Country Case Studies*, Discussion Paper, Africa Regional Series Report No. IDP-130, Washington, DC: The World Bank.

World Bank (1993b) 'Zimbabwe: Economic Update', Paper Prepared For the Consultative Group Meeting for Zimbabwe, Paris, 13–14 December.

World Bank (1993c) *World Debt Tables: External Finance for Developing Countries*, Washington, DC: World Bank.

World Bank (1992) *Zimbabwe: Strategy for Women in Development*, Report No. 9204-ZIM, Washington, DC: World Bank.

World Bank (1991) *Vocational and Technical Education and Training: A World Bank Policy Paper*, Washington, DC: World Bank.

World Bank (1989) *Sub-Saharan Africa: From Crisis to Sustainable Growth*, Washington, DC: World Bank.

World Bank (1987) *Zimbabwe: A Strategy for Sustained Growth*, 2 vols, Washington, DC: World Bank.

World Bank (1985) *Zimbabwe: Country Economic Memorandum, Performance, Policies and Prospects*, 3 vols, Washington, DC: World Bank.

Zaffiro, James J. (1984) 'Broadcasting and Political Change in Zimbabwe 1931–1984', unpublished PhD thesis, University of Wisconsin.

ZANU(PF) (1990) *Election Manifesto 1990*, Harare: Jongwe.

ZANU(PF) (1980) 'Election Manifesto of the Patriotic Front', in Goswin Bauamhogger with Telse Diederichsen and Ulf Engel (eds) (1984) *The Struggle for Independence: Documents on the Recent Development of Zimbabwe (1975[1980])*, Vol. 6, Hamburg: Institut fur Afrikakunde, Dokumentations – Leitstelle Afrika.

ZCTU (1995) *Beyond the Economic Structural Adjustment Programme (ESAP): Framework for a Long-term Development Strategy in Zimbabwe*, Harare: ZCTU.

Zimbabwe Women's Bureau (1998) 'Homestead Development Programme', unpublished report.

Zimbabwe Women's Bureau (1992) *We Carry A Heavy Load, Part II*, Harare: Zimbabwe Women's Bureau.

Zimbabwe Women's Bureau (1981) *We Carry A Heavy Load*, Harare: Zimbabwe Women's Bureau.

Zvogbo, Rungano (1994) *Colonialism and Education in Zimbabwe*, Harare: SAPES Books.

Newspapers and magazines

The Zimbabwe Independent. Harare. (print and electronic editions)
Moto (Harare).
The Parade, Harare.
The New African, 1993, April, London.
BBC, world service www.bbc.co.uk/worldservice/index.shtml.
Daily News, Harare.
DRC War Bulletin, Ministry of Defense, Harare.
The Financial Gazette, Harare.
The Herald, Harare.
The Zimbabwe Mirror, Harare.
Zimbabwe News, Harare.
The Zimbabwe Standard Online [www.thestandard.co.zw].
The Daily Gazette, Harare.
The Daily News, Harare (print and electronic editions).
The Financial Gazette, Harare (print and electronic editions).
The Herald, Harare (print and electronic editions).
The Mail & Guardian, Johannesburg (print and electronic editions).
The Standard, Harare (print and electronic editions).
The Star, Johannesburg (print and electronic editions).
The Sunday Gazette, Harare.
The Sunday Mail, Harare (print and electronic editions).
The Zimbabwe Independent, Harare (print and electronic editions).
The Zimbabwe Mirror, Harare (print and electronic editions).

Index

new society 157–8; and
decline in enrolment 149, 151;
examination performance
151–2; expansion (1980–90)
142–8; gender aspects 143, 144,
151; government/community
commitment 144–5; and
introduction of fees 149;
and literacy rates 143–4;
modernization/alternative
development 156–7; primary
140, 143–5; and provision of
teachers 145, 150; quality of
148, 151–2; in science 146;
secondary 140, 145–7;
stagnation in 148–51;
technical/ practical 153–5;
tertiary 141–2, 147; urban/
rural differences 150;
vocational aspects 152–8;
for work 152–7
Education Act 142, 149
Education with Production (EwP)
system 154–5
Enhanced Social Protection
Programme (ESPP) 67
ESPP *see* Enhanced Social Protection
Programme
Evans, M. 121(7n)
Export Processing Zones 62

family networks/kinship *see* crony
capitalism
farmer organizations 4
Fauré, Y.A. 33(27n)
Financial Gazette, The 205,
206, 207
First Five-Year National Development
Plan (1986–90) 50–3, 86, 166
foreign policy 4–5; and active
non-alignment 185–7;
background 179–80; and
changing global context 185–7;
effect of independence on 180;
future prospects 194;
highest-level setting of 179–80;
importance of Zimbabwe's
location 181–2; increase in
foreign missions 180; and

involvement in DRC conflict
187–93; little change in 193–4;
and multinational enterprises
185–6; principles of 180–1;
reaction to hostile neighbours
182; regional aspects 182–5,
186; and removal of
colonialism 182–3; role in
international politics 193;
security issues 186; and Soviet
Union 185; and support for
liberation in Africa 181–5;
and trade/development
aid 186–7
Foucault, M. 160

Garbett, K. 102(17n)
Gibbon, P. 10, 150
Graham-Brown, S. 145
Grants Allocation Committee (GAC)
67
Group Development Area Schemes
170
Group of 15 (G15) 184
Group of 77 (G77) 184
'Growth With Equity: An Economic
Policy Statement' (1981)
39–40, 43
guerrillas 111–14, 168
Gumbo, P. 10
Gwinyayi, A.D. 121(3n)

Hadeniu, A. 6
Hammar, A. 89
Hanlon, J. 4
Harare Weaving Co-operative 173
Hatchard, J. 12
Henne, J. 175
Herald, The 209
Herbst, J. 3, 5
HIV-AIDS 163
Holtzclaw, H. 121(3n)
Horizon 212
Hove, C. 165, 174
Human Development Report
(1996) 34
human rights 17, 169, 177, 212
Hunzvi, Hitler 116, 117–18
Hyden, G. 33(33n)